MALIGNANT NARCISSISM AND POWER

Using psychodynamic theory and riveting case material, this book dissects the figure of the malignant narcissist leader (MNL). Across the world today, individuals and societies are impacted by unprecedented disruptive influences, from globalization and climate change to economic uncertainty and mass migration. The rise of populists and would-be saviors has promised certainty for anxious populations, but are such leaders suffering from the MNL pathology?

Through the psychoanalytic lens of Otto Kernberg, the authors explain the etiology of the charismatic MNL's clinical features: charisma, grandiosity, criminality, sadism, and paranoia. The book outlines the limitations and complexity of diagnosis, contextualizing the MNL within the transcendental and millenarian movements, and discusses the patho-dynamics of high-pressure groups and totalitarian regimes, including types of groups, methods of mind control, categories of constituents, the corporate totalitarian state, and the authoritarian demagogue. The book looks at a wide range of leaders including Donald Trump, Bhagwan Shree Rajneesh, Roger Ailes, Keith Raniere, Jan of Leiden, and Credonia Mwerinde.

Distinguishing the disordered personality of the MNL from other personality disorders, and presenting a new model of overlapping descriptors to categorize high-pressure group types and identifying types of followers as well, this book represents essential reading for psychodynamically minded psychologists, psychiatrists, social workers, sociologists, political scientists, and those working in organizational development.

Charles Zeiders, PsyD, is the T.S. Eliot Lecturer for Humanities and Spiritual Psychology, Reformed Episcopal Seminary in metropolitan Philadelphia, USA. A clinical and forensic psychologist, Dr. Zeiders is an expert clinician and psychopathologist. His books include *The Clinical Christ, Faith, Forensics, and Firearms*, as well as volumes of depth-psychological poetry.

Peter Devlin, LGSW, is a psychotherapist at Capitol Hill Consortium in Washington, DC. He received his BA from the University of Pennsylvania and his MSW from the University of Southern California. His research interests include trauma and the psychology of power.

MALIGNANT NARCISSISM AND POWER

A Psychodynamic Exploration of Madness and Leadership

Charles Zeiders and Peter Devlin

Routledge
Taylor & Francis Group

LONDON AND NEW YORK

First published 2020
by Routledge
2 Park Square, Milton Park, Abingdon, Oxon OX14 4RN

and by Routledge
52 Vanderbilt Avenue, New York, NY 10017

Routledge is an imprint of the Taylor & Francis Group, an informa business

British Library Cataloguing-in-Publication Data
A catalogue record for this book is available from the British Library

Library of Congress Cataloging-in-Publication Data
A catalog record for this book has been requested

ISBN: 978-0-367-27963-9 (hbk)
ISBN: 978-0-367-27964-6 (pbk)
ISBN: 978-0-429-29895-0 (ebk)

Typeset in Bembo
by Apex CoVantage, LLC

In memory of our friend,

Jaime Robert Triplett,

Poet

CONTENTS

CREDIT LIST

Chapter 1

An earlier version of Chapter 1 appeared as "A 'Psychological Autopsy' of a Malignant Narcissist in Church Leadership: A 'Composite' Scenario with Discussion," published in *The Journal of Christian Healing*, spring/summer 2016, *32*(1). It is reprinted here with edits and additional discussion.

Content in Box 1.1 is adapted from Goldner-Vukov, M., & Moore, L. J. (2010). Malignant narcissism: From fairy tales to harsh reality. *Psychiatria Danubina*, *22*(3), 393.

Text extract (68 words), p. 9, reprinted by permission from SpringerNature: Dunn, M. Mysticism, motherhood, and pathological narcissism? A Kohutian analysis of Marie de l'Incarnation. *Journal of Religion and Health*, *52*(2), 650.

Chapter 2

Content in Box 2.1 is reprinted with permission from Owen, D., & Davidson, J. (2009). Hubris syndrome: an acquired personality disorder? A study of US Presidents and UK Prime Ministers over the last 100 years. *Brain: A Journal of Neurology*, *132*(Pt 5), 1398.

Chapter 4

An earlier version of the section "The Followers: Different Types and Singular Madness" appeared in "A 'Psychological Autopsy' of a Malignant Narcissist in Church Leadership: A 'Composite' Scenario with Discussion," published in *The Journal of Christian Healing*, spring/summer 2016, *32*(1), and it is reprinted here with edits and additional discussion.

Chapter 5

Content in Box 5.1 is reprinted with permission from Lalich, J., & Tobias, M. (2006). *Take back your life: Recovering from cults and abusive relationships*. Richmond, CA: Bay Tree Publishing.

ACKNOWLEDGMENTS

Friends and colleagues whose support, love, and wisdom made this work possible are innumerable.

First and foremost, we bow to our developmental editor Victoria White, principal editor and manuscript consultant of Write Vision Services. If advancing the meaning and integrity of a manuscript was ballet, she would be Baryshnikov. She redacted our impossibly dense copy into clarity and made it appear effortless. All those with writer's block should rush to her door. Thank you for sharing your editorial virtuosity so generously, Victoria.

Heartfelt thanks go to Andrea Klingler of Silverwood Editorial & Communications. Her dedicated efforts as project permissions editor have improved our bibliographic health immeasurably.

We are further grateful for the brilliant source-finding assistance of Joan Wolff, medical librarian of the Bryn Mawr Hospital Medical Library, and for the diligence of our CC Therapy Associates' intern Melissa Stern, whose polymathic approach to translating research summaries into psychodynamic formulations was genuinely impressive.

I thank my colleagues at CC Associates of the Main Line, especially psychotherapists Julie Wegryn and Donna Drennan, whose support and sharing of ideas provided me with deeply appreciated professional scaffolding and psychodynamic insight. I am grateful to the Reverend Doctor Jonathan Riches, Dean of Reformed Episcopal Seminary, for granting me the leave of absence required to research and write this book; I further thank Dr. Riches for being a model of fiduciary leadership and a man for all seasons. I extend gratitude to my patients and students whose courage and curiosity leave me humbled and inspired to press toward answers that heal. I most especially thank my sweet wife, Emily Selvin, who endured a preoccupied husband and brought me espresso as I pored over Kernberg and remarkably thick books. *Te amo diversi generis multa nimis, Emily!* Forever.

Charles Zeiders

I thank my many colleagues from over the years at Green Door and Washington Hospital Center, including two remarkable former clinical directors, Joanne Kim and Kajal Gehi. I am also grateful to thank Pritish Vyas for his invaluable assistance to both Charles and myself, and John Broening for his willingness to listen and provide helpful criticism. I would also like to thank my co-author, Dr. Charles Zeiders, for his friendship and extraordinary support during difficult times. Foremost, I would like to thank my son, Eliott, whose innate optimism and joy is a rebuke to the mad leaders in this volume.

Peter Devlin

Lastly, we thank the anonymous psychoanalyst from Washington, DC, who reflectively stroked his beard and reminded us (in a Viennese accent!) of the speculative nature of our work and its epistemological equivocality. "Ambiguity is endless," he said, and drank all the schnapps.

INTRODUCTION

Across the world, individuals and societies are impacted by unprecedented disruptive influences – globalization, neoliberalism, climate change, war, rumors of war, economic uncertainty, cultural breakdown, and mass migration. Ours is a trepidatious time when anxious people seek certainties in all manner of saviors and would-be messiahs, whose mad interiors are not at first outwardly evident but whose narcissism and criminality pose an existential threat. That is a fact. But what can really be done?

Prior to our graduate work, Peter Devlin and I were earnest young men when we met on Philadelphia's famous South Street in the late 1980s. At some dramatic point amidst our always-animated early discussions, Devlin pulled from his backpack a copy of Erich Fromm's *The Anatomy of Human Destructiveness* (1977) and brandished the tome at me. He declared that Fromm's work would stand the test of time; he described it as a prophetic, poly-display masterpiece. Devlin thus introduced me to an expansive form of psychodynamic, psychosocial criticism that, to varying degrees, has subsequently informed both of our clinical and scholarly pursuits. We stand firm in the Frommian conviction that psychodynamic theory is instrumental to establishing healthful interpretations, not only for the single analysand, but also for the larger society. Like Fromm, we find in the psychoanalytic tradition a body of thought that is comprehensive enough to be critical theory of the human condition – one applicable to the mental phenomena of an individual, a group, or a world.

Operating out of this mindset throughout our clinical lifetimes, we have witnessed an eruption of patients with signs and symptoms immediately emergent from institutional betrayals – antisocial policy, the security state, corporate surveillance, predatory lending, downsizing, cancelled health plans, religious rip-offs, mass fraud, and the extraction economy. They may have dashed hopes from a parade of ingenious, charismatic leaders whose tenure culminated in personal miseries and community calamites. Like Fromm, Devlin and I hold fast to the notion that informed, self-possessed people and professionals have a great deal to offer social elements seeking genuine safety from both disruption and tyranny.

Following in Fromm's footsteps, we are convinced that destructive leadership is a disease that psychodynamic forensics can locate in history, diagnose in the present, and even prevent in the future, especially if placed at the disposal of "healthy" interest groups. In the course of our writing, we have further discovered, perhaps at a new level, the versatile utility of psychodynamic theory as a critical tool applicable to psychopathology, psychohistory, psychobiography, political forensics, psychological autopsy, religious psychology, organizational analysis, and cult studies. But most significantly to our purpose is that our insights about the methods and mind of the mad leader will result in individual, organizational, and social freedom from the subjugating influence of the destructive leader.

As psychotherapists, we find that exposure to a malignantly narcissistic leader can inflict untold psychic damages upon anyone at any stage of development, regardless of their ego strength. As consultants, we find that any organization of any size will lose the bulk of its fineness under the "visionary" executive who ascends to power amid expectations of transformational leadership, but who then purges the critical thinkers, pays her or himself for ruinous management, and makes self-serving decisions that will cripple the organization – all the while injuring external parties with breathtaking criminality. When indictments roll in, this leader will then declare him or herself to be a persecuted genius and a victim of jealous mediocrities in league with perfidious out-groups. Despite our convictions, Devlin and I appreciate the experimental nature of our ideas, so we deploy a range of terms to refer to these leaders – mad, destructive, or malignant narcissist among them. With this range of referents, we demonstrate that a breadth of options exists for how exactly such actors might be interpreted. To us, the reality of a psychodynamic phenomenon falls within an interval, rather than at a point.

We have written this book to explicate the patient zero of mad leadership: the leader whose narcissism, criminality, sadism, and paranoia metastasize from a power position, hurting friends and enemies alike. The mad leader presents ubiquitous health threats out of self-obsession, grandiosity, infectious megalomania, and cancerous hatreds. The malignant narcissist in leadership must be more fully comprehended to stave her or his pathogenic search for unlimited power. We must actualize the promise of psychohistorical, psychobiographical, and psychosocial hunts for the historical, social scientific, and forensic realities that account for the rise of the mad leader – the (mis)leader whose inner sickness has determined so much of humanity's betrayed, heart-sick careening from time immemorial to our uneasy present.

Charles Zeiders, PsyD
Clinical and Forensic Psychologist
The T.S. Eliot Lecturer for Humanities and Spiritual Psychology
Reformed Episcopal Seminary
Clinical Director, CC Therapy Associates of the Main Line
Metropolitan Philadelphia

August 8, 2019
Philadelphia, PA (USA)

1

AN INTRODUCTION TO THE MALIGNANT NARCISSIST LEADER

A psychological autopsy of Bishop Frederick Ladysmith-Jones

An earlier version of this chapter appeared as "A 'Psychological Autopsy' of a Malignant Narcissist in Church Leadership: A 'Composite" Scenario with Discussion," published in The Journal of Christian Healing, spring/summer 2016, volume 32, number 1, and is reprinted here with edits and additional discussion.

How does one account for the rise and fall of a would-be messiah? The preponderance of institutional scandals, crimes, cover-ups, and malfeasance in recent years necessitates an exploration of the concept of malignant narcissism. Although not listed in the current *Diagnostic and Statistical Manual of Mental Disorders* (5th ed.; DSM-5; American Psychiatric Association [APA], 2015), the construct is helpful for understanding the charismatic leader whose attractiveness is predicated on her apparent embodiment of the answer to the deep concerns of a beleaguered group. She grows in fame and influence, only to disappoint with criminal scandals born of grandiosity and megalomania. Combing diverse documentation for malignant narcissist (MN) behaviors exhibited in the past and the present establishes credible inferences about their psychodynamics. The term *malignant narcissism* denotes an assessment of mental operations rather than a medical diagnosis. It is a term applied following assessment, often relying on *information and belief*, a standard legal/forensic phrase that qualifies remarks as believed to be true but without first-hand knowledge (see Chapter 2 for more information on assessment criteria).

In the case of psychobiography or forensic psychology, the phrase *information and belief* implies a higher degree of equivocality than a diagnosis. This is because the assessor cannot directly examine the subject. Various sources, reports, and persons are scrutinized prior to a determination. Nevertheless, there is an urgency to understand the construct because, if left unrecognized, its dangerousness increases exponentially. We address broad assessment criteria, recommendations to screen for these behaviors, the limitations of diagnosis, and the complexity of treatment for such individuals in Chapters 2 and 3 of this book. Chapter 4 explores the patho-dynamics of organizations led by malignant narcissist leaders (MNLs) and recommends treatment options for survivors of high-pressure groups led by MNLs. MNs must be screened and prevented from obtaining leadership or removed from power if they achieve it. Lives are at stake. Perhaps our own.

Religious organizations are particularly vulnerable to destructive leaders. Preying upon the preexistent credulity of the faithful, the MNL claims inspiration and rejects any demands for verification or peer review. He enjoys the flattery afforded to luminaries, and his followers idolize him, revering him as the vessel through whom god reaches their hungry hearts. In such groups, the lack of checks and the plethora of imbalances attract grandiose leaders with unverifiable claims to ultimate truth. Malignant narcissism is especially dangerous when it manifests in a religious leader, because such a leader is trusted with intimate information from their followers, making it easier to manipulate or even blackmail them. New and old religions alike are vulnerable to leaders who aspire to lead the faithful to themselves. They would themselves be god.

When a narcissistic cleric assumes church leadership, the matter is intrinsically problematic. But when the leader's narcissism is *malignant*, it is catastrophic. Such a destructive cleric will injure not only her detractors but also her followers and eventually herself. She will be charismatic and grandiose, offer infectious oratory, and gain followers. She will become the adored champion of a disaffected group looking for recognition in a world populated by "enemies." She will use convincing theological rationalizations to gratuitously and sadistically injure the enemies of her "divine" agenda. Her followers will continue to buy in and love her. Her grandiosity will delude her into thinking that providence has vouchsafed her to be incapable of mistakes. Wildly overconfident, she will engage in criminal overreach and when called to account, demonstrate enraged paranoia. To preserve her legacy and avoid accountability, she will blame former allies, run away, or die by suicide. If she ends her own life, she will depict this last destructive act as a kind of victory. In some cases, the MNL will encourage followers to co-suicide. This is especially true when the destructive leader cultivates apocalyptic paranoia among followers.

Individuals with this pathology may be male or female. But the broad professional consensus is that this affliction is predominately a male one, and the existing literature focuses on analysis of male behaviors and male case histories. There are many possible reasons for this, including the fact that sexism has historically prevented women from reaching equivalent positions of power. As a result, the male pronoun is used throughout the remainder of the book except in Chapters 6 and 7 where equally menacing examples of female MNLs are addressed.

This chapter presents a cursory literature review followed by a profile of a malignantly narcissistic leader (MNL), sketching a composite to form an "as if," but clinically accurate, psychological autopsy. Thus, the autopsy's patient is a fiction, but his psychodynamics are not.

Review of the literature

Psychology's great thinkers have concerned themselves with this characterological disease. After World War II, psychoanalyst Eric Fromm introduced the term "malignant narcissism" in 1964 and described it as a severe mental illness which represented the quintessence of evil (Fromm, 2010, p. 33). Fromm used *evil*, an import from the theologians, as a referent for socially cancerous authority motivated by hate, likely to culminate in terror, horror, and death. He reserved the malignant narcissist label for grandiose, charismatic leaders whose psychopathology accounted for a broad destructiveness that devours enemies, proponents, and the individuals themselves. Writing in the wake of the world wars, with genocide and total warfare finalizing in nuclear devastation, Fromm saw the negative visionaries behind these repulsive behaviors as lovers of death, or *necrophilic* personalities. These were the MNs, "the root of the most vicious destructiveness and inhumanity" (Fromm, 2010, p. 33).

Others have noted that this cancerous form of narcissism is built around aggression and idealizes the destructive aspects of the self. Herbert Rosenfeld, a German-British analyst and Kleinian, postulated a destructive form of narcissism, whereby the ego merges with an aggressive, idealized self-image and surrounds itself in grandiosity expressed in self-evidently "virtuous" violence (Steiner, 2008). Cornell University psychiatrist Otto Kernberg (1970), celebrated for his theories on borderline personality organization and narcissistic pathology, described the MN as fundamentally narcissistic and criminal. More specifically, Kernberg delineated the most salient features of MN into a quaternity: a narcissistic personality disorder (NPD) with predominant grandiosity, antisocial features, ego-syntonic sadism, and paranoia. George Pollock (1978), a professor of psychiatry who taught at Northwestern University, characterized the MN as an actor who evinces diseased grandiosity, amorality, and unregulated behavior with traits of sadism. His definition very much mirrors that of Kernberg – a bit of interrater reliability, to say the least.

A more recent peer-reviewed exploration of this pathology was conducted by Mila Goldner-Vukov and Laurie Jo Moore in 2010. Reiterating the *Kernbergian Quaternity* (KQ) (a term I use for convenience sake) for the 21st century, they pinpoint the four criteria essential to the KQ form of malignant narcissism: (1) narcissistic personality disorder, (2) antisocial features, (3) ego-syntonic sadism, and (4) paranoid tendencies (Box 1.1).

When these four elements of malignant narcissism constellate in a single leader, the profile that emerges is of a monstrous personality who will devolve into an impaired professional and imperil his organization. Sam Vaknin (2016), an Israeli expert on psychopathic narcissism, wrote:

> The malignant narcissist invents and then projects a false, fictitious, self for the world to fear, or to admire. He maintains a tenuous grasp on reality to start with and this is further exacerbated by the trappings of power. The narcissist's grandiose self-delusions and fantasies of omnipotence and omniscience are

supported by real life authority and the narcissist's predilection to surround himself with obsequious sycophants.

The narcissist's personality is so precariously balanced that he cannot tolerate even a hint of criticism and disagreement. Most narcissists are paranoid and suffer from ideas of reference (the delusion that they are being mocked or discussed when they are not). Thus, narcissists often regard themselves as "victims of persecution."

The narcissistic leader fosters and encourages a personality cult with all the hallmarks of an institutional religion: priesthood, rites, rituals, temples, worship, catechism, mythology. The leader is this religion's ascetic saint. He monastically denies himself earthly pleasures (or so he claims) in order to be able to dedicate himself fully to his calling.

The narcissistic leader is a monstrously inverted Jesus, sacrificing his life and denying himself so that his people – or humanity at large – should benefit. By surpassing and suppressing his humanity, the narcissistic leader became a distorted version of Nietzsche's "superman."

n.p.

BOX 1.1 GOLDER-VUKOV AND MOORE'S FOUR ELEMENTS OF MALIGNANT NARCISSISM

First criterion: narcissistic personality disorder	"The core features of NPD that are recognized in malignant narcissism (MN) are a grandiose sense of self-importance, preoccupation with fantasies of unlimited success, a sense of power and brilliance, a belief in being special or unique, a strong need for excessive admiration, a sense of entitlement, interpersonal exploitativeness, a lack of empathy, and prominent envy" (p. 393).
Second criterion: antisocial features	"[Malignant narcissists] are contemptuous of social conventions and show a . . . tendency to lie, steal and mismanage money. They may commit burglary, assault or murder, and they may even become leaders of sadistic or terrorist groups. They are capable of feeling concern and loyalty for others . . . but primarily for their disciples or blind followers. They realize that others have moral concerns, but they easily rationalize their antisocial behavior" (p. 393).
Third criterion: ego-syntonic sadism	"Individuals with malignant narcissism have a tendency to destroy, symbolically castrate, and dehumanize others. Their rage is fueled by the desire for revenge" (p. 393).
Fourth criterion: paranoid features	"The paranoid tendencies in malignant narcissists reflect their projection of unresolved hatred onto others whom they persecute" (p. 393).

Source: Goldner-Vukov & Moore, 2010.

// context (location, yr?)

Psychological autopsy of a malignant narcissist[1]

That Bishop Frederick Ladysmith-Jones ended his own life was sad but not surprising. Rumors were that the indictments issued against him by the State Attorney General's Office were damning. A list of charges leveled against Ladysmith-Jones and his Faith Cathedral included defamation, fraud, illegal detention, harassment by communication, and perjury. At the same time, his estranged (and excommunicated) lover, Margot Van Buren, provided a damning interview to Dan Truth, an important religion journalist. According to Ms. Van Buren, the beleaguered Bishop was a frighteningly insecure child-man who compensated for his inferiority by cultivating a messianic persona, surrounded himself with yes-men and sycophants, and brutally denounced and injured the reputations and fortunes of his detractors. The interview further exposed Ladysmith-Jones for illegally disbursing Faith Cathedral's money in order to finance his lavish lifestyle and reckless lawsuits. Complicit in his crimes, Van Buren turned state's witness and cooperated with investigators to expose the once popular churchman's malfeasance.

Bishop Frederick Ladysmith-Jones, a religious leader who felt entitled to speak for God and to control virtually any agenda that interested him, was finally confronted with a situation he could not control. After firing several legal teams (dubiously financed by Faith Cathedral endowment monies to which he was not personally entitled), Ladysmith-Jones simply had no good options. The law appeared ignorant to his "special" status as the self-proclaimed "Reformed Catholic Prophet to the Sacramental Communions of Christendom," and his group of formerly blind followers now looked upon Ladysmith-Jones with dismay. The newscasts of his preposterous grandiosity, rhetorical meanness, and cruel treatment of his detractors caused a precipitous falling away of his flock and a ruinous drop in tithing.

Unable to afford more counsel, and on the heels of a grueling, humiliating deposition, Bishop Ladysmith-Jones returned to his rectory, prepared certain documents, drank a half gallon of communion wine, and shot himself in the head. Authorities found his body adorned with his vestments, wearing his Bishop's cross and ring. His "final epistle" was a rambling document in which he affirmed that God had chosen him for a prophetic ministry to the Sacramental Communions of Christendom. He blamed the failure of his mission on "revisionists in the greater church, atheists in secular society, and Judas Iscariots within Faith Cathedral."

For a brief but poignant time, Bishop Ladysmith-Jones had been the darling of the Reformed Catholic Movement. He was a charismatic, persuasive speaker who embodied the hopes of Christians from various sacramental denominations. They desired ecclesial unity and the affirmation of a conservative, resolutely orthodox faith to counter a spiritual lassitude perceived to have crept from contemporary culture into the church. He had been the Golden Boy of theologians, seminary deans, and laity. He was the protégé of the venerable Bishop Augustini.

The news of his suicide made me reflective. What were the extenuating factors in Ladysmith-Jones' learning history that created his sick, attractive character? Why was he successful? Did his ministry have to conclude so ignominiously?

The origins of narcissism: shame, neglect, and trauma

Fred Jones was born into a poor family in Lincoln, Nebraska. His father, Fred Jones, Sr., spoke neither about his own family history nor about his family's origin. His father did not seem to want a past. He also possessed no outward signs of piety. But he did insist that his wife and son attend a non-denominational church, despite the fact that his wife was Catholic. Fred, Sr., was often too hung over to attend services with his family. A welder by trade, he spent money as soon as he earned it. He gambled it away or bought drinks at dive bars near the rundown home he rented on the poor side of Lincoln where he kept his family. Records indicate police arrested Fred Jones, Sr. on numerous occasions for domestic abuse of his wife and young son. Charges were always filed and always dropped by Mrs. Anne Marie Jones. Evidence suggests Mrs. Jones was afraid of her husband and was depressed. She told pastoral counselors that neither her father nor her husband had been any good to her. She could only depend on the Pope and God the Father. She resented her son, Fred, for keeping her in an unsatisfactory marriage. Blind to Fred's trauma and neglect, she lacked the insight that Fred required love, care, and treatment. While neglecting young Fred for being his father's son, she also made the boy the object of various fantasies based on imagery from the Catholic faith her spouse forbade her to practice. Vamik Volkan (2004) described a similar, religiously-laden developmental driver of narcissism:

> A Catholic mother fantasized that her son would grow up to be the Pope (i.e., an idealized father to replace the bad father she herself had experienced as a child), while her routine mothering functions left the child deprived of ordinary affection and approval for just being an average child. This perception of her child as unique was conveyed into the developing self of the small child and became the foundation for the child's future sense of his own grandiosity.
>
> *p. 313*

As in this scenario, young Fred's value depended on an unreality. His mother did not value him for himself, but as a toy savior. In an early psychological defense, Fred repressed his need for love and attention and instead assumed a grand persona. After he became Bishop Frederick Ladysmith-Jones as an adult, he wore magnificent vestments to cover his unimpressive physique. While yet a little boy, Fred traded the reality of shame for the glory of spiritual importance. What else could he have done when his mother attended to him only when he was quoting Scripture with flourishes like the TV priests and preachers? She only brightened and praised her son when he played the "minister game."

Joseph Burgo (2016) pointed out that future cult leaders like Fred Jones develop narcissistic defenses in reaction to the sense of defectiveness sustained from trauma, neglect, and abuse.

> The belief that one is exceptional and superior betrays a defensive sense of self out of touch with reality. In order to escape from feelings of core shame – of being small, needy, and defective – the cult leader takes flight from himself

and seeks refuge in a grandiose self-image meant to "disprove" all the damage. *I'm not defective. I'm a supremely important person.* It comes as no surprise that Charles Manson, David Koresh, and Jim Jones all emerged from horrific backgrounds.... In denial of early trauma and the resulting psychological damage, all three men eventually came to view themselves as exceptional and superior, projecting a grandiose self-image that persuaded others to do their bidding.

pp. 117–118

From a developmental viewpoint, it is important to note that the mothers of some cult leaders maintained quasi-delusional notions that their sons were messiahs. But of course, there will always be variations on the parental theme and the manner in which care-failures deform the budding character.

Elementary and middle-school years

Fred Jones performed well in school, and enjoyed praise from teachers for excelling academically. He presented with superior verbal ability, perhaps an outcome of having imitated preachers at home. His essays were generally excellent, and he enjoyed lead roles in school plays and musicals. Social adulation from academic achievement and starring roles sustained his sense of specialness.

It is noteworthy that he performed poorly in gym class. Not being particularly athletic, Jones simply refused to play sports. Phobic of appearing inadequate, his will to power required another route. Instead he played army with his friends, inevitably choosing the role of a beleaguered combat commander who vanquished enemies against incredible odds. During this imaginary play, Fred offered stirring speeches to his playmates, mustering them to charge into combat with him and kill imaginary enemies.

His growing charm empowered him to make friends easily. But he also lost friends quickly due to his inflexibility, his insistence on having his way, and his unwillingness to be vulnerable to others. He also gained a reputation for telling tall tales; he said he had helped his father invent a medical instrument that saved lives and earned his family a fortune. These fictions elevated his mood above the depression, trauma, and shame at his core.

A family friend observed that 12-year-old Fred would stand before the mirror wearing his mock military uniform, and pose by himself for long periods of time. He also read Superman comics avidly and enjoyed collecting the magazine that offered stories of the mundane, mild-mannered Clark Kent transforming into the Man of Steel.

High school and early college

At his father's insistence, Fred attended a high school sponsored by a consortium of Bible churches, which was also a feeder school for a strict Protestant fundamentalist college. Staff was drawn from among male seminarians and pastors associated with the fundamentalist churches.

In one of his unpublished memoirs, Fred wrote that the teachers saw him as a threat, especially in matters of religious doctrine. He read precociously and ecumenically and earned enemies among the staff by quoting passages from Church Fathers in class, literature with which his teachers were unfamiliar. To them he sounded "too Catholic" and culturally alien to be appropriate for their school.

But many of the students celebrated Fred for his ability to hold his own, challenging authority figures in matters of doctrine. To the chagrin of his instructors, this fueled Fred to advance more "Catholic" beliefs in his religion classes. Eventually there was a blowup between Fred and an instructor in which Fred and the instructor accused each other of apostasy and heresy. The students rallied around Fred while the administration supported the instructor.

To keep order, the administration suspended Fred and put him under investigation for insubordination. This deliberately isolated him from the rest of the student body. Students and faculty alike speculated that Fred might be expelled. Without support from other students, frightened for his future, and bedeviled by unredressed resentments toward the school leaders, Fred became depressed and tense. He wrote:

> Without the support of my friends, suffering mightily under accusatory interrogations with the hawk-nosed headmaster and his inquisitors, I began to feel bereft and numb. My appetite collapsed, and I became gaunt like the ascetics of the early Church. I was sure to be expelled, despised by men, and hopeless for a meaningful future. To myself I was as an insect. Nightmares plagued me, and I awoke screaming from images of winged giants descending from thrones to devour me.

Clearly, Fred's narcissistic defenses were collapsing. Depressed, unable to feel pleasure, or even to eat, his core shame born of maternal deprivation manifested in his image of himself as an insect. Paternal abuse caused core trauma, here manifested in hyperarousal and nightmares of malevolent authority figures.

Fred's memoir continued:

> In desperate fervor, I prayed that in my weary and heavy-laden state God would grant me rest. Then, to my amazement, all grace came upon me. In a flash the Great Commander seized me in soothing brilliance. Sorrow turned to joy, darkness to sight of inner light. So close was I held by Deity that I felt at one with the Source who loved me utterly. Nervousness vanished in the face of charismatic streams of divine energy. I understood myself to be of profound importance to the paradisiacal Father who set before me a providential path to advance His kingdom with powerful authority. My confidence completely returned. My sense of myself as unique among men caused me to exalt within my spirit. I told no one about the experience.

This mystical experience drove Fred's acute psychopathology into spontaneous remission. It was affirming, kind, and reparative. Nothing about the experience is bizarre or suggestive of a psychotic process. This brief unity with the divine radically rebalanced Fred's psyche. Mary Dunn (2013), professor of theological studies at St. Louis University, described "mystical union" as:

> an archaic desire for merger with an idealized other "who possesses wisdom, kindness, vast knowledge, unending strength and a capacity to soothe . . . and maintain emotional balance" . . . for the Christian mystic – as for the pathological narcissist – the quest for union with the divine . . . attests to an effort to maintain the wholeness of the self against the threat of its fragmentation.
>
> *p. 650*

Dunn (2013) further believed that spiritual encounters (like Fred's) offer the possibility of mystical re-parenting through God's divine omnipotence, a reparative balm to counter parental neglect. To the extent that Fred met divine empathy, his mother-wound – born of maternal neglect – would have been addressed toward repair, thereby ameliorating some of his depression and shame. To the extent that Fred met divine protection, his paternally inflicted trauma would have been repaired – the divine blessing breaking the curse of paternal abuse. But it was not to be.

Although the potential for repair and health was implicit in Fred's mystical experience, the encounter instead inflated his grandiosity. He saw himself as "unique among men" and felt superior, special, and entitled. A good spiritual advisor might have mentored the future Bishop to appreciate his encounter as a healing grace that facilitated a healthy narcissism (a self-valuation sufficient for effective functioning). But the paternal figures in Fred's world at the time reprised his traumatizing father. No safe authorities existed in his psychosocial universe. He had undergone a rare, beautiful encounter with the divine, but he missed its meaning and placed the experience in service to his narcissistic defenses.

From Protestant fundamentalist college to Reformed Catholic seminary

Following his mystical experience, school authorities solved the problem of their precocious student by graduating him early. He attended Calvin and Luther College, a Protestant fundamentalist school, where he majored in Religion and minored in English Literature. He joined the debate team and demonstrated a unique talent for making even the most ludicrous position viable. He excelled in his classes, demonstrating a grasp of every subject and expressing himself with a quick wit. A fellow alumnus described him as a "riveting monologist with opinions about everything. People loved being around him; he was so engaging. He never reached out; we all just came to him. I think he took it for granted."

In the course of his studies, Fred encountered Anglo-Catholic writers. He attended several services and became "hooked" on the liturgy and captivated by the pageantry, the solemn intonations, and the authoritative poetry of *The Book of Common Prayer*. He thrived on the Gothic context and soaring music. Most of all, he was drawn to the role of the priest. The priest wore the most resplendent vestment, read the most important texts, and officiated at the changing of bread and wine into the body and blood of the Savior of the world. Fred decided that he would seek ordained ministry.

When he graduated from the Protestant fundamentalist college, he flew to the United Kingdom and spent the summer reading Anglican and Roman Catholic works while exploring cathedrals and shrines. A dean's discretionary grant for an extraordinary student funded his transatlantic adventure.

When he returned to the United States to begin his studies at Reformed Catholic Seminary, he was more polished than ever. His pale blue eyes had the arresting knowingness of the mystic, and his Midwestern twang had given way to a slight but durable British accent. Not only did Fred change his voice, he legally changed his name to Frederick Ladysmith-Jones. Fred/Frederick morphed his persona from that of a poor Midwesterner from an alcoholic family into that of an Englishman with a pedigree and a future in a church that purported to defend the very soul of Christianity.

Divinity training

Classmates describe Frederick's seminary years with both envy and disgust. He gained notoriety as a brilliant, radically conservative theologian with no tolerance for ambiguity. Widely read and annoyingly confident, he gave no ground in theological debates. He backed his arguments with excellent points drawn from Scripture, tradition, and reason. One contemporary stated:

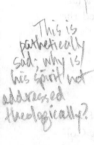
This is pathetically sad; why is his spirit not addressed theologically?

> Frederick spoke with amazing authority. He came off like some guy from *Downton Abbey* or the House of Lords. He dazzled people with brilliant linguistic skills while oozing a messianic sense of himself. Faculty and students gravitated to him; they felt they could be adjunct saviors with him. They gave him a lot of attention and in return he made them feel special and important. His grandiosity was infectious. It was in seminary that his charisma really heated up. The faculty fed into it, too. Frederick was easily their favorite student, and he received special treatment. The seminary dean, who went on to become Faith Cathedral's Bishop Augustini, began to groom Frederick for an important role in the Reformed Catholic Movement. What Augustini didn't get was that Frederick was grooming him, too. Augustini didn't see Frederick's lethal ambition and megalomania. All he saw was this brilliant high church guy who would be invaluable in the Reformed Catholic Movement and who would help win the culture war.

Interestingly, the seminary dean was psychologically minded. Prior to receiving Holy Orders, each seminarian endured a mandatory psychological examination. Dean Augustini consulted regularly with Dr. Roosevelt, the seminary psychologist, and generally followed the expert's recommendations.

Dr. Roosevelt administered a battery of standard psychological assessments to priest-candidate Ladysmith-Jones. On a well-respected test of character pathology, Ladysmith-Jones scored positive for narcissistic personality disorder and evidenced elevations on a scale of antisocial or criminal traits. Dr. Roosevelt also felt that Frederick suffered from a latent mood disorder (plus trauma and shame) that he defended against with pathological grandiosity.

When interviewed for this psychological autopsy, Dr. Roosevelt disclosed the following:

> Until I tested Ladysmith-Jones, Dean Augustini and I enjoyed an excellent working relationship. I figured that I'd just tell the dean that – while brilliant – Frederick shouldn't be a priest. He tested out with narcissistic personality disorder, and his clinical presentation supported that. His grandiosity was more pronounced than any I'd ever encountered. So, I compared the way he presented with the diagnostic criteria for narcissistic personality disorder in the *DSM-5*. He had fantasies about becoming a historically important church figure and saving the Western world from spiritual death. He disclosed that providence chose him during a high school mystical experience. Ladysmith-Jones presented himself as an exaggeratedly self-important young man, preoccupied with fantasies of unlimited success. He had a reputation for being interpersonally exploitive. He indicated that he could only be understood by others who were "also culturally and spiritually elite." He threw the words "high church" and "Anglo-Catholic" around a lot. He was obviously put off that I was not buying into his greatness and providing him with excessive admiration. He made some dismissive remarks about psychology not really being a science, and his sense of entitlement got under my skin. I lost my cool, which is rare for me.

Dr. Roosevelt informed Dean Augustini that Frederick's character pathology made him a poor priest candidate. He expressed his concerns that Frederick's spirituality was likely to involve de facto self-worship, that he had the personality of a cult leader, and that he had criminal tendencies. Dr. Roosevelt presciently predicted that Frederick presented a suicide risk if the "narcissistic supplies that keep his grandiosity charged up over his hidden depression were ever to be interrupted." Sadly, Augustini simply did not believe him. Dr. Roosevelt further observed:

> Augustini was childless, and I think he had deeply paternal feelings toward Ladysmith-Jones. But Jones fed on the old man's affection in service to his grandiosity, so his injured core went unrepaired. It was obvious that the protégé was not exactly introjecting Augustini's humane values into his unreceptive super-ego. FLJ's concealed egomania, combined with his immature conscience, was a leadership cancer waiting to spread. I knew it was just a matter of time, but Augustini just could not abide my determination about Fred's psychopathology. No father wants to hear that his son is a malignant narcissist. When Augustini told me he would put Ladysmith-Jones forward

for ordination, I flipped and went over Augustini's head to the Seminary Board. Ladysmith-Jones was an impaired professional in the making and an obviously bad choice for a church leader. He also represented a threat-in-the-making to the credibility of the Reformed Catholic Movement. Frederick had an ability to develop a theory of mind about any person who was useful to him. He lacked empathy, but he could read people. This made him a master manipulator. Despite my efforts, he convinced the Seminary Board that he was as pure as the driven snow. With that fake English accent, he piously announced that I was an apparently well-meaning psychologist, deleteriously enlisting the tools of so-called social science upon a population of holy people called to religious life. He asked the board if they valued the instruments of nasty secular humanism over the still, small voice that guides the hearts of men to become priests, etc., etc. The board got all worked up. They fired me, and Ladysmith-Jones went on to ordination.

Speaking in a tone of regret and bitterness, Dr. Roosevelt concluded, "I wish Augustini and the board had listened to me. Ladysmith-Jones went on to destroy Augustini, Faith Cathedral, and the faith of innocent people. Decision makers should heed the advice of their experts."

At Faith Cathedral with Augustini

Faith Cathedral was the jewel in the crown of the Reformed Catholic Movement. It boasted Gothic architecture, Anglo-Catholic worship, a huge endowment, a dedicated staff, and a host of ministries. Augustini, who left Reformed Catholic Seminary to lead this extraordinary place, administered all of this with his ambitious young protégé by his side. The venerable old man and his brilliant young spiritual scion must have impressed the distinguished parishioners. Parishioners tended to be wealthy and smart, and successful in either academic or business careers. For newly ordained Father Ladysmith-Jones, the grandeur and success of the institution reflected and affirmed his own specialness.

By tradition, Faith Cathedral was led by a Bishop. Thus, when Augustini came into leadership there, the Archbishop of London flew to the United States specifically to ordain Monsignor Augustini a Bishop. To the chagrin of senior priests, Father Frederick Ladysmith-Jones played a prominent role in the ceremonies. During the celebratory dinner, he sat on the left of the Archbishop of London and drew more time and attention from the Archbishop than Augustini, who sat on his right. During their animated conversation, Father Ladysmith-Jones learned of the Archbishop's grand plans for the Reformed Catholic Movement, as well as his worries about church finances in the United Kingdom and his personal struggles. Part of Ladysmith-Jones' success was his ability to make people and groups feel deeply understood, accepted, and safe. The Archbishop of London must have succumbed to that part of the young priest's character and over-confided in him. One professional described Ladysmith-Jones as possessing "psychopathic charm."

Once ordained, Bishop Augustini put his young priest forward on every front. Unwisely, Augustini appointed him Cathedral Chief of Staff and allowed him the role of diplomat in internal and external affairs. Frederick played a prominent role in all areas of church administration. Augustini trusted him implicitly. Frederick was condescending and impatient when interacting with administrative staff. But his interactions with vestrypersons, wardens, and wealthy donors were cordial, warm, interesting, and fun. One church administrator said:

> The second he arrived, he went on a charm offensive with the leaders and the wealthy people. He also made himself indispensable to Bishop Augustini, who was suited to the role of father figure and patriarch but definitely not CEO. It was kind of irresponsible to give such an inexperienced priest so much power so fast. Nobody knew if he could handle it. But we all learned quickly that scandal slid off of Father Ladysmith-Jones; we learned to put up with him and did what he said.

Charisma

For the next 12 years, the career of Frederick Ladysmith-Jones soared. Throughout the Reformed Catholic Movement, he became a household name. His sermons and opinions were all over the Internet. Even his detractors acknowledged that he was a brilliant theologian and speaker who inspired and persuaded when articulating the conservative orthodoxy of the movement. A delighted Bishop Augustini continued to dote on his now-famous priest. After all, Ladysmith-Jones perfectly espoused the important positions of the movement concerning the inerrancy of Scripture, male priesthood, moral theology, culture wars, and so forth. He had made several well-received television appearances that raised the profile and prestige of the Reformed Catholic Movement. One member of Faith Cathedral reflected:

> During the 12 years Ladysmith-Jones was on the ascent, he demonstrated the most astonishing charisma. He held us spellbound every time he spoke. His sermons and addresses were always greater than the sum of their parts. Hearing him preach changed the way we felt. He was like a drug to us. The more we adored him, the more he glowed. The more he glowed, the more we idolized him. At the time, the idea that he was an egomaniac and a criminal was inconceivable to us. He gave voice to everything we believed, and for that we adored him. He controlled our smiles and our tears. Now people say it's obvious that he was bad. But we saw him as representative of God Himself.

[handwritten margin note: They're all looking at him, not Christ]

Regarding the mass credentialing of such disturbed characters as Ladysmith-Jones, Burgo (2016) observed:

> Human beings apparently have an innate need for leaders or role models they can look up to and aspire to emulate. The Grandiose Narcissist who appears

to embody our ideals, often by manipulating his public persona, plays into that need by presenting himself as a hero, and by nature, we are easily seduced.

p. 37

From documentary and interview data, it is clear that a reciprocal relationship existed between Ladysmith-Jones' adoring coreligionists and his grandiosity. His radiating rightness and messianic self-confidence were cause for his culturally beleaguered followers to shower him with ever more adoration – which fueled the fires of his sense of election and infallibility. Volkan (2004) affirmed,

> It is generally when a large group's identity is threatened and when the group is regressed that the "fit" between a community and an individual with exaggerated self-love is likely to be the strongest: the leader's belief in his or her own omnipotence . . . creates comfort for followers in search of a savior.
>
> *p. 193*

Integral to understanding Ladysmith-Jones' success is the profundity of spiritual experience that some of his followers experienced. Occasionally during his ritualistic healing services, followers experienced streaming energy that correlated with psychosomatic relief. They attributed this relief to a divine force flowing through to Ladysmith-Jones, and they complimented their minister's specialness all the more. Ladysmith-Jones absorbed these narcissistic supplies into his ever-increasing grandiosity. A Jesuit acquainted with this element of his ministry explained:

> Ladysmith-Jones possessed something uncanny in terms of his person and ministry. . . . His moving healing rituals combined elements of Roman Catholic and Anglican healing liturgies, which he celebrated incanting soaring liturgical poetry accompanied by stirring music. People loved it. As a celebrant, the man was a rock star . . . so it's not surprising that suggestible people benefitted. . . . He choreographed these events with himself as the amazing central figure who eventually anointed supplicants with oil while dramatically droning ancient prayers of healing. Don't get me wrong, I know that God can work through a broken vessel. And I definitely believe in the legitimacy of healing. But I'm sensitive to the fact that cult leaders can engender healing experiences that mimic genuine charismatic healing. After Ladysmith-Jones fell from grace, I reread *Feet of Clay* by Anthony Storr (1996). The chapter on Jim Jones made it clear that a self-obsessed cult leader, who is undoubtedly headed for destruction, can inaugurate electrical sensations in followers that are construed as divine transmissions from the cult leader to the people. It's documented.

This same interviewee remarked that Ladysmith-Jones seemed to encourage dependence among his followers, a phenomenon not uncommon to cult leaders (see Chapter 4).

The dark side

Ladysmith-Jones espoused a "perfect" theology that eloquently identified enemies of the "good." Reviewing his writings, sermons, and YouTube videos, we see how he used embodied evils – critics of the Reformed Catholic Movement, Muslims, immigrants, billionaires, women, homosexuals, the media, pornographers, the lazy poor, secular globalists, theological revisionists – to explain the anxiety and unhappiness of so many of his followers. Finnish Jungian analyst Harri Virtanen (2013) explained the function scapegoating plays in the psychology of narcissistic defenses:

> Certain kinds of personality structures may be supported by ideologies that seem to cure the narcissistic wound. An extreme ideology coupled with low self-esteem may cause inflation of the ego. Ideology is the answer to the narcissistically wounded ego – the pain, frustration, fury and hatred find an explanation and reason. And, most importantly, ideology helps the wounded ego to find an enemy. Extreme ideology is what fills their existential vacuum and provides some sense of meaning and purpose.
>
> *p. 672*

Volkan (2004) added that narcissistic extremism has properties created by the pathological leader's defenses:

> It can be recognized in the hatred of uncertainty; the revulsion against anything imperfect, impure, or bodily; the rage and violent retaliation against perceived attack, unbearable humiliation and shame; destructive envy and the arrogant disregard for humble limits . . . the evasion of vulnerability; the presence of self-deception and the denial of the harm that one has done to others; the moral condemnation for those who do not share the same beliefs; and ultimately in the negation of love.
>
> *p. 160*

As Ladysmith-Jones' followers learned whom he despised, they understood whom God must despise. The minister's sermons and fireside chats implied the message that God had elected Ladysmith-Jones and his followers to live out divinely revealed truth and to flourish in pure metaphysical certainty. Those outside Reformed Catholic belief were an existential threat to the people of God, a threat to the pure and the good, and to truth itself as expressed through Ladysmith-Jones and, thus, his followers. But God would not allow His elected to be destroyed by evildoers. Ultimately, all threats would have to be destroyed. With gratuitous punishments, God would obliterate them in this life *and* the next. This was divinely ensured and supported by reasonable theology. The God of Reformed Catholicism would roast the impure in endless, ever-burning infernos, while the elect would enjoy protection, prosperity, and divine congratulations.

Analysis of Father Ladysmith-Jones' rhetoric heightens our understanding of the malignancy of his narcissism, and at the same time accounts for the tenure of his success as a social phenomenon. He evacuated his core sense of inadequacy with projective defenses. Once he identified the object of his projections, he feared their return in terms of some kind of attack that would injure the perfection embedded in his grandiose self-fantasy. To the extent that he experienced anxiety, it was paranoid anxiety. He conflated internal threats to his psychic balance with external enemies. To quell the fear that he would be devoured by externalized enemies that bore his projected inferiorities, he cultivated sadistic fantasies of gratuitous torment for them, the plausibility of which he upheld through theological rationalizations and apocalyptic imagery. The public adulation he received strengthened these grotesque psychodynamics, and their ongoing operation amplified his grandiosity, his projective identification, and his sadistic scapegoating across a large cross-section of the Reformed Catholic Movement.

A disillusioned follower of Ladysmith-Jones, Daniel Dickenson, who later became director of the Shaker Committee for Human Rights, inveighed:

> Initially Ladysmith-Jones organized our upset and disappointment in terms of an orthodox Christian worldview. We believed in him and his message. He told us we were the light of the world, and he pointed to where the spiritual, cultural, and economic darkness resided. He gave hope to those of us who felt betrayed by our institutions. But, ultimately, he was toxic. His message contained far too much in-group flattery and a mean message to hate the out-groups. Plus, his enemies consisted of a lot of terribly vulnerable populations that would have benefitted more from ministry than vilification. When I watched a documentary on European dictatorships of the '30s and '40s, I realized that Ladysmith-Jones was cut from the same cloth, so I left. Demagoguery and fascist psychology have no place in a Christian movement. Somehow, I knew the guy was an impaired professional, and a tyrant, and that he would, sooner or later, fall apart.

Dickenson's intuition was prescient. Ladysmith-Jones' career indicates that the narcissistic accolades he received from his followers swelled his grandiosity to the point where he believed he was incapable of making mistakes. At that juncture, the criminal element of his character may have begun to express itself. Regarding what she calls the "tyrant," Professor Betty Glad (2002) wrote, "The tyrant [easily recognized as a malignant narcissist in leadership] is one who exercises powers for his own rather than the general interest." She explained that although his persuasive traits provide initial advantages when gaining power, other elements of his personality (criminality and lust for absolute power) are his downfall (Glad, 2002, pp. 1–2). Then she added:

> For those [leaders] with the malignant narcissistic disorders noted above, the achievement of absolute power can act as a kind of narcotic. As Volkan has

noted, the narcissistic leader in certain historical circumstances may be able to structure an external world that supports his grandiose claims. Unlike the ordinary narcissist who experiences repeated frustration of his grandiose claims in a world he does not control, the tyrant can minimize his frustrations and thus the experiences that can lead to depression. In short, he can construct a world that provides him with temporary relief from his internal conflicts. But . . . this structuring has long-term consequences that are apt to prove detrimental to his psychic balance.

Glad, 2002, p. 25

This was certainly the case with Frederick Ladysmith-Jones.

Criminality

After 12 years of remarkable success, and while at the pinnacle of his career and influence, Frederick Ladysmith-Jones began his sad and destructive days of over-reach. A Cathedral bookkeeper with whom he was having an affair commented one day that despite Ladysmith-Jones' celebrity and ability to raise vast monies for the movement, he had not received any advancement in his ecclesial rank. Further, she continued, the benign Bishop Augustini laid claim to the bishopric, while Ladysmith-Jones, the de facto leader, was without a prestigious title. Her point pierced the priest between the eyes.

For some time, Ladysmith-Jones had worked to consolidate power both within the Cathedral administration and in the worldwide Reformed Catholic Movement. For years he had quietly purged influential board members who objected to his heavy-handed control of Cathedral administration. Eyewitnesses describe his leadership style as increasingly tyrannical and intolerant of power sharing.

Felix Benjamin, Esq., the former Faith Cathedral Chancellor and chief legal advisor, describes his tenure under Bishop Augustini and Father Ladysmith-Jones:

> When Augustini was ordained bishop, he called and asked me to be his Chancellor. As a religious and cultural conservative, I jumped at the chance to contribute to the Reformed Catholic Movement. For me it was a vocation. But I became increasingly frustrated with Augustini's shirking of meaningful leadership. He kept shrugging things off to this very young, cocky priest who operated almost independently of supervision. At first, I tried to make the best of it. But then, I had to speak up, because genuine matters of law were involved. Ladysmith-Jones was impulsive and impatient with the checks and balances of Cathedral administration. Like any large institution with a not-for-profit-status, the Cathedral administration and the Board of Directors have to abide by procedures that are determined both by bylaws and by state and federal law. Departure from those statute-determined procedures opens the institution to lawsuits. For instance, when a donor tithes big money to Faith Cathedral, he has the right to specify what the donation will be used

for, such as missions. Once we get a donor-specified gift, we can't divert the funds, say, to buy the popular priest-in-charge a better car, or remodel his residence, or increase his discretionary budgets. But that is exactly what Ladysmith-Jones did. He trampled all over due process as it pertained to authorizing his access to money. He was having an affair with the cathedral bookkeeper, and she set up all kinds of "discretionary funds," the monies of which had been diverted from the board-approved budget and donor directives. He would also hustle extremely large sums from philanthropists for an expressed purpose, like the Cathedral school, which he promised to name after them; then, he would spend it for another purpose, like hiring a minor army of IT workers to promote him all over the Internet or produce his videos. It was unethical and illegal. When I alerted Augustini and the board, I thought they would sack him. Little did I suspect that I myself would lose my job and my reputation.

Documents reveal that Ladysmith-Jones paid IT workers to decimate Mr. Benjamin's reputation on social media. Using fraudulent identities, the IT workers spread allegations on LinkedIn and Facebook that Benjamin was under investigation by the State Bar Association. They mentioned felonies and misconduct. Then links to the slanderous and libelous allegations were sent to Bishop Augustini and the board. Alarmed that the Cathedral Chancellor faced imminent indictment, Augustini asked the board to dismiss Mr. Benjamin. They readily complied, and Ladysmith-Jones had purged the one person in Cathedral governance who might have checked his larcenous overreach.

He continued using social media to injure his enemies both within and without the Cathedral. Sadly, his benefactor and boss, Augustini, was to fall victim to this criminality too. Sally Lightfoot Tipton, a former Cathedral administrator, recalls:

> Father Frederick had just received a huge check for a Christian Education Building from Grover Vancouver, chair of the Vancouver Custard Foundation, when several panicked board members entered his office. They were upset and asking for advice. They said they saw a post from a mother with a baby – they did not recognize her name – who was appalled to see Bishop Augustini in the Cathedral garden acting strange and confused and exposing himself. They had also received emails from several parties indicating concern that the Bishop was demented. Father Frederick affirmed that he had been covering up for Bishop Augustini out of loyalty, but now, because the old man's impairment was so obviously advanced . . . he had to take action. I don't know what happened, but the Bishop just went away – it happened fast – and Father Frederick was acting head of the Cathedral.

After Ladysmith-Jones' suicide, investigators learned that the priest had placed a stack of official papers before the Bishop for signatures. Augustini, who eschewed the work of CEO, signed the documents perfunctorily and thanked his protégé for his excellent administrative work. Unbeknown to the Bishop, he had effectively signed his powers of Cathedral governance over to Ladysmith-Jones – and had legally granted the priest power of attorney in all his financial and medical affairs. A lead police investigator remarked:

> There were illegalities in numerous ways. Augustini had been tricked into signing documents that caused him to lose his job but also his liberty and civil rights. Once Ladysmith-Jones had power of attorney, he retired Augustini to a monastery affiliated with Faith Cathedral, where he kept the old man imprisoned and drugged. Every week a nervous looking neurologist – a man blackmailed by Ladysmith-Jones with information about illegal drug use gleaned from a sacramental confession – would come, inject the patient with a mind-numbing drug, and write bogus notes about the Bishop's dementia. Finally, a nun trained in nursing transferred to the monastery and recognized that Augustini had medically induced delirium, not dementia. She alerted the authorities. We investigated and sorted it all out, but it was too late. Augustini's mind was chemically wrecked, and Ladysmith-Jones had committed his crimes. Ladysmith-Jones was the bad actor, but Augustini does not get a pass. He was asleep at the switch.

Ladysmith-Jones' trespass against Bishop Augustini came to light later, but at the time of Augustini's loss of power, the priest lost no time pursuing more power and rank. He arranged to purchase an ordination as bishop.

Seized email correspondence between Ladysmith-Jones and the Reformed Catholic Archbishop of London reveal that Ladysmith-Jones diverted $600,000 from the Vancouver Custard donation to the London Bishop's UK foundation. Correspondence further shows that the London Archbishop was also "tithed" $100,000 for his personal "discretionary fund." It is believed that the Archbishop of London was all too happy to sell the rank of bishop to Ladysmith-Jones. Poor financial management of his UK foundation combined with a variety of expensive personal problems made him Ladysmith-Jones' willing confederate.

The fall

Ladysmith-Jones's ordination celebration took place at Faith Cathedral. The event was impressively luxurious and expensive. Important media outlets covered the event, and Ladysmith-Jones' IT department used the event to plaster social media with positive propaganda for their master. On the outside, the moment appeared as another predictable triumph for the Teflon prophet of Reformed Catholicism. But events began to unravel the minister's momentum.

Just prior to Ladysmith-Jones' ordination, Felix Benjamin, Esq., filed suit against Ladysmith-Jones, Faith Cathedral, and board members for defamation and numerous damages that all but wrecked his reputation and legal career. The suit was all the more alarming in that Mr. Benjamin's own attorney was the former Provost of an Ivy League law school, and was reputed for his relentless aggression in matters of civil litigation. During this period, several members of Ladysmith-Jones' IT department defected Faith Cathedral as a matter of conscience. They had come to regret their complicity in the destruction of so many reputations and livelihoods on behalf of their boss's ambition. As part of discovery, they provided Benjamin's legal team with damaging depositions as well as evidence on flash drives and damning memoranda. Bishop Ladysmith-Jones dismissed the veracity of the evidence and, with fanfare and bravado, promised to submit to a deposition.

Coevally, Daniel Dickenson published a critique of the Reformed Catholic Movement in the popular Shaker Committee Human Rights' blog. Calling for a different approach to the solving of the problems of postmodern Christendom, he chastised Ladysmith-Jones for teaching against Christian baptismal vows:

> Bishop Ladysmith-Jones fails to call for "serving Christ in all persons and loving one's neighbor as oneself." His scapegoating theology does not "strive for justice and peace among all people" and it fails to "respect the dignity of every human being" (Episcopal Church, 1979, p. 304). To the contrary, to the extent that he calls us to despise our neighbor but love ourselves, he calls us to participate in the life and doctrine of Antichrist. The Bishop's doctrine is uncharitable and is therefore unsupported by the Gospels into which we were baptized.

Dickenson's post went viral and as an avalanche of similar critiques followed, tithing at Faith Cathedral went into free fall.

Next, attorneys representing the incensed Vancouver Custard Foundation sent threatening inquiries. Grover Vancouver wanted an accounting for the small fortune his fund donated for the explicit purpose of building a Christian Education Building on Faith Cathedral's campus. A disillusioned insider had tipped off the philanthropist that the donated monies were spent on Ladysmith-Jones' phony ordination and his team of expensive lawyers.

Then concerns about the handling of the Augustini matter broke. Federal and state authorities opened an investigation and Ladysmith-Jones was a person of interest facing serious charges. Bishop Ladysmith-Jones hired another team of the best and most expensive attorneys. To pay their fees, he raided Faith Cathedral's endowment fund without board authorization.

In the midst of this fury of changing fortunes, the Bishop had a falling out with Margot Van Buren, his longtime bookkeeper and with whom he had been having an affair. When she learned her hero had become dissatisfied with her recent weight gain and had spent a weekend "spiritually advising" a young triathlete from a Seven Sisters college, Ms. Van Buren grabbed her laptop and marched into the state Attorney General's Office. For immunity, she turned state's witness. She also gave several damning interviews to Dan Truth, an important religion journalist who followed Ladysmith-Jones and the Reformed Catholic Movement. The interviews depicted

Ladysmith-Jones as a deluded con man and a fraud. Of Bishop Ladysmith-Jones' reaction, a Faith Cathedral intern said the following:

> When Ms. Van Buren gave her interview, the Bishop lost it. Against the advice of everyone, he went on TV and excommunicated her. It was so bizarre that the media coverage proliferated into a circus. Story after story about his crimes came out. The Bishop could not manage the damage to his office and ministry. I think he turned to heavy drinking, which only fueled his erratic behavior. In his public rants, he accused lots of people of disloyalty and heresy and anti-Christian conspiracies. He insisted God would get them. And he kept proclaiming that he represented the authentic soul of the Western world. He looked desperate and silly, declaring holy war against – well – everybody while insisting on his virtue and importance.

This observation of the Bishop's behavior under duress is consistent with an unhealthy narcissistic coping style under pressure. In a study of narcissism and the use of fantasy, Robert Raskin and Jill Novacek (1991) found:

> Narcissists cope with stressful experiences by imagining themselves in more ideal situations. In particular, narcissistic persons who are experiencing higher levels of daily stress tend to experience (1) power and revenge fantasies in which they see themselves in a powerful position able to impose punishment on those who have wronged them, and (2) self-admiration fantasies in which they imagine themselves and others admiring their fine qualities of competence, consideration, wisdom, greatness and attractiveness.
>
> *p. 496*

Bishop Ladysmith-Jones was suddenly in immense trouble. His public airing of revenge and self-admiration fantasies demonstrated aggravated paranoia and his weakened grasp on reality. His attorneys advised him to keep a low profile and adhere to sensible legal strategies. Heated arguments ensued and the Bishop fired several excellent, incredulous teams of top legal advisors. One attorney put it this way:

> Whenever we discussed with the Bishop the realities of his legal disadvantages, he either embarked on violent declamations that devolved into rambling non sequiturs, or he accused us of not being for him, arguing we were against him. Eventually he fired us, which was remarkably stupid, because we're among the profession's best, and we really could have helped him – not to escape reality, which he apparently wanted – but to cut a very good deal with the prosecution.

Two events precipitated Bishop Ladysmith-Jones' suicide. First, he rushed unprepared to a deposition with the attorneys working on behalf of Mr. Benjamin's civil suit. Meticulously prepared, the plaintiff's side asked questions to which they already knew answers. Besides appearing arrogant and hung over, the Bishop answered several questions in such manner that his perjury was obvious. Second, the religion journalist Dan Truth invited Bishop Ladysmith-Jones to participate in an interview to rebut the interview given by his estranged, excommunicated lover. Ladysmith-Jones made the mistake of allowing Mr. Truth to film the interview. Once released, the video revealed an exhausted, furious man incapable of providing clear answers to reasonable questions. Dan Truth said:

> I gave him ample opportunity to clear himself. Why wasn't he a hatemonger? Was he having an extramarital affair? Was he a serial cyber stalker? Where did the Custard donation go? What really occurred in the Augustini matter? Was it false that he purchased his Bishop's ordination from the Archbishop of London? If there were reasonable explanations, Bishop Ladysmith-Jones did not provide them. He ranted, alluded to enemies, and showed lots of anger. Then he referred to himself as the Reformed Catholic Prophet to the Sacramental Communions of Christendom. That was quite a big title for a very naughty boy to give himself. Ladysmith-Jones was a cartoon. My readers laughed him off the web.

Bishop Ladysmith-Jones left the interview, returned to his rectory, adorned himself with his vestments, prepared documents, drank communion wine, and shot himself in the head. Authorities reported that Ladysmith-Jones described himself as a martyr "who died for an unutterably beautiful vision of what the world could be" in his final epistle.

It is a matter of psychoanalytic wisdom that the trapped MN will use suicide in service to his grandiosity. Goldner-Vukov and Moore (2010) explained that narcissists use suicide as a mechanism to control their own fate while twisting it into a type of victory (p. 394). The psychodynamic logic of suicide resides in the MNL's antipathy of accountability, which is tied to a wild dread of prestige loss. Death before dishonor becomes the guiding cognition, even if dishonor serves a truly corrective function. Philippe Cotter (2009) wrote:

> The powerful dynamics of cognitive and paranoid degeneration the ... [malignant narcissist] ... is caught up in is proof that the ... [defenses] ... he resorts to are inadequate. ... [His defiant attitude] ... is, in the end, always defeated by the forces he himself has unleashed. Martin Luther King once wrote that "evil contains the seed of its own destruction."

On a final forensic note, blood spatter evidence on an open comic book in the rectory study indicates that Ladysmith-Jones was, strangely, reading from a section of a Superman comic at some point prior to his suicide.

Final notes on the psychological autopsy

An excerpt of a recent study of the dimensionality of narcissism could begin the obituary of Bishop Ladysmith-Jones. Back et al. (2013) found that the narcissist brings to the world a host of tendencies which:

> involve a grandiose view of the self, a strong sense of entitlement and superi-
> ority, a lack of empathy, and a need for social admiration, as well as tendencies
> to show dominant, charming, bragging, impulsive, and aggressive behav-
> iors. . . . [R]esearch has revealed a complex mix of . . . [narcissistic features] . . .
> including traits such as extraversion, self-esteem, need for power, and domi-
> nance, but also disagreeableness, aggressiveness, low need for intimacy, and
> hostility. . . . With regard to interpersonal behaviors, narcissism is related to
> charming, self-assured, and humorous behaviors . . . but also to selfish, hostile,
> and arrogant behaviors. . . . Narcissism is related to popularity . . . and leader-
> ship and celebrity status. . . . It is, however, also related to negative evaluations
> in long-term acquaintance . . . and conflict in romantic relationships.
>
> *p. 1014*

The late Bishop Ladysmith-Jones was all of the things that these researchers say about narcissism, while his leadership status, combined with his criminality, morphed him into malignancy. He demonstrated the bio-psycho-social-spiritual problems that narcissists inflict upon their relationships. What separated him from manifesting merely annoying narcissism, or discrete NPD, was his malignancy. Overwhelming evidence shows that his personality contained criminal, sadistic, and finally paranoid features. His tenure as a prominent minister, then bishop, in the Reformed Catholic Movement destroyed careers, reputations, tithing, institutional credibility, relationships, and faith.

That police, social workers, and pastoral counselors did not rescue him from the paternal abuse and maternal neglect of his childhood is sad. His childhood required defenses for his psychological and perhaps even physical survival. His unconscious impulses formed narcissistic defenses, using his latent social skills and brilliance toward disarming charisma, and led to a socially compelling grandiosity. That his seminary mentors and Cathedral bosses did not address his identifiable and escalat-ing psychopathology is a tragedy not easily measured. Bishop Frederick Ladysmith-Jones is easily identifiable as an MN and a criminal. However, perhaps those who might have interrupted the formation of his destructive character, his entrance into ministry, and his freewheeling ways as a pastor, share culpability for his pestilential leadership and his grandiose suicide (see Chapters 2 and 4 for further detail).

Conclusion

Malignant narcissism is an extreme character pathology that may afflict clerical leaders in addition to other types of leaders. The pathology is defined by core narcissism, criminality, sadism, and paranoia. The trajectory of this madness involves initial success, grandiosity, overreach, decline, and possible suicide. Durably successful leaders with this issue will closet their narcissism and not engage in overreach. This phenomenon can no longer go unaddressed.

Note

1 As noted earlier, this is a fictional biography. Undocumented quotations are composite material. All names of persons and organizations are fictitious.

References

American Psychiatric Association. (2015). *Diagnostic and statistical manual of mental disorders* (5th ed.). Arlington, VA: American Psychiatric Publishing.

Back, M. D., Küfner, A. C., Dufner, M., Gerlach, T. M., Rauthmann, J. F., & Denissen, J. J. (2013). Narcissistic admiration and rivalry: Disentangling the bright and dark sides of narcissism. *Journal of Personality and Social Psychology, 103*(6), 1013–1037. doi:10.1037/a0034431

Burgo, J. (2016). *The narcissist you know: Defending yourself against extreme narcissists in an all-about-me age.* New York, NY: Touchstone Books.

Cotter, P. (2009). The path to extreme violence: Nazism and serial killers. *Frontiers in Behavioral Neuroscience, 2010*(3), 61. doi:10.3389/neuro.08.061.2009

Dunn, M. (2013). Mysticism, motherhood, and pathological narcissism? A Kohutian analysis of Marie de l'Incarnation. *Journal of Religion and Health, 52*(2), 642–656.

Episcopal Church. (1979). *The book of common prayer and administration of the sacraments and other rites and ceremonies of the church together with the psalter or psalms of David according to the use of the Episcopal Church.* New York, NY: Church Publishing.

Fromm, E. (2010). *The heart of man: Its genius for good and evil.* Riverdale, NY: American Mental Health Foundation. (Original work published 1964)

Glad, B. (2002). Why tyrants go too far: Malignant narcissism and absolute power. *Political Psychology, 23*(1), 1–37.

Goldner-Vukov, M., & Moore, L. J. (2010). Malignant narcissism: From fairy tales to harsh reality. *Psychiatria Danubina, 22*(3), 392–405.

Kernberg, O. F. (1970). Factors in the psychoanalytic treatment of narcissistic personalities. *Journal of the American Psychoanalytic Association, 18*(1), 51–85. doi:10.1177/000306517001800103

Pollock, G. H. (1978). Process and affect: Mourning and grief. *International Journal of Psycho-Analysis, 59*(2–3), 255–276.

Raskin, R., & Novacek, J. (1991). Narcissism and the use of fantasy. *Journal of Clinical Psychology, 47*(4), 490–499.

Steiner, J. (Ed.). (2008). *Rosenfeld in retrospect: Essays on his clinical influence.* London: Routledge.

Storr, A. (1996). *Feet of clay: Saints, sinners, and madmen: A study of gurus.* New York, NY: Free Press.

Vaknin, S. (2016, November 2). Narcissistic and psychopathic leaders (article online). *Healthy place.* Retrieved from www.healthyplace.com/personality-disorders/malignant-self-love/narcissistic-leaders/

Virtanen, H. (2013). The king of Norway: Negative individuation, the hero myth and psychopathic narcissism in extreme violence and the life of Anders Behring Breivik. *Journal of Analytical Psychology, 58*(5), 657–676.

Volkan, V. (2004). *Blind trust: Large groups and their leaders in times of crisis and terror.* Charlottesville, VA: Pitchstone Publishing.

2

ASSESSMENT OF THE MALIGNANT NARCISSIST LEADER

Clinical features, selected psychodynamic epidemiological items, and interdisciplinary observations

Whatever the configuration of abuse, neglect, and role modeling, the malignant narcissist leader (MNL) will reach maturity with pernicious assumptions about themselves, the world, and others; these assumptions will be charged with high voltage libido and portend poorly for the people and projects the leader will touch. Stakeholders may never fully appreciate that so much of the leader's "genius" grew from a trauma-driven attempt to become his own savior, an avenging god, and/or a prophet leading his followers to the Promised Land.

In the main, however, it is the learning history that is predicted to be developmentally deforming. From infancy to young adulthood, traumatic stimulation will derange physical, sexual, intellectual, and relational functioning. Affective intensity, replete with hatred, will conjure denial, splitting, projection, and dissociative defenses. Traumatic relations will set forth a relational style of unbearable loneliness combined with a pitiful ambivalence toward intimacy. Storms of despair and rage will occur that derail an often-formidable intelligence.

Psychobiographers will find that the MNL defends against the torments of tender years by compensation and reaction formation. In cases where malignant leadership has a dynastic quality, such as North Korea, the tyrant father simply role models MNL behavior, and his heir fits to the tyrant-template upon assuming power. In other cases, the etiology may be idiopathic or mystifying, or offer an uncanny quality.

Mercifully, not all malignant narcissists become leaders. Some aspire to leadership but fail. Some career through life loveless, furious, and impotent. Others live out their spiritual megalomania[1] via the predations of serial killing and sadism. Some intrigue for position, miscalculate, and go to prison – not the intended C-suite or bishop's palace. A frustrated aspirant may burn out from drugs or write an unreadable manifesto prior to suicide. And, in some instances, MNLs are circumvented from obtaining leadership. It is important to equip assessors with adequate screening tools and the insight to see past the charisma to the destruction a malignant narcissist in power portends.

Malignant narcissism in a leader: broad assessment and analytic recommendations

Due to the demonstrated destructive nature of the MNL, we contend that formalizing the diagnosis would represent an advance psychopathology, one with preventative and therapeutic implications for society. Community samples demonstrate that the prevalence of narcissistic personality disorder may be as high as 6.2 percent DSM-5 (APA, 2013), and given NPD's significant comorbidity with antisocial personality disorder and other personality disorders, and given the tendency for sociopathic narcissists to gravitate to positions of power, the notion that the construct validity of MNL might be statistically established is more than within grasp and will illuminate a variety of institutional failures and health threats. Formal recognition of MNL would not only represent an advance for psychopathology but also improve the effectiveness of leadership analysis, police forensics, political science, psychohistory, and like specialties.

Criteria

A *Destructive leader:* a person of interest, who may hold himself in high regard, shall qualify for the term destructive leader if he

   1 Holds a leadership position, or aspires to one, and
   2 According to information and belief or other evidence, has or may inflict injury on persons or groups, or violate relevant norms, or offend against human dignity.

B *Malignant narcissist leader:* a person of interest, already qualified for the term destructive leader (DL), shall qualify for the term malignant narcissist leader (MNL)[2] if he evinces, according to information and belief or other evidence,

   1 A narcissistic personality disorder, characterized by grandiosity, and specific signs and symptoms recommended by diagnostic manuals, or relevant criteria, and
   2 Antisocial behavior, delimited by such terms as psychopathy, sociopathy, criminality, or specific signs and symptoms recommended by diagnostic manuals.

C *Kernbergian Quaternity:* a person of interest, who qualified for the term malignant narcissist leader (MNL), shall qualify for the term Kernbergian Quaternity Positive (KQ+) if he evinces, according to information and belief or other evidence, the additional items of

   1 Ego-syntonic sadism, characterized by pleasure, gratification, or elation derived from the infliction of pain on an object(s) consonant with the subject's ideals and self-concept, and

2   A paranoid outlook, characterized by unwarranted suspicion that malevo-
    lent objects intend to harm the subject via plots, exploitation, untrustwor-
    thiness, attacks, or betrayals.

Qualifying criteria: if the individual is an MNL with an added feature of the Kernbergian Quaternity, consider specifying this as MNL, with ego-syntonic sadism,
or MNL, with paranoia. If the MNL is likely positive for ego-syntonic sadism and
paranoia, but has not fully assessed, consider specifying as MNL, unspecified.

Diagnostic features of the malignant narcissist in leadership

The malignant narcissist leader (MNL) diagnosis pertains to a destructive character
style distinguished by narcissistic personality disorder, criminality, ego syntonic sadism, and a paranoid disposition. Malignant narcissism (MN) involves a persistent
pattern of grandiosity, a need for narcissistic supplies, and clear demonstrations of
self-aggrandizement.

Individuals will identify with an ultimate value like a god, a principle, the nation,
a historical force, an economic theory, a political ideal, an ideology, and so forth.
Embodying an ultimate ideal is part of MN and represents a reaction formation
against shame and worthlessness. It is also a form of self-justification. Egomania and
megalomania indicate narcissism.

Criminality is also a criterion. Relevant features include crime, fraud, lying,
theft, false imprisonment, betrayal, dismantling polity, procedure violations, creation
of unjust laws, impingement upon human dignity, and human rights violations.
Measurements of Machiavellianism fall into this category. Criminality may appear
merely sociopathic, but psychodynamically the criminal behavior is in service to a
"great mission" that guides the individual's acts. Criminality may be thus narcissistically, rather than instrumentally, motivated.

Ego-syntonic sadism (non-conflictual cruelty) is requisite to MNL. This entails
enjoying the suffering of others, often identified as enemies of the MNL's great mission. As a trait, sadism occurs in conjunction with narcissism, sociopathy, and paranoia. For the MNL, sadism redresses the Caine-like envy felt for an Abel, warrants
utilitarian torture of political threats minus moral considerations, and neutralizes
perceived critics of MNL power or position. Sadism also provides a victim-object
whose torment represents the happy expiation of the MNL's inadequacies, self-
doubt, and ubiquitous hatreds.

Last, paranoia accounts for the individual's suspicion of political enemies, groups,
or persons viewed to detract from the ideal with which the individual conflates his
identity. Paranoia leads to enemy identification, which enables the MN to bond
with the group in shared scapegoating. This malignant psychodynamic evacuates conflictual material from individual and group psychological processes and
advances group cohesion at the expense of an out-group.

An MNL meets some or all of these criteria. Leaders that may be MNL, but cannot be fully assessed, are termed destructive leaders (DL), whereas leaders with narcissistic character disorder, combined with criminality, are designated MNLs. MNLs that fill all four items (i.e., narcissism, criminality, ego syntonic sadism, and paranoia) are designated Kernbergian Quaternity Positive (KQ+). Specifiers for MNL that fail to qualify as KQ+ are designated as follows: MNL with ego-syntonic sadism, MNL with paranoia, or MNL, unspecified.

Non-exhaustive list of overlapping constructs relevant to assessment

Investigators might reference this list of overlapping constructs to hone their assessment of a person of interest who qualifies for the terms DL, MNL, or KQ+ and who may evince additional features of disturbance, including but not limited to:

Grandiosity in combination with aggression
Egomania
Ego inflation
Megalomania
Loyalty to ideological supporters
Invented worldview
Idealization of destructive facets of the self
Destruction or rejection of love for superiority maintenance
Inability to negotiate or compromise for superiority maintenance
Manipulative object relations
Uncanniness
Oratory giftedness
Charisma
Criminality in service to the ego

Etiology

Genetic for individuals who become MNL

Relevant etiological childhood factors include a traumatic learning history, disorganized attachment, orphan psychology, neglect, abuse, paternal/maternal violence, paternal/maternal neglect, pernicious role modeling, or disruption to Eriksonian stage negotiation. Shengold (1989), Miller (1980), and Masterson (1981) explicate early etiological factors via concepts of soul murder, child abuse, and abandonment depression (rage) in relation to caregiver object relations. Environmental violence is likely to bring genetic predispositions to expression.

Role modeling and generational transmission play a causal role in MNL development, especially in dynastic malignancies. Acquired MNL may emerge as an especially virulent form of Lord Owens's (2008) hubris syndrome (e.g., a narcissistic predisposition, combined with prolonged leadership, sycophancy, and other factors).

Genetic for individuals and groups dominated by MNL

Transitions or chaos in the life of an individual, organization, or society provides opportunities for the MNL to gain control and metastasize pernicious elements of their malignant narcissism to the greater society. Vulnerable individuals include idealists, reactionaries, and pilgrims, as well as the economically motivated, and persons in search of a savior. Groups seeking social stability combined with a tradition (authoritarians) anxious to regress to a norm, groups frustrated from lack of social progress (revolutionaries) anxious to transcend to the next level, or groups otherwise imperiled may succumb to MNL influence.

> Intelligent and manipulative people form with a predisposition to develop psychopathic traits and other features of malignant narcissism, as well as the ruthlessness to eliminate their competition on their way to the top, not only take advantage of chaotic political and social situations, they view them as opportunities. . . . Stalin was one of the most successful tyrants in the twentieth century and a prime example of someone capable of exploiting such opportunities.
>
> *Haycock, 2019, p. 84*

Associated features supporting MNL determination

Ideation

Leaders assessed with an MNL diagnosis demonstrate ideation supportive of the principal malignant traits. Ideation supportive of narcissistic traits include unconscious, preconscious, or conscious cognition such as:

- "I am an infallible visionary with unlimited scope."
- "I am a special case."
- "I know everything."
- "I alone can solve this problem."

Ideation supportive of criminal traits include:

- "The ends justify the means."
- "Might makes right."
- "History demands this."
- "Nothing I do can be wrong."

Ideation supportive of ego-syntonic sadistic traits include:

- "This is justice."
- "They deserve this."
- "Diseases must be eradicated."
- "Better them than me."

Ideation supportive of paranoid traits include:

- "That group intends to harm us."
- "No one can be trusted."
- "They plot against us."
- "Agents are everywhere."

Affectivity

Elation from affirmation, praise, and adulation especially distinguishes the MNL. Narcissistic supplies are essential to MNL self-esteem regulation and sustained grandiosity. Praise and success drive elation. Critique and failure drive rage. Notions of personal accountability trigger distain. Defiant death is preferred to account-ability. Internal rivals and external enemies galvanize wrathful emotions. Items that contradict the MNL ego ideal trigger fear and loathing.

Object relations

The MNL is the center of a given object universe. The individual demands loyalty, with taking outweighing giving. But loyalty to loyalists will be present, as well as a degree of self-serving morality that distinguishes the MNL from the pure psycho-path. Split object relations characterize MNL interpersonal style. Out-groups and enemies split to "all bad" objects, and the MNL and his "people" split to "all good" objects. Anyone in proximity to the MNL will experience his uncanniness, other-ness, or charisma. The individual triggers emotional extremes from even "unsug-gestible" individuals. Variant expressions of a "messiah complex" will delineate good and bad objectification.

Impulse control

Early career success, attributed to genius, may stem from impulsivity. Relying on defensive omnipotence rather than hard work, the MNL will "go from the gut" and rush to resolve issues more suitably lent to study and input by experts. Under pressure, decision making becomes catastrophically rash, with failure blamed on underlings. Poor impulse control regarding public statements, financial propriety, and sexual behavior will undermine MNL credibility. Substance use, declining health, and psychiatric comorbidity increase impulsivity and lend a bizarre flavor to leadership behavior.

Culture-related diagnostic issues

Malignant narcissism is a trans-historical and trans-cultural character configuration. Historians and psychobiographers find no shortage of DL, MNL, and KQ+ personages from which to draw. Political psychiatrists identify numerous heads of state with narcissistic and criminal traits (Burkle, 2016), and organizational psychologists establish grandiose psychopaths as persistent derailers of corporate flourishing (Kilburg, 2012). Since Fromm (1964) coined the term following World War II, it has been retroactively applied to ancient rulers and tribal chiefs. In addition to achieving general face validity, the MNL construct has gained informal inter-rater reliability in its application to such figures as Adolf Hitler, Joseph Stalin, or the Kim Dynasty. Informal interrater reliability exists among groups of American psychiatrists who believe Donald J. Trump demonstrates MNL (see Chapter 4) (Gartner, 2017; Gartner, Reiss, & Buser, 2019; Lee, 2017).

Gender-related diagnostic issues

Some controversy exists around MNL and gender. Some experts insist that MN afflicts only men. For instance, Tudoroiu (2016) writes, "Masculine pronouns are used to designate totalitarian dictators, because no woman has ever occupied such a position" (p. xiii). Such statements, however, may stem from stereotypes which have now deteriorated. We find evidence of malignant narcissism in the leadership styles of Elizabeth Holmes, an egomaniacal American entrepreneur and CEO of Theranos[3] who was indicted for billion-dollar fraud regarding specialty blood tests, and Credonia Mwerinde, Ugandan visionary leader of the Movement for the Restoration of the God of the Ten Commandments who was implicated in a mass murder of devotees when her apocalyptic prophecies failed to materialize.[4]

Development and course

Martin Luther King Jr. (1986/1996, as cited in Cotter, 2010) remarked that evil (in this case a pathology) carries the seeds of its own destruction. This disease has a predictable course. Power and malignant narcissism interact in such a way that we can theorize a meta-trajectory to describe the likely unfolding of the career of an afflicted person. According to Glad, this trajectory includes:

1 Grandiosity and ability to employ antisocial tactics provide advantages in securing political power in certain situations.
2 Political power [is] used to buttress grandiose self-image, defend against external criticism, provide company, [and] bolster splitting and paranoiac defenses.

3 But consolidation of absolute power is apt to lead to a vicious cycle:

    a Orchestrated adulation and friendships feel false [intimating increased paranoia].

    b Grandiose plans lead to rash behavior; this and ruthless political tactics create new enemies . . .

    c Project overreach and [the] creation of new enemies leads to increasing vulnerability, a deepening of paranoiac defenses, and volatility in behavior.

                                     Glad, 2002, p. 6

Professor Glad (2002) offers that overreach increases the list of enemies but drains resources required to contend with escalated vulnerability. Despite furious, destructive efforts to maintain control, and desperate gambles born of grandiosity and magical thinking, the MNL exhausts his options. He wrecks himself and his movement, and, in the end, both his friends and enemies find shambles about them.

Not all MNLs overreach. Some, instead, enjoy long tenures in office and die of natural causes.

Comorbidities

The MNL construct conceptually overlaps with personalities who are determined to be demagogic, authoritarian, revolutionary, and necrophilic. The constructs of the Dark Triad and Machiavellianism suggest MNL. Terms indicating a dictatorial role in an organization are comorbid with MNL. These include autocracy, Caesarism, caudillo, cult of personality, despot, supreme leader, messiah, and president for life.

Comorbid mental health issues may include depression, mania, delusions, psychosis, trauma, hypochondriasis, and substance use disorders. Declining physical health may potentiate destructive MNL manifestations. For example, in the final years of World War II, Hitler's Parkinson's disease and prescription drug addiction constricted his mental focus and promoted unrealistic fantasies of military success (Ohler, 2017). Similarly, Stalin's strokes combined with alcoholism and pronounced paranoia activated criminal purges punctuated by sadism (Stal, 2013). Mao's progressive paranoia is linked to tobacco addiction, COPD, and cardiac disease associated with late slippage of his leadership competencies (Retief & Wessels, 2009).

Thanatological features of MNL

A person with MNL traits is at heightened risk for homicide and/or suicide, and a mortality risk exists, not only for an MNL's enemies, but also for friends and followers. Any entity or group within the MNL purview may be subject to his death drive. Thanatological considerations regarding MNL lethality include, but are not limited to, the following:

1   Ideological dehumanization of others may precede murder, persecution, or genocide. Because individuals with "malignant narcissism consistently attempt to destroy, symbolically castrate, and dehumanize others, their sadism is often expressed in ideological terms" (Akhtar, 2009, pp. 163–164).

2   Because individuals with MN demonstrate "ego-syntonic suicidal tendencies that do not [always] reflect sadness and inner guilt, but a megalomaniac triumph over the ordinary fear of pain and death" (Akhtar, 2009, p. 164), irreversible changes of fortune, credible threats of accountability, or catastrophic disruption to the grandiose self, represent credible risk factors for MNL suicide.

3   An MNL's apocalyptic vision and threats to human life correlate positively. A leader self-identified to play a special role in a post-apocalyptic reconstruction may order followers to hasten an apocalypse via mass murder. Equally dangerous, a depressed, defeated, or defiant leader may order the mass suicide of followers to demonstrate apocalyptic triumph over identified "evil" forces, and as fantasized denial of death, in anticipation of heavenly reward.

Types of cults formed by an MNL

Any organization is vulnerable to potential takeover by an MNL or like leader. Over time, such organization will become cult like. Terms such as cult, high-pressure group, totalistic organization, totalitarian regime, and the like, all have overlapping meanings and indicate the presence of an MNL, or MNL archetype organizing governance. We use the broad categories spiritual/human potential, commercial, and political to assess and analyze high-pressure groups. However, because no leader or organization presents in an ideal form, we view these broad categories as overlapping (see Chapter 5 for further detail and examples). Alternatively, Lalich and Tobias (2006) organize specific cult types according to their theme and malignant leader characteristics, and the website of the International Association of Cultic Studies is populated by public domain articles proposing methodologies.

Clinical features and interdisciplinary observations of the malignant narcissist leader profile

The following sections exposit MNL features from a clinical perspective and offer interdisciplinary perspectives on that madness. Some material reflects accepted psychodynamic theories of psychopathology, and other material innovates to advance analytic power. Some material is of a depth-psychological nature. Mindful that analysts have traditionally drawn images, ideas, and narratives from the humanities to enrich concept formulations, several sections have been rendered in that spirit. Readers are reminded that findings concerning the psychodynamics of specific leaders are made in good faith, but fall short of scientific certainty, given the conjectural nature of such determinations. That notwithstanding, the following represents a trove of heuristics and hypotheses which add interdisciplinary heft to the profiling of dangerous leaders.

The god drive

To compensate against the psychic deformity of the formative years, the subject will launch an audacious defensive project, one that expresses teleology of apotheosis – of becoming a god.

Because this defensive drive toward divinity is implicit in the tenure of the malignant leader, I have taken the liberty of coining a term "god drive" to distinguish it from mere primary or secondary drive. The god drive is a Will to Divinity that sets destructive leaders and their followers on a hero's journey that begins with optimism and concludes in hell. The poet W.H. Auden ("September 1, 1939," 1939/2019) referred to such men as "psychopathic gods." Obvious examples include Adolf Hitler, Pol Pot, and Jim Jones.

The god drive represents a specific form of reaction formation, whereby the MNL identifies himself as an ultimate value, an ultimate authority, and entitled to the prerogatives of a god. Secular expressions of the god drive include, but are not limited to, claims to embody the ultimate value of a business activity, political party, or culture. The destructive leader lives in holy terror of his core-level shame, deformity, or perceived inadequacy. Throughout his career he spends considerable energy defending against narcissist injury. Shame is the shadow of the grandiose persona, and any experience that threatens to expose this psychic deformity to the full light of consciousness is hypervigilantly detected and ruthlessly addressed. Like the maniac, the malignant narcissist enjoys the expansiveness, the "high," of the fully funded self-image. But disruptions to the plausibility of superiority threaten the destructive leader with exposure to his lovelessness, ugliness, and incapacity. Threats to the narcissistic mask, either from criticism or failure, are met with defensive fulminations.

Inadequacy, disturbed reality testing, and defensive apotheosis

Seeking to escape the hell of infantile shame, powerlessness, neglect, and abuse, the destructive leader aspires to power and prerogatives that can only be associated with the divine. Failing to experience love during their infancy and early development, the mad leader adapts to a relational universe where faith in god or others is impossible. Unconsciously, he fears that genuine relational love will activate the powerless vulnerability from which he will spend his life defensively fleeing. For this pathetic, pained individual, human relationships will be characterized by a demand for narcissistic supplies to strengthen their grandiosity – a grandiosity which barricades the MNL's inadequacy from even his own self-perception.

The sacrifice of the followers: power over love

Although the mad leader may speak brilliantly on spirituality, he will envy his god, ultimately usurping his god's place in the lives of his followers and in the face of his god. This is his primordial Faustian bargain: to choose power over love. Importantly, the mad leader can never fully defend against his unloved core, preconsciously perceived as unlovable, and thus presenting a heightened risk for self and other murder. To remain a god, the leader orders sacrifice in service to the god drive. Such sacrifice includes the sin eaters of old, comrades killed in purges, the Greek official whose death warrant Alexander the Great signed for giggling at his un-Macedonian expression of godhood. This lethality can be expressed in apocalyptic fantasy, group suicide, and mass killing. Potential targets of negrophilic libido are enemies, friends, institutions, nations, economies, and the self. If cornered by an unbeatable force that threatens to overturn his apotheosis, the MNL may sharpen his blade to sacrifice his "babies" and then himself. The inner logic is: death before dishonor; suicide before accountability; preposterous personae over discovered defect. Anyone associated with the malignant leader suffers a heightened mortality risk.

Organizations reflective of a malignant leader's homicidality and suicidality include the Waffen SS, the ISIS infantry, the Solar Temple, and Marshal Applewhite's Heaven's Gate (see Chapter 5 for analysis). The historical reality of these death-mongering fanatics credentials Freud's theory of the death drive – and the ancient admonition that idolatry is an abomination that careens toward desolation. A contemporary MNL in corporate culture will express the god drive in terms of self-promotion that renders him an *icon* of the highest value of the culture's stakeholders. As a phenomenon of mental life apotheosis is limited to neither theistic epochs nor religious groupings. The religious instinct takes many forms. See Chapter 4 for a complete discussion of the patho-dynamics of organizations led by MNLs.

But such a leader is not initially recognized as an equivalent of a metaphorical antichrist. To the contrary, he rises to power, because supporters perceive him as a genius who solves intractable problems. Followers applaud him as a messianic figure, likely to provide spiritual security, immense wealth, or national salvation. Between ovations, the leader is further protected from the pathos-of-the-ordinary by appropriating into their identity the highest value of the culture: divine right, warlord, or market maker. But this leader is spiritually mad. Deluded by the godishness of their personae, he deploys their giftedness via deeds that fulfill the definitions of evil: he may oversee cruel acts, acts preceded by malice, acts that outsource suffering from the MNL and his acolytes, who glow in reflected glory; and these acts – if beheld by healthy conscience – are morally appalling, atrocious, and beyond empathic comprehension (Stone, 2017, p. 22).

Necrophilous character: an aspiring god with a license to kill

Implicit in the god drive is denial, not merely of limits, but of mortality. Formative trauma may have caused an early fear of death, but ordinary humanness, believes the

MNL, is insufficient to create existential security. An arrangement must be made. Unlike ordinary men, the Great Man identifies with a perfect vision of himself, his ego ideal. This perfection provides authority, and authority is power, and power protects the Great Man himself and the life of his plans. As a living ideal, he unleashes his destructiveness as a defense against death, or any of death's cousins, like ego injury. His destructiveness assumes the role of a life strategy. He prefers earthly death to death of his sacred sense of himself as a perfect prodigy, and thus the rough beast of necrophilous character is born. Like a criminal, the malignant narcissist deploys his destructiveness to shore up treasure against external threats and to achieve his ends. But unlike the criminal, the malignant narcissist also destroys from the vantage of perfection. His destructiveness is self-evidently moral and congruent with his conscience. The necrophilous element of the destructive leader involves the preservation of mortal body and grandiose mind from even fantasized harm. Such a character is dangerous because such a character is a living god with a license to kill.

Narcissism

Due to traumas of early development, the future destructive leader will be a narcissist, one especially prone to grandiosity. Narcissism repairs a deficient sense of worthiness. Lingiardi and McWilliams (2017, p. 46) explain that "people with narcissistic personalities at the more pathologic levels . . . suffer from identity diffusion (often concealed behind a grandiose self-presentation), lack an inner-directed morality, and behave in a way that is highly destructive and toxic to others." At core, the afflicted mind of the narcissist suffers from a catastrophic absence of love, accompanied by the unconscious fear that their humiliating inner deformity will be witnessed by another. This is the essence of shame.

Chief narcissistic indicators

To compensate against a sense of shame, the individual requires infusions of acclamation and applause to ward off the pain of the abandonment depression and its swirl of destabilizing affects. According to Lingiardi and McWilliams,

> When the environment fails to provide . . . evidence [of the narcissist's grand nature, they may feel] depressed, ashamed, and envious of those who succeed in attaining the power they lack. They often fanaticize about unlimited success beauty, glory, and power, and their lack of real pleasure in either work or love can be painful to witness.
>
> *2017, p. 46*

Chief indicators of this deformed character include:

- Grandiosity, or a preoccupation with unfeasible superiority and lack of a healthy sense of limitations

- Omnipotence, or a sense of god-like power
- Omniscience, or a sense of god-like authority on knowledge

Louis de Canonville, 2018

Attributes relevant to the mad leader's narcissism involve an addiction to experiences that inflate their self-esteem, a concerted avoidance of shame, a core sense of inadequacy, an envious contempt of more successful people, and the fantasy that unlimited success (to which entrenched, defensive cognition entitles them) will result in secular or spiritual salvation.

According to the *Psychodynamic Diagnostic Manual*, the pathological narcissist preoccupies himself with self-image; feels predominantly shame, contempt, and envy; strives to experience self-perfection to feel well; and pathologically believes that possessing the riches, power, and fame that others enjoy will cure their discontent. The destructive leader will idealize himself and devalue others (Lingiardi & McWilliams, 2017, p. 48).

By the time the MNL exits his formative years, he will evince a sense of self-importance that will impress targeted parties, even if the MNL's achievements fail to match his persona. Fantasies of ongoing triumphs, special powers, and personal brilliance will populate his day dreams. He will hold the notion that his thunderous uniqueness can be comprehended only by other elites and their institutions. To feed his admiration hunger, he will orchestrate, consciously or unconsciously, scenarios in which he is the vital center of impressed attention. While ascending to his heights, he will steal others' thunder and ascribe their achievements to himself; failures and setbacks, he will disavow. Exuding importance, his presentation will trigger undefended parties to credential his authority and do his bidding. Cognizant of conventional morality, he views himself as a Great Man, one who transcends mass mores and who heroically achieves his ends, even at another's expense. Often exquisitely aware of the feelings of others, he will exploit his emotional intelligence to manipulate, but not to console or to assume culpability for inflicting injury. His arrogance will reveal itself in a condescending attitude and adornments of prestige.

Whereas the MNL flees a childhood sense of inadequacy, he will ever run, in adulthood, toward esteem-raising resources. Fighting the identity-annihilating properties of his traumatic learning history, the MNL will require adulation like a medicine, but if events interrupt a steady dose of that ego-strengthening medicine, then the MNL will deflate and develop depression; it is axiomatic that: as goes the MNL's self-esteem, so goes his emotion. Low self-esteem and intolerable affects are positively correlated. Hence, maintaining a heighten sense of self is indispensable to his well-being and basic security. To gain approval, the MNL will pursue great achievements; he will even ignore his experts and embark upon risky ventures to become the face of a great deed. So great is his hunger that he issues his orders against sensible protests, and without complete information. If his recklessness meets with success, he will bask in the stakeholders' approval, believing that the favorable outcome was because of his genius and not despite his sloppy haste and lack of forethought. Relationally, the MNL will be capable of a degree of superficial intimacy with unchallenging people; these relationships will lack depth and prop his self-esteem. An irony of the MNL character is the trait-like desire to stand above others – to lord as superior person, a Great Man, a magic entity – while requiring narcissistic supplies and applause from parties who witness that he advances himself at the expense of others (Ronningstam, 2016). Thus, the destructive leader populates his immediate circle with people who – regardless of their merits – are sycophants, ready to administer pharmaceutical grade blandishments and exculpations, like insulin to a self-esteem diabetic.

What happens when the destructive leader's ideal self-image is contradicted?

When failure interrupts the mad chief's exalted self-image, narcissistic rage will overwhelm his intellect and behavior. Saddam Hussein, for example, defended the shame of defeat in the first Gulf War with immense narcissistic rage. When U.S.-led forces drove him from Kuwait, the dictator's dreams of glory collapsed, and he retaliated by burning the nation's oil fields in an act of catastrophic eco-terrorism. Post muses,

> If he could not have Kuwait's oil, then neither could the United States. To passively bend the knee and submit to superior force was impossible for Saddam; he was compelled to take action to restore his sense of efficacy and power, defending against passive powerlessness with redemptive and powerful action.
>
> *Post, 2015, p. 23*

Whereas Saddam's offended narcissism drove his ecological crime, Idi Amin's narcissistic defenses determined his domestic persecutions. Amin's aggression toward Ugandan intellectuals cannot be understood without understanding his character pathology. The presence of educated people in the body politic threatened to confront Amin with the realization that his limited intelligence and lack of education placed him out of his depth as head of state. A former CIA profiler opined that Amin's persecutions expressed a

> narcissistic rage in retaliation for the narcissistic shame of having one's grandiose self confronted, this revealing of the underlying inadequacy that produces a painful narcissistic wound that then leads to narcissistic rage. In Amin's case, this led to a purge of the intellectual class.
>
> *Post, 2015, p. 25*

In cases where the destructive leader endures a narcissistic injury against which he cannot retaliate, he may simply become psychotic. After firing on unarmed protestors during the 2011 Arab Spring, Muammar Gaddafi could not tolerate the humiliation of being unloved by a population tired of his sponsorship of terror and domestic repression. His final days were spent in delusion. The tyrant insisted his people loved him and would protect him. A mob of furious Libyans, however, pulled him from hiding in a drainpipe, sodomized him with a bayonet, and shot him dead (Post, 2015). Similarly, cult leader Shoko Asahara, architect of the 1995 sarin gas attack in the Tokyo underground, became psychotic when, during court proceedings that found him guilty of 27 murders, a disciple testified against him for the prosecution. Deprived of adulation and unable to restore psychic balance via narcissistic retribution, the cult leader sank into shame and went mad (Akimoto, 2006).

Criminality

In early life, the malignant narcissist will have witnessed the success of violence, criminality, and perpetration. Resultantly, the future MNL identifies with the aggressor. Despite an intact ability to formally discern right from wrong, the MNL's superego will not have introjected the full conventions of accepted morality. Rather, the *good* is determined by fulfilling ambition, even at the expense of others. The MNL will use "cold empathy" and a charming, often riveting interpersonal style to manipulate individuals, and entire societies, to do their bidding.

The MNL's criminal traits include suboptimal moral anxiety, manipulation skills (like a con artist's), rage from unfulfilled desires, self-permission to fulfill any desire, and a steady march to push back limits and extend power. Total control defends the destructive leader from the pathologically perceived threat of injury – and ensures that they can act with impunity (Lingiardi & McWilliams, 2017, pp. 50–51). Avarice, concupiscence, and envy also comprise the criminal impulse. Whereas the MNL's psychodynamic structure contains a partially functioning super ego, predicable ego defense mechanisms will on occasion activate; these will transfigure the individual's crimes into virtues.

Criminal organizations reflective of sociopathic leadership leanings include Soviet Russia, the Rajneesh cult, and Enron. Interestingly, the successful criminality of the corporate sociopath may be attributed to a larger prefrontal cortex than those enjoyed by less neurologically endowed criminals (Gabbard, 2014). The probability that the same holds true for the successful MNL is high.

Paranoia

Formative experiences leave the MNL with unbearable emotions, deep humiliation, frightening urges, and horrific ideas that are defensively disowned and then protectively attributed to another person or group.

> Because pathologically paranoid individuals tend to have histories marked by felt shame and humiliation, they expect to be humiliated by others and may attack first in order to spare themselves the agony of waiting for the inevitable attack from outside. Their expectation of mistreatment creates the suspiciousness and hypervigilance for which they are noted – attitudes that

tend to evoke the hostile and humiliating responses they fear. Their personality is defensively organized around the themes of danger and power (either the persecutory power of others or the megalomanic power of the self).

Lingiardi & McWilliams, 2017, pp. 48–49

The paranoid element of the MNL's character involves projecting unacceptable elements of the mind onto external others. The leader senses danger from these projectively identified targets, and he takes emergency measures to destroy the threats. The destructive leader will defend against his pathological sense of endangerment with preemptive strikes against innocents.

Endpoints of the MNL's paranoia include hate crimes, religious persecution, hits against corporate competitors, organizationally debilitating micromanagement, and war crimes. Malignant paranoia is not always obvious. Combined with socially intelligent manipulation, the destructive leader's charisma may disarm the defenses of those identified as dangerous and therefore targeted for metaphorical or real liquidation. The MNL's gift for grandstanding while rationalizing atrocities born from these paranoid endowments frustrate prosecutors and institutions of justice alike.

As an example, during the Balkan wars, at the close of the last century, in splintering Yugoslavia, former president of the Bosnian Serb Republic, Radovan Karadzic, rallied his military behind the suspicion that Muslim and Croatian communities posed an existential threat to the Bosnian Serbs, and that the Islamic presence threatened to extinguish Western civilization. Karadzic was convicted of the crime of genocide in 2016 when the court proved that he ordered the Siege of Sarajevo – in which 10,000 people were killed – and the Srebrenician slaughter of 7,000 Muslim boys and men. On appeal, he depicted the war crimes tribunal as a stooge-institution for evil international interests, and he vowed to fight on against the enemy's civilization. But Karadzic's conviction was upheld, and he received a sentence of 40 years to life. Given that he assumed office with a clear intention to "ethnically cleanse" his jurisdictions (Donia, 2014), his sentence partially gratified champions of international justice. The result of this paranoid nationalism was mass murder unseen in Europe since World War II. Karadzic had ordered his troops to devastate the city so that inhabitants would find it "unbearable with no hope of further survival" (Borger, 2019, n.p.). The paranoid process originating this order devastated scores of non-combatants, as did the order to shell the Sarajevan hospital, where he once practiced medicine.

From his cell in Dutch a prison, the lethal politician and former psychiatrist continues to charm journalists, write publishable poetry, and eloquently justify the extermination of defenseless communities 20 years prior to his conviction by the International War Crimes Tribunal in the Hague. American psychiatrist colleagues of Karadzic profiled him as a malignant narcissist (Dekleva & Post, 1997). Then, the echo of Karadzic's heroic, paranoid hate speech posed international risk, and the threat still continues. Many of his countrymen hail him as a hero, and his delusional declamations against Muslims inspired the slaughter of 50 worshippers in a Christ Church, New Zealand mosque. A survivor of Karadzic's atrocities lamented that the leader's "virulent dehumanization" of out-groups "inspires extremists world-wide" and demands an international effort "to deconstruct and delegitimize Karadzic's ideology and methods" (Borger, 2019, n.p.). Although paranoia like Karadzic's illustrates a particular pathogenesis toward violence, the wellspring from which it flows – rewarding him with pleasurable elation in afflicting others – is sadism.

Sadism

The destructive leader's lifelong reaction formation against the furies of the abandonment depression include a pre-psychotic preoccupation with dominating others.

> Internally, the sadistic person may experience deadness and affective sterility, which are relieved by inflicting pain and humiliation. . . . In search for total control over another – a project Fromm (1973, p. 323) called the turning of "impotence into omnipotence" – the sadistic person always chooses as a target those who are subordinate, weaker, and comparatively powerless. . . . The hallmark of sadism is the emotional detachment or guiltless enthusiasm with which domination and control are pursued. This detachment has the effect [and intent] of dehumanizing the other.
>
> *Lingiardi & McWilliams, 2017, pp. 51–52*

Often preoccupied with avenging indignities or desirous to obtain a mood altering "high," the destructive leader will experience glee in godlike power while inflicting suffering on others. The goal is to revel in omnipotent control over a threat, real or imaginary. To the sadist, kindness is weakness; the sadist identifies with powerful, heartless role models, and derives pleasure via object domination and the infliction of pain. The sadist surmounts self-contempt by assuming the superior position. Sadists are argumentative, caustic, malicious, and quick to anger. The MNL tilting toward sadism cultivates contempt and glories in controlling and dehumanizing others. The harm happy leader will not only flourish injuring others, but he will contrive rationalizations for sadistic behavior, convincing stakeholders that sadistic perpetrations against targeted groups are not only justified but a high ideal. For the MNL, sadism is an expression of the god drive metastasizing. Unconsciously identified with divinity or its secular equivalent, the MNL behaves bestially, but he enjoys paradisiacal gratification.

For such individuals, sadism is genuinely transportive, even therapeutic. Victimizing others triggers a welcome rush, like cocaine or methamphetamine. One physiological explanation is that traumatic learning ushers a physiological cascade that degrades the MNL's neurochemistry, terminating in low arousal, blue mood, and joylessness. But inverting this unwelcome dysphoria is as simple as a quick visit to the torture chamber, or shooting the children of dissidents in front of their mothers. For some MNLs, sadistic activity threatens to escalate into a process addiction like gambling or binge eating. Such sadism results in euphoria – along with vengeful satisfaction – and godlike power conferred by homicide and hate. Perhaps these mechanisms account for Adolf Hitler's energization when authorizing nightmarish Reich policy against Jews, or Josef Stalin's delight in details from NKVD extractions of teeth and confessions from dismembered comrades.

An exemplar of sadism among destructive leaders involves Shaka Zulu, supreme leader of the Zulu from 1816 until his assassination in 1828. He was known for meeting the slightest opposition with instant death. During his rise to power he deployed his soldiers to terrorize his enemies – and his subjects – and he took special care arranging the gratuitously cruel deaths for populations he blamed for tormenting him in youth for his illegitimacy; some he impaled on stakes sharpened from their own fence posts. He even orchestrated a creative, gruesome death for the priestess-mother of a political rival by placing her overnight in a locked house with devouring jackals and hyenas. Zulu's sadistic policies were born from spiteful bereavement and malignant envy of others' liveliness.

> In 1827 Nandi [his mother] died, and with his mother's death Shaka became openly psychotic. About 7,000 Zulus were killed in the initial paroxysm of his grief, and for a year no crops were planted, nor could milk – the basis of the Zulu diet staple – be used. All women found pregnant were slain with their husbands, as were thousands of milk cows, so that even calves might know what it is to lose a mother.
>
> *Morris, 2019*

Suspicious at every turn, Shaka consolidated his power by assuming the epicenter of a centralized state. Zulu appointed himself as chief executive, legislature, supreme court, and high priest. In this last role, he divined who plotted against him and legitimized the use of state power to humiliate and kill enemies, all of which was based on unprovable, mystical evidence (Kets de Vries, 2009). Eventually these overreaches were a catalyst for the priest-king's assassination.

Speaking psychodynamically, Shaka Zulu's punitive policies cannot be understood without reference to core hatred and vengeful motivation. Like any leader in this dismal category, Zulu's humiliating childhood ignited misanthropic hatreds that burned behind his policy formation. One might (un)safely observe that hatred is the emotion of the MNL in sadistic mode, revenge is his goal, and perpetration is, if not a joy, an antidepressant. That is until assassination, or extradition to the Hague, changes the dynamic.

Caligula Complex

Upon gaining executive control and dismantling checks on his imbalanced leadership, the MNL is susceptible to abandoning himself to polymorphous perversity in a broad sense. Dismantled checks correspond to internal checks. Without concern for accountability, the MNL may act upon infantile whims and fantasies, heretofore unimaginable, even for him. The process may occur suddenly following a Nietzschean realization of infernal freedom. Or, manifestations may occur gradually, as it dawns upon the MNL that everything is permissible. Perverse acts consistent with the Caligula Complex involve cruel and unusual forms of sexual rights violations, extreme torture of a bizarre nature accompanied by sadism, preservation of the frozen remains of executed enemies, the forcing of legislators to kill in cold blood colleagues suspected of disloyalty, and cannibalism. Specific examples of the Caligula Complex are to be found in the biographies of Muammar Gaddafi, Saddam Hussein, and Idi Amin. Manifestations of the Caligula Complex demonstrate that MNL pathology has escalated to an extreme dimension, and that the leader believes that he is scandal-proof and beyond accountability.

Other psychopathological features

The destructive leader may be afflicted with additional psychopathologies. Often responsible for providing a group with a raison d'etre, the MNL will offer novel augmentations to preexisting ideologies or creatively spin complete world views from whole cloth. In terms of perception and decision making, they may experience random events and weird intuitions as providential signs and locutions from cosmic forces that ratify their infallibility and importance. The destructive leader's creativity and intelligence will be derailed by the ideas of reference, bizarre fantasies, and strange beliefs indicative of the schizotypal personality disorder. In addition, despite their charisma and emotional intelligence, some destructive leaders' lack of genuinely close relationships suggests a schizoid interpersonal style. From a methodology involving historians rating tyrants for character disorders, it was determined that Kim Jong-il, Saddam Hussein, and Adolf Hitler not only met Kernberg's criteria for malignant narcissism, but they also scored high on schizotypal and schizoid traits as well (Coolidge & Segal, 2009).

Bipolarity may also afflict the malignant narcissist. The destructive leader Kaiser Wilhelm, for example, is described by psycho-historians as a mercurial monarch whose grandiose and paranoid tendencies were fueled by mood extremes. These mood extremes "were as infectious and as virulent as a deadly microbe, and can easily infect those in thrall of the host figure. It is a phenomenon known as induced psychosis" (Lieb, 2008, p. 888).

One reading of the bipolar hypothesis is that mood extremes infuse the destructive leader's characterological malignancies with profound emotional energy that attracts various constituencies to their dangerous doctrines – and destructive decisions. Warmongering followers of Kaiser Wilhelm contributed to the destruction of World War I, including 9 million dead and 21 million wounded. Their actions also set the stage for the atrocities of Nazism and Bolshevism. Other destructive leaders believed to have had underlying character malignancies nourished by bipolar disorder include Napoleon, Hitler, and Stalin.

Vengeance is mine, saith the MNL

For the MNL, vengeance is a central impulse and a revenge-ready posture that informs the entirety of the MNL's narcissism, criminality, paranoia, and sadism. Masterson (1981) once remarked that the suffering child possesses limited defensive options when suffering deprivation, violence, and degradation. In observing that the perpetrator enjoys the superior position in the dynamics of abuse, Masterson theorized that the child will envy the perpetrator and fantasize about inflicting similar injuries on an inferior person until the fantasy restores the child's self against the narcissistic injury. In reverie, the abused child finds a strategy of transcendent value. No longer will he be passive or helpless. Revenge is active and potent. How satisfying to pay back the perpetrator and charge interest. In adulthood, vengeance will more than tinge damaging deeds toward friends and enemies. Masterson explained, "Instead of being weak, small, helpless, a passive object, the individual is strong, active, and meting out just punishment for the trauma and thereby undoing the past" (p. 183).

The vengeful mind is also a political mind. In adulthood, the MNL will draw on past wrongs to certify the rightness of private and official aggressions. During his tenure, the destructive leader's river of megalomaniacal libido will be fed by tributaries of vengeful energies. But despite triumphs and retributive successes, a part of the MNL's sense of self will ever ache with a sense of victimization.

The blessing of cursing

Like Cain of the Book of Genesis, the MNL envies the Abel who enjoys the goods of life more than he. Like Cain, the MNL will avenge himself against the brother in the envied position; and like Cain, the MNL will severe relational ties – to moral agents or love objects – that might mitigate his soul's wretchedness, or allay his destructiveness.

The story is this: Cain envied Abel, because God favored the younger brother's ritual sacrifices over his own. Cain connived, with malice aforethought, to murder Abel, and thereby remove the object whose thriving diminished his sense of prestige. Cain lured Abel to a field and killed him. Aware that the earth cried out with Abel's spilled blood, God confronted Cain with the fratricide, but Cain's posture was one of damage control. Under divine investigation, Cain failed to acknowledge Abel's existential entitlement to live and thrive despite Cain's envy, and this demonstrates Cain's narcissism. Cain failed to acknowledge the gross immorality of fratricide, and this demonstrates Cain's criminality. Cain evinced no remorse for the enjoyment of tension discharged during of the murder, and this demonstrates his ego-syntonic sadism. Protecting his interests, Cain plea bargained *post facto* to the Judge's sentence of (a) banishment from the divine presence, and (b) roaming the earth. Following God's pronouncement, Cain exclaimed, "My punishment is more than I can bear. Today you are driving me from the land, and I will be hidden from your presence; I will be a restless wonderer on the earth, and whoever finds me will kill me" (Genesis 4:13–14, NIV Study Bible).

To this, God responds with a mixture of exasperation and indulgence, affects ascribable to the parent of an obdurate child or a compassionate authority. Impatient for closure, God enabled Cain to avoid several consequences of his criminality. To Cain's protest that he, a killer, could be killed, God exclaims, "Not so; if anyone kills [you] Cain, he will suffer vengeance seven times over." Then the Lord put a mark on Cain so that no one who found him would kill him (Genesis 4:15, NIV Study Bible). This mark is not a mark of shame, and although Cain is banished from God's presence, it is also not a curse. The mark "is a protecting sign: it indicates that Cain is a member of a clan that will exact blood for blood" (text notes on Genesis 4:15, New Jerusalem Bible). With the mark, God leaves Cain to defend his vulnerability with the same unrehabilitated violence that led to Abel's murder and alienation from God Himself.

In similar strangeness, a later part of the story shows Cain standing in contempt of God's judgment. Condemned to roam the earth, Cain never serves his sentence; he simply refuses to wander the world. Instead he enjoyed "intercourse with his wife . . . and . . . became the founder of a city" (Genesis 4:17, New Jerusalem Bible). His city, like the organization of any destructive leader, becomes prosperous and violent, and Cain's legacy is that of an inventive but inhuman culture.

The ancient story has psychodynamic significance. The moral learning history of the MNL culminates in partial introjection of the cultural morality, at best. To the extent that the culture's moral agents, represented by the MNL's super ego or corresponding external authorities, might punish the MNL, the destructive leader will be activated to self-justify. Whether defending intrapsychically against a damning conscience or publicly against prosecution, he will mobilize his ego defenses and defend his bad behavior convincingly. His narcissism will cause him to argue that his case is special, for he himself is special, and that extenuating circumstances, which interrupt the lives of special people, render his normally immoral acts defensible, even laudable. His defensiveness and narcissistic self-righteousness will undermine effective punishment from his harangued conscience and his super ego will leave him alone, just as God left Cain. Similarly, his intense energy and remorseless self-concern may cause external objects, whether family, followers, or authorities, to determine that the resources required to rehabilitate, punish, and enforce justice upon the destructive leader are simply too dear to muster. Like God with Cain, they run the risk of leaving him alone to build his prosperous, violent city at human cost.

The mad leader is a sadistic leader, one whose destructive behavior is a function of childhood wretchedness mentally associated with punitive objects. In adulthood, he protectively applies this diseased dynamic onto unhappy entities whom he will enjoy injuring from the vantage of his adult authority. Of this dynamic, vengeance and envy will be prime movers, while the constraints of conscience and convention will be diminished, neutralized, or ignored. In mythic terms, the mark of Cain symbolizes the bizarre sense in which the sadistic, vengeful, envious leader delights in the blessing of cursing.

Other psychopathological considerations

The abandonment depression and trauma may predispose a future destructive leader to psychic gifts and spiritual perception

Within a subgroup of abused children, a sixth sense activates that predisposes them to uncanny knowing of the psychic states of others, direct perception of spiritual phenomena such as angels and ghosts, and a proneness to profound intuitions and uncanny insights.

For a narcissistic leader, mystical experiences confirm a sense of destiny that drives grandiosity and infallibility. For a criminally disposed person, the opening of such perceptual doors is used in service of manipulation of others and power procurement. For the paranoid and sadistic leader, spiritual evidence ratifies pathological suspicions and baptizes the humiliation of enemies. Destructive leaders with mystical gifts are especially dangerous to any religious population or institution.

The abandonment depression and trauma may predispose a future destructive leader to a creative illness that appears to "cure" them but damages society

Intermittently demonized by the developmental agonies set forth by the abandonment depression, the aspiring leader broods upon some special truth with which to enlighten his soul's dark night. Depth psychologists find that mystical experiences erupt from the unconscious to transform the ego's torment into transcendence. It is a self-generated therapeutic experience that turns the destructive leader into an evangelist of sorts. One psychiatrist explains that

> When the guru's dark night has been ended by his new vision of reality, he usually appears to become convinced that he has discovered the truth. The fervent certainty with which he proclaims this accounts to a large extent for his powerful effect upon others; his persuasiveness, his charisma. . . . [The charismatic leader exudes] . . . a special magical quality of personality by virtue of which the individual possessing it was set apart from ordinary men and women, and treated as if endowed with supernatural or superhuman powers.
>
> *Storr, 1996, p. XIV*

Emerging from their curative epiphany, the leader will defy convention and be bound by neither precedent nor law. Made special by his epiphany, the charismatic leader no longer answers to human beings. Cosmically chosen and in possession of the "Truth" delivered with conviction, the MNL is "accorded the right to direct every aspect of his followers' lives. For example, he may dictate where they live, with whom they form sexual relationships, and what should be done with their money or to their possessions" (Storr, 1996, p. XV). In possession of riveting, messianic energies, the charismatic leader attracts people and groups needful of his inspired solutions to their problems.

> These may be relatively minor problems, such as running a business or a church . . . or there may be huge problems such as leading a nation through crisis or war. The charismatic leader may actually solve the problems, but there is always a risk, because he has problems of his own, *and sometimes he is not in great psychological shape.*
>
> *Oakes, 2010, p. 10; italics added*

While the mystical experience of the MNL will be authentic, he will unconsciously desecrate it in service to his false self. He benefits from the experience but misses its meaning. Disallowing his narcissism to shrink in relation to the Truth, he diminishes the experience in service to his grandiose ego. He halts the process, say, of the flame of cosmic love from burning through his shame-concealing defenses to illuminate to him the lovability he shares with the human family. Such surrender would require a return to the vulnerability of his early life. And this is unacceptable. Hence, assuming the posture of greatness, he will live and lead for himself, unconscious that his narcissistic defensives enslave his "illumination" in service to his inflated ego.

Hubris syndrome: explicating malignant leadership by exploring a lesser form of narcissism in office

Informing the understanding of the destructive leader is David Owen's (2008) construct of hubris syndrome (see also Owen & Davidson, 2009). A statesman and psychiatrist, Owen proposed this diagnostic category for application specifically to leaders impaired by pride in high office. From his tenure as the United Kingdom's Foreign Secretary and his psycho-historical research, he observed that democratically elected leaders, endowed primarily with normal mental health, may acquire leadership characteristics not dissimilar to the presentation of the more pathological MNL. A factor which predisposes leaders to hubris syndrome is the presence of at least moderate narcissism. Once in office, however, the presidents and prime ministers Owen studied did not succumb to hubris syndrome immediately. Rather, the length of their tenure predicted symptom onset, while the strain of responsibility combined with power were stressors driving morbidity. Once a narcissistically vulnerable leader exercises power in high office over time, vulnerability to hubris syndrome increases. The disorder is diagnosed by the presence of three or four of the symptoms in Box 2.1 with at least one symptom selected from those marked "unique" to differentiate hubris syndrome from mere narcissistic personality disorder (Owen & Davidson, 2009, p. 1398).

Malignancy in leadership is an especially virulent form of hubris syndrome, one in which the mad leader's narcissistic predisposition interacts with the full force of criminal, paranoid, and sadistic traits. Once in office, the MNL's pathology will blossom more quickly and awfully than the more compensated Hubristic Leader. Although vulnerable to the stressors as the Hubristic Leader, the MNL enters office with a sicker core and carries the dangerous defensive style of a leader enthused to lead from the fantasy that he is incapable of mistakes. Unlike the merely Hubristic Leader, the MNL assumes power with an already impaired character. His traumatic learning history has so deformed his psyche that he is immediately dangerous and ready to play god.

Special gifts that credential the MNL to himself and his followers

The early success of the MNL is abetted by a degree of real talents. Examples include the Italian cleric Savonarola's spellbinding sermonizing, packed with apocalyptic

BOX 2.1 SYMPTOMS OF HUBRIS SYNDROME

- A propensity to see the world primarily as an arena in which to exercise power and seek glory
- A predisposition to take actions which seem likely to cast the individual in a good light – taken in part in order to enhance their image
- A disproportionate concern with image and presentation
- A messianic way of talking and a tendency to exaltation in speech and manner
- An identification with the nation or organization – to the extent that they regard the outlook and interests of the two as identical (unique)
- A tendency to speak of themselves in the third person or use the royal "we" (unique)
- Excessive confidence in the individual's own judgement and contempt for the advice or criticism of others
- Exaggerated self-belief, bordering on a sense of omnipotence, in what they personally can achieve
- A belief that rather than being accountable to the mundane court of colleagues or public opinion, the real court to which they answer is much greater: history or god
- An unshakable belief that in that court they will be vindicated (unique)
- Loss of contact with reality; often associated with progressive isolation
- Restlessness, recklessness and impulsiveness (unique)
- A tendency to allow their "broad vision," especially their conviction about the moral rectitude of a proposed course of action, to obviate the need to consider other aspects of it, such as its practicality, cost and the possibility of unwanted outcomes (unique)
- Incompetence in carrying out a policy, where things go wrong precisely because too much self-confidence has led the leader not to worry about the nuts and bolts of a policy

Source: Owen & Davidson, 2009, p. 1398. Used with permission.

rhetoric, which offered thought leadership to late 15th century Florentines anxious from Renaissance-related economic and cultural disruptions. He attracted them with his teaching on how they might avoid divine judgment. He also made accurate predictions about late medieval geo-politics that were hailed as prophesies. For a time, he ruled the city-state as a theocracy before his overreach incited a mob to demand his hanging and burning.

Until mid-late-career Adolf Hitler was also a gifted orator whose ability to address post-war shame, economic depression, and military evisceration were hailed as evidence that the Chaplin-esque ranter was a demi-god. Jim Jones and David Koresh capitalized on well-developed rhetorical gifts, genuine spiritual insight, and – in Jones' case – healing gifts, later undermined by charlatanism. Rhetorical panache delivered with confidence, combined with an impressive success, will credential a destructive leader to himself and his constituents.

The MNL's tendency to fabricate: Pseudologica Fantastica

Despite actualizing real ability in indisputable accomplishments, the destructive leader will fabricate reality when it suits him. This tendency, known as *Pseudologica Fantastica*, is a syndrome characterized by interesting lies and fabulous exaggerations; these may be partially believed by the teller. *Pseudologica fantasitica* serves the function of strengthening grandiosity via fraudulent attainments, and manipulating stakeholders such as diplomates, investors, or competitors. These fictions are geared to increase the teller's sense of importance while impressing the listeners. *Pseudologica Fantastica* extends beyond the lies of the sociopath; the strategy represents an infantile attempt to make the leader's magisterial persona plausible to himself and others.

The more fantastic the story, however, the more prognostically damning it is for the leader's reality testing. At times the reality orientation of an entire society will be impaired, as state sponsored propaganda inflicts *Pseudologica Fantastica* upon a citizenry. In North Korea, the Kim Family dictators outsource fabulous, aggrandizing narratives to the state media, who serve as proxies for the protection of the Kim dictators' personae. After hearing years of broadcasts that the Kims possess superpowers, perform miracles, and are sung to by exotic sea creatures on special occasions, some North Koreans functionally worship the Kims as gods. This amounts to a variation of a shared psychotic disorder on a grand scale.

Sexual life of the MNL

As a rule, the sexual life of the MNL presents a hazard to his sex objects. The bizarre bisexual, communist evangelist Jim Jones, for example, had sex with congregants as a way to subjugate them and also to provide them with the "privilege" of closeness to his person. Similarly, Branch Davidian David Koresh enjoyed sexual access to the wives of his male disciples and "married" (read: statutorily raped) a number of their daughters. In addition to keeping a wife and mistresses, Mussolini engaged in compulsive sex with an endless stream of women, whose experience with Duce ranged from libido-drenched patriotic joy to the dismal degradation of the rape survivor. Gaddafi deployed a special security squad to kidnap university women, subject them to gynecological exams, and guard the tyrant's underground pleasure bunkers where he raped them. Gaddafi's secret services also abducted a succession of boys for pedophilic rapes. The malignant corporate executive will sponsor sex parties for other "elites" whose smiles fade when films surface that turn business negotiations to blackmail.

Perversion and objectification regularly characterize the sexual life of the MNL. Reacting to the permanent trauma of the abandonment depression, the individual will simulate love and intimacy but depth is precluded by the need to escape core shame. Hence, the vulnerability implicit in true love is reflexively anathema. Unsurprisingly, the status of the MNL within a group provides no shortage of partners – both willing and unwilling. Although promiscuity is the mainstay of this individual's sexual style, the male MNL's Don Juan-ism reveals hatred of women and insecure masculinity. Etiological origins of this empty sexual style lie in fear of engulfment by the mother, fear of castration from the father, and/or a defense against the dread of an inner sexual deformity. Stoller notes, "His unending, frantic need to prove himself – his gratification only in numbers of conquests – reveals that his body is more in the service of power than eroticism" (1975, p. 57). A paucity of published examples makes it difficult to opine about the corresponding sexual projects of the female MNL.

Although this phallic narcissism is the predicable sexuality of the destructive leader, it is not the final story. Variability within the MNL's sexual life involves dehumanization of partners, misogyny, auto-eroticism, sadomasochism, gender instability, pedophilia, and assorted paraphilias. The fantasy that partners are "whores" or animals justifies their use as soulless toys. The individual is bogged in unconscious incest fears, and he views the wife as "virgin" and disposable sex objects as "whores," which is a workable, if complex, solution to Oedipal concerns. Masturbation predictably retroflects libido upon the self-loved self. Sadism confirms control and consummates revenge fantasies. Masochism ritualizes victim status and justifies the sense of betrayal that nourishes entitled hatred, later acted out as cruel public policy, instituting anti-human theology, or self-evidently just theft of investor cash.

Stein's (2005) observations of the psychodynamic aim of perverse sexuality are especially applicable to the MNL. Beneath the leader's sexual grotesqueries lie pain, dread, and hatred. Dynamic analysis makes transparent

> the lacerating memories and fantasies that animate [his] perverse scripts . . . [that] not only forestall [his overwhelm from] nameless dread and deep shame, but also transmutes them into triumph and revenge. This is done by turning tables on the other who represents the child's original adult object, who once, in gratifying their own needs . . . humiliated and betrayed the child.
>
> *p. 780*

Importantly, for the MNL, his erotically organized hatred exists not only as a vile co-occurrence with his professional tenure, but as an element of MNL itself. Simply, the destructive leader may demand that his constituents submit to his sexual perversion to remain in good standing with him or his organization. But whether his sexuality is expressed privately or professionally, coercively or consensually, the teleology of his sexuality is identical to the goal of his leadership per se: to hover god-like above the inferno of the abandonment depression and allow the other to be consumed.

Preventative and epidemiological measures

Public education regarding the signs and symptoms of malignant narcissism is vital to prevention. To increase awareness of destructive leadership and exploitive, high-pressure groups, state departments of health might design programs appropriate to specific demographics, affinity groups, and vulnerable populations, and point the public to online resources as well as to vetted, non-partisan consultative services. Boards of directors, management teams, and human resources departments related to commercial and non-profit organizations would prophylactically benefit from obligated education related to all dimensions of their legal and ethical fiduciary responsibilities and provision of specific strategies for identifying and removing destructive and malignant narcissist leaders. Mandated reporting requirements would further decrease the social epidemiological risks related to malignant management and reduce its prevalence.

For leaders considered for socially impactful, high-level roles, such as bishop, CEO, or political appointee, investigation-based profiles are recommended. Past behavior predicts future behavior, but aspiring MNs artfully conceal previous destructiveness and deftly bamboozle interviewers; thus, disinterested third party consultants comprised of former intelligence personnel, sophisticated law enforcement, and forensic psychopathologists are ideal to conduct not mere background checks, but investigation-based profiling comparable to those assembled by MI5, the Mossad, or KBG. Such investigative efforts improve the preventive likelihood of organizational and societal catastrophes emergent from the secondary, or metastatic, effects of malignantly narcissistic leadership. Corporations, global churches, and governments would further benefit from requisite mental health examinations for leaders every five years. Whereas a full physical examination is recommended annually, a full psychological examination bi-decennially is geared to rule out hubris syndrome (Owen, 2008), acquired MNL, and emergent destructiveness. Although this standard is likely to fall short of an actual best practice, for early detection and intervention, it remains a solid starter-standard that will lower MNL prevalence and metastasis, with reductions in legal expenses, damages, and absenteeism, while also increasing organizational reputation, revenue, and quality of life – as well as escalating social security in the most literal sense.

Conclusion

Grandiose leaders with the mentioned characteristics, personal problems, and leadership styles exist as a type. A survey of world history will confirm this, as will the literature on leadership studies, the psychology of religion, or even the daily news. To promote testable hypotheses and use full heuristics, this chapter provides a short-list of important psychodynamic considerations regarding the malignant narcissist in leadership. Although this type of individual will be prevalent in any population, ongoing delineation of the phenomenon from psychological, organizational, and policy perspectives will sharpen awareness and facilitate preventative actions among relevant professions and the larger public. Over a century ago Dostoyevsky remarked, "While nothing is easier than to denounce the evil doer, nothing is more difficult than to understand him."[5]

Notes

1 Spiritual megalomania pertains to the mad leader's conscious or unconscious self-identification with an ultimate value that thus entitles the MNL to unlimited jurisdiction over domains relevant to the theme of that self-identification. Ideation consistent with spiritual megalomania might include such cognitions as, "I am Germany, and Germany is me," or "I am the future of the economy," or even "I am god."
2 Alternatively, malignantly narcissistic leader.
3 "In 2004, Elizabeth Holmes dropped out of Stanford to start a company that was going to revolutionize healthcare. In 2014, Theranos was valued at $9 billion, making Holmes, who was touted as 'the next Steve Jobs,' the youngest self-made female billionaire in the world. Just two years later, Theranos was cited as a 'massive fraud' by the SEC, and its value was less than zero" (*The Inventor*, 2019).
4 A prostitute turned mystic, "Ms Mwerinde was claiming to receive messages from the Virgin Mary through a hidden telephone system that spoke through objects such as cups and plates" ("The Preacher," 2000).
5 This apt unreferenced quote is to be found in Robert Simon's famous *Bad Men Do What Good Men Dream: A Forensic Psychiatrist Illuminates the Darker Side of Human Behavior* (2008), p. 247.

References

Akhtar, S. (2009). *Comprehensive dictionary of psychoanalysis*. London, UK: Karnac Books.

Akimoto, H. (2006). The Aum Cult leader Asahara's mental deviation and its social relations. *Psychiatry and Clinical Neurosciences, 60*(1), 3–8.

American Psychiatric Association. (2013). *Diagnostic and statistical manual of mental disorders* (5th ed.). Washington, DC: American Psychiatric Association.

Auden, W. H. (1939/2019, September 1). Poetry for students. *Encyclopedia.com*. Retrieved from www.encyclopedia.com/arts/educational-magazines/september-1-1939

BBC News. (2000). The preacher and the prostitute. Retrieved from http://news.bbc.co.uk/2/hi/africa/694729.stm

Borger, J. (2019, March 20). Radovan Karadžić war crimes sentence increased to life in prison. *The Guardian*. Retrieved from www.theguardian.com/law/2019/mar/20/radovan-karadzic-faces-final-verdict-in-bosnia-war-crimes-case

Burkle Jr., F. M. (2016). Antisocial personality disorder and pathological narcissism in prolonged conflicts and wars of the 21st century. *Disaster Medicine and Public Health Preparedness, 10*(1), 118–128.

Coolidge, F. L., & Segal, D. L. (2009). Is Kim Jong-il like Saddam Hussein and Adolf Hitler? A personality disorder evaluation. *Behavioral Sciences of Terrorism and Political Aggression, 1*(3), 195–202.

Cotter, P. (2010). The path to extreme violence: Nazism and serial killers. *Frontiers in Behavioral Neuroscience, 3*, 61. Retrieved from http://journal.frontiersin.org/article/10.3389/neuro.08.061.2009/full

Dekleva, K. B., & Post, J. M. (1997). Genocide in Bosnia: The case of Dr. Radovan Karadjzic. *Journal of the American Academy of Psychiatry and the Law, 25*(4), 485–496.

Donia, R. J. (2014). *Radovan Karadžić: Architect of the Bosnian genocide*. Cambridge, UK: Cambridge University Press.

Fromm, E. (1964). *The heart of man: Its genius for good and evil*. Riverdale, NY: American Mental Health Foundation Books.

Fromm, E. (1973). *The anatomy of human destructiveness*. New York: Fawcett.

Gabbard, G. O. (2014). *Psychodynamic psychiatry in clinical practice* (5th ed.). Washington, DC: American Psychiatric Association.

Gartner, J. D. (2017). Donald Trump is: (A) bad, (B) mad, (C) all of the above. In L. Bandy (Ed.), *The dangerous case of Donald Trump: 27 Psychiatrists and mental health experts assess a president* (pp. 93–109). New York, NY: St. Martin's Press.

Gartner, J. D., Reiss, D., & Buser, S. (2019, May 31). President Donald Trump's poor mental health is grounds for impeachment. *USA Today*. Retrieved from www.usatoday.com/story/opinion/2019/05/31/donald-trump-should-impeached-because-his-bad-mental-health-column/1260781001/

Glad, B. (2002). Why tyrants go too far: Malignant narcissism and absolute power. *Political Psychology, 23*(1), 1–37.

Haycock, D. A. (2019). *Tyrannical minds: Psychological profiling, narcissism, and dictatorship*. New York, NY: Pegasus Books.

HBO. (2019). The inventor: Out for blood in Silicon Valley. Retrieved from www.hbo.com/documentaries/the-inventor-out-for-blood-in-silicon-valley/about

Kets de Vries, M. F. R. (2009). Leadership by terror: Finding Shaka Zulu in the attic. In *Reflections on character and leadership: On the couch with Manfred Kets de Vries* (pp. 167–192). West Sussex, UK: John Wiley & Sons.

Kilburg, R. (2012). *Virtuous leaders: Strategy, character and influence in the 21st century*. Washington, DC: American Psychological Association.

King, Jr., M. L. (1996/1986). *A testament of hope: The essential writings and speeches of Martin Luther King, Jr.* (Ed. J. M. Washington). New York, NY: HarperCollins.

Lalich, J., & Tobias, M. (2006). *Take back your life: Recovering from cults and abusive relationships*. Richmond, CA: Bay Tree Publishing.

Lee, B. (Ed.). (2017). *The dangerous case of Donald Trump: 27 Psychiatrists and mental health experts assess a president*. New York, NY: St. Martin's Press.

Lieb, J. (2008). Two manic depressives, two tyrants, two world wars. *Medical Hypotheses, 70*(4), 888–892.

Lingiardi, V., & McWilliams, N. (Eds.). (2017). *Psychodynamic diagnostic manual* (2nd ed.). New York, NY: Guilford Press.

Louis de Canonville, C. (2018). The narcissist's addiction to grandiosity. *Narcissistic Behavior*. Retrieved from https://narcissisticbehavior.net/the-narcissists-addiction-to-grandiosity/

Masterson, J. (1981). *The narcissistic and borderline disorders: An integrated developmental approach*. New York, NY: Brunner/Mazel.

Miller, A. (1980). *For your own good: Hidden cruelty in child-rearing and the roots of violence*. New York, NY: Farrar, Straus & Giroux.

Morris, D. R. (2019). Shaka: Zulu chief. *Encyclopedia Britannica*. Retrieved from www.britannica.com/biography/Shaka-Zulu-chief

Oakes, L. (2010). *The charismatic personality*. Bowden Hills, Queensland: Australian Academic Press.

Ohler, N. (2017). *Blitzed: Drugs in the Third Reich*. New York, NY: Houghton Mifflin Harcourt.

Owen, D. (2008). Hubris syndrome. *Clinical Medicine (London, England), 8*(4), 428–432.

Owen, D., & Davidson, J. (2009). Hubris syndrome: An acquired personality disorder? A study of US Presidents and UK Prime Ministers over the last 100 years. *Brain: A Journal of Neurology, 132*(Pt 5), 1396–1406.

Post, J. M. (2015). *Narcissism and politics: Dreams of glory*. New York, NY: Cambridge University Press.

Retief, F., & Wessels, A. (2009). Mao Tse-tung (1893–1976): His habits and his health. *South African Medical Journal, 99*(5), 302–305.

Ronningstam, R. (2016). *NPD basic: A brief overview of identifying, diagnosing and treating narcissistic personality disorder* (2nd ed.). National Education Alliance for Borderline Personality Disorders. Retrieved from https://borderlinepersonalitydisorder.org/wp-content/uploads/2013/11/NPD-Basic-Second-Edition-In-Print-03-2016.pdf

Shengold, L. (1989). *Soul murder: The effects of childhood abuse and deprivation*. New York, NY: Fawcett Columbine.

Simon, R. (2008). *Bad men do what good men dream: A forensic psychiatrist illuminates the darker side of human behavior*. Washington, DC: American Psychiatric Association.

Stal, M. (2013). Psychopathology of Joseph Stalin. *Psychology, 4*(9A1), 1–4.

Stein, R. (2005). Why perversion? "False love" and the perverse pact. *International Journal of Psychoanalysis, 86*(Pt 3), 775–799.

Stoller, R. J. (1975). *Perversion: The erotic form of hatred*. New York, NY: Pantheon.

Stone, M. H. (2017). *The anatomy of evil*. Amherst, NY: Prometheus Books.

Storr, A. (1996). *Feet of clay: Saints, sinners, and madmen – A study of gurus*. New York, NY: Free Press.

Tudoroiu, T. (2016). *The revolutionary totalitarian personality: Hitler, Mao, Castro, and Chávez*. New York, NY: Palgrave Macmillan.

3

SYMPATHY FOR THE DEVIL

Application and limitations of the malignant narcissist diagnosis

Diagnoses are used to frame the symmetry of a client ("How dare frame thy fearful symmetry," saith William Blake). Nevertheless, it is important to note that these diagnoses are contested: "It (the DSM-5) makes it seem like an anxiety disorder doesn't have any mood symptoms and a mood disorder doesn't have any anxiety symptoms. But it isn't that simple. It's just not the way people present" (Greenberg, 2013, p. 54). With several caveats and dictums always in consideration, this chapter uses the cluster of symptoms designated as malignant narcissist leader (MNL) to describe and therapeutically address a client named Mr. John Green (a pseudonym).

Although not a discrete category in the DSM-5, malignant narcissism is a shorthand description for individuals who share the comorbidities of narcissism and antisocial personality disorders – that is, an "individual who is both pathologically narcissistic and anti-social, where self-justifiable violence, sadistic cruelty and self-destructiveness are in service to a very fragile and unstable self-esteem" (Logan, 2009, p. 92). However, in the preface to his book *The Man Who Mistook His Wife for a Hat: And Other Clinical Tales* (1998), Oliver Sacks writes of the case history: "There is no 'subject' in a narrow case history; modern case histories allude to the subject in a cursory phrase . . . which could apply to a rat as a human being" (Sacks, 1998, p. VIII). To counter this, he further writes: "To restore the human subject at the centre – the suffering, afflicted, fighting, human subject – we must deepen a case history to a narrative or tale; only then do we have a 'who' as well as a 'what,' a real person" (Sacks, 1998, p. VIII). This chapter, building upon the criteria developed in Chapter 2, attempts to present a case history of a client while mindful of Sack's dictum. It acknowledges that human beings are messy, flesh and blood creatures.

A DSM diagnosis, even if useful, is always reductive and perhaps inaccurate. In a very profound way, a diagnosis distances both the clinician and patient from the existential dread. She or he fails to address the greater questions of the ultimate meaning and complexity of the patient's life. It presents a permanent statement about a human being when, at best, it is a description and a story.

In his book *Heart of Man: Its Genius for Good and Evil* (1964), the psychoanalyst Eric Fromm first described and coined the term *malignant narcissism*. He wrote that "such individuals are self-centered, grandiose, sadistic, suspicious, and disregard the rights of others. They also lack empathy and seek power through exploitation and abuse" (Sperry, 2016, p. 660).

However, there is a certain tension with this description. Diagnoses are based on storytelling. The clinician listens to a tale told by a client. Yet, as Kurosawa's *Rashomon* so poignantly illustrates, stories are subjective. Moreover, interpretations are rooted in a clinician's biases. David Rosenhan's Thud experiment still illustrates this point even though it took place almost 50 years ago (see Rosenhan, *Being Sane in Insane Places*, 1973). Then, as Gary Greenberg points out in his book on the DSM-5, *The Book of Woe*, diagnoses are not "natural" in the way diabetes or the common cold is natural. People diagnosed with schizophrenia are different from those diagnosed with schizophrenia and depression. Therefore, human beings are an amalgamation of different states of being (Greenberg, 2013).

If this client contains multitude diagnoses, then several therapeutic approaches should be proffered toward treating him. In this chapter, these therapeutic perspectives include self psychology, a part of dialectical behavior therapy, as well as Eye Movement Desensitization and Reprocessing Therapy. Multiple perspectives are essential. Human beings who manifest these symptoms are possibly the most distressed clients a psychotherapist or social worker will encounter (Sperry, 2016). Their therapeutic outcomes are considered impossibly grim.

The client: Robert Green

Robert Green was born in the southeast section of Washington, DC, an economically distressed neighborhood separated from the city by the Anacostia River. He is a 44-year-old African-American male who is currently on parole for drug possession. He is also a known leader of a drug gang that flourished in southeastern DC in the mid- to late '90s. He has been diagnosed by a community mental health center with antisocial personality disorder and post-traumatic stress disorder, and he has been assigned to court-stipulated outpatient counseling there. During the intake interview (for which this writer was present), he was asked for a history of his life.

A patient history

During his childhood and adolescence, Mr. Green had multiple caregivers. First his single mother, then an aunt, and finally, by his sixth birthday, foster care. He lived in a series of foster homes where he reported that he was repeatedly raped and beaten. He stated that as a youth he was short and diminutive and, therefore, a target of older, larger, predatory children. During adolescence, Mr. Green began selling drugs and mugging people. He also gained a reputation for violence. He spent most of his adolescence in juvenile detention centers for assault and robbery.

As an adult, Mr. Green became a leader in one of southeast DC's drug gangs while going in and out of the federal prison system. Mr. Green tightly controlled the gang and, in his own words, his leadership style was "religious" – meaning under Mr. Green's reign, new gang members pledged oaths to him in secret, elaborate ceremonies. These ceremonies had manifold purposes. They created an aura of both secrecy and allegiance to Mr. Green and to the gang. During this induction, new gang members were presented with rules that Mr. Green wrote that were strict and allowed him tight control over members. He felt this control was necessary for his gang to thrive and avoid prosecution. However, he admits he violated many of these rules while enforcing them upon others.

The trajectory of his life culminated in his murder conviction of his 3-year-old daughter. A murder, he claims, was an accident. He served ten years in prison for the crime, but he was released on a technicality based on a mistake made by the prosecutor. The irony of this circumstance is that, while waiting for his release, he threw a vat of boiling water at another inmate's face. Mr. Green permanently blinded the inmate. Therefore, he had to serve additional time despite the discovery of the technicality.

It should also be noted that during the patient history Mr. Green discussed the murder of his daughter in a flat, factual manner. He lacked emotional display or response when he discussed the crime, which may have been a revenge killing to punish an ex-girlfriend or an accident (he admits he shook his daughter because he was angry with the mother).

Mr. Green reported he has had many altercations upon release from prison. He stated that he pursued an ex-girlfriend by car and, instead of catching up to her car, smashed his own car. He was also rearrested for having a trunk full of cocaine in a friend's car, but he was somehow able to have those charges reduced. Mr. Green proudly stated that he was one of the most important drug distributers in Washington, DC. He explained he enjoys physically hurting those he perceives as betraying him, and his daughter's murder may not be the only murder in his past.

He also has an unusual hobby. Mr. Green reported that he keeps salt water tanks in an ex-girlfriend's basement and cares for and breeds lobsters. He stated he is fascinated by these creatures – the way they look and move about, "prancing" on the bottom of the tanks like spiders. Lobsters have rigid exoskeletons that protect fleshy bodies. Mr. Green may have a rigid exoskeleton of grandiosity and criminality. He may also be unwilling to confront what is underneath his exoskeleton. The exoskeleton symbolizes the journey a therapist and Mr. Green might undergo because, in order to grow, both the lobster and Mr. Green must relinquish their rigid exoskeletons so they can develop. There are several possible theories and therapeutic techniques one may derive about Mr. Green from this history.

A neurobiological hypothesis based on Mr. Green's history

Mr. Green's brain, much like that of every other human being, has been uniquely shaped by not only biology, but also his attachments (or lack thereof) and social environment. The human brain is a social brain, and it is shaped by discrete experiences and human interactions (Lieberman, 2013). In his case, he experienced severe attachment and social deprivation during his infancy, childhood, and adolescence.

Ideally, early interaction with caregivers creates a secure attachment bond that also influences "the development and expansion of the infant's regulatory system" (Schore, 2003, p. 19). The absence of a significant caregiver means Mr. Green's "development of the ability to cope with stress" may have been impaired (Schore, 2003, para. 20). This impairment in turn means that he may have "hippocampal atrophy," which, as the hippocampus is the seat of memory in the brain, may affect learning (Cozolino, 2010, p. 250). This impairment happens because "sustained higher levels of metabolism (due to prolonged stress) continue to pump sodium into neurons, eventually overwhelming the cell's ability to transport it out again" and "results in the death of the cell membrane and cell death" (Cozolino, 2010, p. 250). Stress also releases cortisol, and prolonged stress means that cortisol could have diminished Mr. Green's immune system, his brain plasticity, dendrites, and remyelination. Cortisol also kills cells and "inhibits neurogenesis and neural growth" (Cozolino, 2010, p. 251).

Furthermore, Mr. Green's impaired attachment history may have had an impact on the development of the right hemisphere of his brain. According to Bowlby, the mother and infant bond is filled with intense emotion (Holmes, 2014). This bond is critical to the development of the right brain which is "deeply connected into the emotion-processing limbic system" (Narvez, Panksepp, Schore, & Gleason, 2013, p. 46). It specifically impacts the child's "visual emotional information, the infant's recognition of the mother's face, and the perception of arousal-inducing maternal facial expressions" and is "attuned to the mother's right hemisphere" (Narvez et al., 2013, p. 35). In fact, an infant's emotions are almost solely stored in the right hemisphere during the infant brain's formation, but the caregiving bond is necessary for this to fully develop.

If this communication between mother and infant is disrupted, it may "have a long-lasting yet hidden impact on our self-esteem" and "may create a bias toward shame, guilt, and pessimism" (Cozolino, 2010, p. 107). Furthermore, "infants cope with the emotional distress caused by unresponsive mothers through self-regulation behavior associated with greater activation of the right hemisphere" (Narvez et al., 2013, p. 37). Greater activation or "extreme right frontal activity" can lead to adults who are "more fearful and defensive, and have higher levels of stress hormones" (Cozolino, 2010, p. 106). If "the mutual gaze between caretaker and child is a primary mechanism for promoting brain growth and organization," then Mr. Green may have suffered significant obstruction of these qualities (Cozolino, 2010, p. 186). Although this obstruction does not excuse his criminal and violent behavior, it may offer insight into why he has behaved in an antisocial manner. There are, however, also other ways to analyze and assess Mr. Green's life.

There is no way to know if the turmoil in Mr. Green's early life created the neurological distress described except perhaps with magnetic resonance imaging.

However, Mr. Green's behavior is indicative that, at least, part of this hypothesis may be true.

Mr. Green and attachment theory

Two types of attachment experiences contribute to narcissism: overindulgence and neglect (Campbell & Miller, 2011). If Mr. Green's account of his childhood is true, then he experienced the severest form of neglect. When a child experiences "repeated rejection or maltreatment," it "may suggest that one is unworthy of consistent care and nurturance" (Campbell & Miller, 2011, p. 435). If so, then

> defensive narcissism may thus emerge in response to parental coldness, rejection, and disapproval.... Consequent acknowledgement of being "deserving" of aversive treatment would be emotionally overwhelming and, as a consequence, the developing narcissist may evolve inflated self-views in order to ward off fears of being unworthy.
>
> *Campbell & Miller, 2011, pp. 435–436*

The neglect stunts the child's ability to develop and to have an examined life and an authentic personality. Instead, it can lead to lifelong distress due to a distorted and false understanding of who they are, which means they will struggle forming intimate bonds.

Mr. Green's history of impaired attachments may have contributed to his violent and antisocial history, compounding his neglect. In his youth, he never had a stable attachment figure, which means he lacks security in intimate relationships and reacts violently when he perceives he is being abandoned. His "lack of felt security arouses a simultaneous wish to be close and the angry determination to punish the attachment figure for the minutest sign of abandonment" (Fonagy, 2001, p. 7). Furthermore, Mr. Green's proclivity for violence, not just in his business, but also in his personal life, may be tied or related to the insecure-ambivalent stage defined by psychologist Mary Salter Ainsworth (Salter Ainsworth, Blehar, Waters, & Wall, 2015). In relationships with others, especially intimate relationships, he is hyper-vigilant and expects abandonment and betrayal, lacks the capacity to self-soothe or have others soothe him, and then responds violently. This hyper-arousal or -vigilance has destroyed all his intimate relationships and may have contributed to violence against his family members, including the murder of his daughter.

This attachment impairment is compounded by the trauma he experienced as a youth and also his cultural socialization toward violent behavior. These violent, traumatic experiences potentially lead to a "persistent expectation of violence and exploitation; destruction of capacity for social trust" and a "persistent mobilization of the body and mind for lethal danger, with the potential for explosive violence" (Shay, 1995, p. XX). There is also a possibility that the physical violence he experienced throughout his life caused neurological damage although the attachment impairments described may have shaped his neurological makeup too.

Treatment for Mr. Green

As discussed earlier in this chapter, treatment outcomes for people who manifest this particular cluster of symptoms are bleak. However, this chapter proposes several discrete therapeutic approaches that may improve Mr. Green's prospects for staying out of prison, possibly forming stable, reciprocal relationships, and ceasing the use of physical and emotional violence.

Mr. Green and self psychology

Heinz Kohut's theory of self psychology rejected the primacy of innate sexual drives and emphasized the importance of empathy in human development (Banai, Mikulincer, & Shaver, 2005). He illuminated the psychic phenomena of self-object others or self-object experiences: psychic interactions that nourish the psyche or self and impact a person's experience of themselves and their self-esteem. Kohut declared, "The most fundamental finding of self psychology is that the emergence of the self requires . . . the presence of others designated as objects" (Wolf, 2002, p. 16). Kohut theorized that, through bonding between human beings, the development of the self transforms through three states or axes: the grandiosity axis, the idealization axis, and the alter ego-connectedness (twinship) axis (Banai et al., 2005). The grandiose axis delineates a person's ability to sustain self-esteem and to be able to display dedication to meaningful tasks. The idealization axis describes and delineates a person's ability to develop and sustain goals and principles. Finally, the alter ego-connectedness axis delineates a person's ability to relate to other human beings, perform well in groups, communicate feelings, and form intimate bonds (Banai et al., 2005, para. 5).

Kohut further theorized that a disruption in this "narcissistic sustenance" through these self-objects leads to "disorders of the self" (Banai et al., 2005, para. 7). A well-adjusted child "learns to soothe himself rather than collapsing in despair . . . comes to experience internal strength despite defeat" (Mitchell & Black, 1995, p. 160). A child lacking stable self-objects "displayed an underlying lack of self-cohesion, serious doubts about one's sense of continuity over time, lack of confidence in one's ability to deal with life's hardships, and vulnerable self-esteem" (Banai et al., 2005, para. 9). The distressed child then becomes an adult lacking the ability to regulate emotion and more likely to lash out at others over the most minor provocation.

As an infant and child, Mr. Green lacked stable self-objects. Because his caregivers were unable to offer him the attention a child requires for healthy development, he would have unsuccessfully incorporated the three axes and developed a stunted and unrealistic conception of his selfhood. His early life may have emulated the foundlings psychoanalyst Rene Spitz studied in his seminal book, *Hospitalism* (Mitchell &

Black, 1995, p. 38). Spitz observed children who were living in a foundling home who had their physical needs met, but who were deprived of a nurturing presence. Tragically, children who were deprived of a nurturing presence became stunted emotionally and physically, with more than one-third dying if that state of being continued for several years (Mitchell & Black, 1995, p. 38).

This emotional stunting and inability to begin developing a cohesive self may have led Mr. Green to meet and develop malignant self-objects. He may have envisioned himself with misplaced grandiosity as a major drug dealer whose idealized goals were solely criminal and whose peers were fellow drug dealers or other criminals. This conception of his selfhood combined with an inability to process stunted, fragmented emotions may have contributed to Mr. Green's history of violence.

Mr. Green's self-object needs in therapy

A therapeutic relationship with Mr. Green might be a tempestuous, daunting, and even dangerous undertaking. Kohut theorized that clients "treat their analyst and envision themselves, as intensely needed, functional aspects of their own subjective experience" (Mitchell & Black, 1995, p. 160). Moreover, Kohut delineated three types of object transference that mirror the three self-object axes mentioned. The first is called mirroring transference whereby the therapist reflects and displays understanding of the client's "experience of themselves, their excitements, their perceptions as well as their disappointments" (Mitchell & Black, 1995, p. 160). During this transference, the therapist offers the client a nurturing space for his self to be appreciated, understood, and fostered. Kohut called the second object transference the idealizing transference. Here, the therapist is held in supremely high regard by the client, which permits the client to also view himself in higher regard because of his connection with the therapist. Kohut described the third transference as the alter ego or twinship transference whereby the client wishes to be like the therapist in some way "not in terms of external resemblance but in significance of function" (Mitchell & Black, 1995, p. 161).

In Mr. Green's case, these transferences might be fraught with distrust, anger, and even, as a form of self-protection, abuse toward the therapist. Mr. Green would initially, and may never, accommodate the "holding environment" of the mirroring transference. He may likely have a negative self-conception of himself further compounded by his lack of awareness of how he regards himself. To add to this potentially difficult transference and countertransference, psychoanalyst Otto Kernberg listed the characteristics of malignant narcissism as having "any or all of the following: (1) paranoid regressions in the transference . . .; (2) chronic self-destructiveness . . . as a triumph over the analyst; (3) major and minor dishonesty in the transference; and (4) overt sadistic triumph over the analyst, or malignant generosity" (Kernberg, 1993, p. 290). See Chapter 2 for additional details and analysis.

To overcome these difficult transferences, Mr. Green would have to reflect emotional despair and traumatic symptoms in ways that did not destroy the therapeutic relationship. If he and the therapist were able to contend with his problematic selfhood, the therapist might become a nurturing presence that allows Mr. Green to foster and grow empathy and emotions. This transference might be buttressed by the idealizing and twinship transferences. If Mr. Green were able to identify with the therapist and hold the therapist in high regard (thereby bolstering his own positive self-regard), the therapist might be able to use these transferences from Mr. Green to identify with another way of being and living. However, the therapist will have to contend with his or her own countertransferences that may manifest in a multitude of ways – none positive. With a client so deeply distressed, even an experienced clinical social worker should seek supervision and counsel.

Mr. Green and dialectical behavior therapy

Dialectical behavior therapy (DBT) is an evidence-based therapy for people who have been primarily, although not exclusively, diagnosed with borderline personality disorder (Linehan, 2014). However, it is also increasingly applied to other types of diagnoses. It includes both individual and group therapy and incorporates cognitive behavioral therapy and meditation.

There is a psychoeducational group that is solely devoted to developing compassion within individuals titled *Compassion-focused Group Therapy*. This group happens within the context of a DBT program (Parker, Woods, & Gilbert, 2009). The group incorporates meditation, guided imagery, role playing, and psychoeducational lectures on compassion.

The outline of the program is

1. Introduction to the basic ideas and approach – learning how our minds work and why they are difficult to regulate; 2. Looking at what compassion is and how it can help with our difficulties; 3. Outline and practice various exercises that help us with our difficulties; 4. Looking at and working with our fears, blocks, and difficulties in developing compassion.

Parker et al., 2009, para. 48

A psychoeducation program like this might provide Mr. Green with a framework to conceptualize how he needs to cultivate healthier relationships.

For Mr. Green to begin this program, he would need to be already beginning to develop ego strength, to display the beginnings of a positive relationship with his therapist, and to show signs of a regard for others. Without this progress, he would not be able to psychically tolerate the group as he would attempt to dominate the group and, when that failed, would then become abusive. Moreover, the group would not tolerate his grandiosity and intimidation tactics. However, if he was able to participate in the group, it might be a life-changing experience. The group rubric addresses therapeutic growth both cognitively and somatically. If he learned to exist within a group and relate to others without being destructive, he may have an opportunity for a less destructive life.

EMDR and treatment outcome results

With a human being so deeply distressed as John Green, therapy would be extraordinarily difficult for both client and therapist. Otto Kernberg writes: "Patients with narcissistic personalities who are undergoing resolution of the pathological grandiose self frequently present complications so severe that the treatment may be stalemated or prematurely interrupted . . . because the clinical picture is of a condensation of grandiose and sadistic strivings" (Kernberg, 1993, p. 290). Mr. Green's malignant narcissism is the reason for addressing his circumstance with self psychology. If Mr. Green is to have a minimally productive life, he must receive healthy narcissistic sustenance from his therapist (as opposed to the severe neglect he received through most of his life). Moreover, through therapeutic relationships (both in individual and group therapies), he might be able to learn to form healthy attachments with other human beings. It is important for a therapist to keep in his mind's eye, however, that Mr. Green is both a predator and a victim, that, in his youth, he was violently assaulted and raped.

With a client like Mr. Green, so psychically twisted and aggressive, it might be helpful to circumvent talk therapy and use a technique like Eye Movement Desensitization and Reprocessing Therapy (EMDR) to treat his trauma. EMDR is a comparatively new therapy that "uses eye movements or other forms of rhythmical stimulation, such as hand taps or tones, in a way that seems to assist the brain's information-processing system to proceed at a rapid rate" (Shapiro & Forrest, 2004, p. 5). EMDR may be an effective treatment for Mr. Green because it appears to work directly on our pre-literate selves or default selves. This technique would detour around Mr. Green's grandiose claims and verbal aggression.

If all these techniques were used, it would be important to measure Mr. Green's progress quantitatively. One way to measure his progress would be the Compassion Measurement Tool (CMT), which was developed from empathy research at Syracuse University. It includes 64 questions and "4 sub scales: cognitive compassion, emotional compassion, strong compassion, and barriers to compassion" (Hoisington, 2013, para. 9). CMT could be implemented at the beginning and the termination of Mr. Green's therapy. At the termination of his therapy, it would be important for Mr. Green to have a support network in place, even if it was minimal. If psychotherapy is successful with someone like Mr. Green, the therapist might be the first and only healthy, boundary-setting relationship he has ever had. Losing it might be deeply distressing without other relationships blossoming.

Therefore, if the therapist and client were able to accomplish the goals of ending Mr. Green's criminal behavior, infusing and expanding his ability to be empathic and compassionate, and engaging in positive relationships, it would be time, perhaps, to end the therapeutic relationship. However, there is a caveat to this hopeful note. In his book *The Anatomy of Human Destructiveness*, Eric Fromm writes:

> This fallacy lies in the belief that a thoroughly destructive and evil man must be a devil – and look his part; that he must be devoid of any positive quality;

that he must bear the sign of Cain so visibly that everyone can recognize his destructiveness from afar.

Fromm, 1973, p. 432

Fromm further writes: "The destructive person will show a font of kindness; courtesy; love of family; of children; of animals; he will speak of his ideals and good intentions" (Fromm, 1973, p. 432). Therefore, a therapist or social worker needs to be careful and skeptical as they work with clients so deeply distressed.

Conclusion

In October 2005, neurologist James Fallon examined the brain scans of serial killers. While he did so, he also had brain scans of his own family on his desk. One of these scans displayed "low activity in certain areas of the frontal and temporal lobes linked to empathy, morality, and self-control" (Stromberg, 2013, para. 3). To his surprise, the brain scan that indicated sociopathy was his own.

In the ongoing and maybe never-ending debate between nature and nurture, neurological discoveries are illuminating personality tendencies. But these tendencies are, at best, just tendencies. Even though James Fallon discovered he had these tendencies and, indeed, had difficulty throughout his life mustering empathy for others, he became a "pro-social sociopath" (Stromberg, 2013, para. 6). Fallon credits a loving mother and a happy childhood for this outcome.

Therefore, even if Mr. Green inherited an irenic lineage, the deprivation and trauma he experienced as a child also shaped the makeup of his brain and his notion of his selfhood. Sadly, for Green: "Although brain development is guided and controlled to some extent by genetic information, a not insignificant portion of brain structuration and neural patterning is thought to occur through interaction with the child with the environment" (Cicchetti & Cohen, 2006, p. 7). Mr. Green tells us that he has been horrifically violent, has lacked empathy for those he has destroyed, has been a leader who exhibited totalistic control over his followers, and has been one of the most notorious leaders of a drug gang in DC. In person, he appears to be articulate, charming, and charismatic unless you listen to what he is saying about how destructive he has been. These are all character traits that fall under the diagnostic rubric of malignant narcissism. Many mental health professionals believe people diagnosed with psychopathy, which would include malignant narcissism, are untreatable and that psychopathy is a discrete brain disorder. They are often portrayed as secular demons and their nightmarish presence overpopulates our popular culture (Jalava, Griffiths, & Marun, 2015).

The question for the therapist, the neurologist, the courts, and society is: can a human being with Mr. Green's violent history, as a fully formed adult, learn to be empathic and even foster a richer emotional life that includes reciprocal love? If such a transformation did take place (as may happen as a result of many religious conversion experiences in prison, most famously perhaps with Malcolm X), would there be discrete changes to his brain? One source of hope is the knowledge that neural plasticity occurs throughout the lifespan of a human being even though it occurs at a slower pace in older adults (Liou, 2010). Moreover, perhaps by opening the self to others (beginning with the therapeutic process), the need for relatedness (which Kohut explained is innate) can be fostered and nurtured and, possibly, redeem a life.

Mr. Green is no devil, but, instead, flesh and blood. It would be easy to obscure his humanity, as ugly as it can be, in a metaphysical cloak. A case study of a human being like Mr. Green isn't the study of theodicy or abnormal personality, but instead the story of how one human being contends with the vicissitudes of the human condition or is psychically broken by those vicissitudes (particularly those vicissitudes that are rooted in childhood neglect and deprivation, predation, and emotional and physical abuse). The easy path would be to disown Mr. Green's humanity and portray him as a "super predator" or demon. It would sanitize what it means to be human. It is much more difficult to view Mr. Green on the continuum of what it means to be human: a continuum that includes cruelty, violence, sorrow, racism, poverty, and anguish.

This psychological suffering then becomes like a stone dropped in a pool of water, sweeping other people in its wake. It includes, in Mr. Green's case, self-loathing masked as grandiosity, self-harm, rage, violence, paranoia, and a powerful need to control the people in your life. But with only a sliver, if that, of empathy, relatedness, love – those other very human attributes that Freud and Fromm and Rogers and the perennial philosophers asserted were essential for a satisfying life. In the end, stripping away all the diagnostic language, Mr. Green's suffering is directed inward and outward. Ignoring it, reducing it to a metaphysical or diagnostic formula, obscures the nature of human suffering and its catastrophic impact on the human psyche.

References

Banai, E., Mikulincer, M., & Shaver, P. R. (2005). "Selfobject" needs in Kohut's self psychology: Links with attachment, self-cohesion, affect regulation, and adjustment. *Psychoanalytic Psychology, 22*(2), 224–260. doi:10.1037/0736-9735.22.2.224

Campbell, W. K., & Miller, J. D. (2011). *The handbook of narcissism and narcissistic personality disorder: Theoretical approaches, empirical findings, and treatments.* Hoboken, NJ: John Wiley & Sons. doi:10.1002/9781118093108

Cicchetti, D., & Cohen, D. J. (Eds.). (2006). *Developmental psychopathology* (2nd ed., Vol. 2, *Developmental neuroscience*). Hoboken, NJ: John Wiley & Sons.

Cozolino, L. (2010). *The neuroscience of psychotherapy: Healing the social brain* (2nd ed.). New York, NY: W.W. Norton.

Fonagy, P. (2001). *Attachment theory and psychoanalysis.* New York, NY: Other Press.

Fromm, E. (1964). *The heart of man: Its genius for good and evil.* New York, NY: Harper & Row.

Fromm, E. (1973). *The anatomy of human destructiveness.* New York, NY: Holt, Rinehart & Winston.

Greenberg, G. (2013). *The book of woe: The DSM and the unmaking of psychiatry.* New York, NY: Penguin Group.

Hoisington, W. D. (2013, October 19). Measuring compassion: From theory to application. Paper presented at the New England Psychological Association Annual Meeting, Bridgeport, CT. Retrieved from www.academia.edu/3215500/Compassion_Measurement_Tool_-_CMT

Holmes, J. (2014). *John Bowlby and attachment theory*. New York, NY: Routledge.

Jalava J., Griffiths S., & Marun, M. (2015). *The myth of the born criminal: psychopathy, neurobiology, and creation of the modern degenerate*. Toronto, Buffalo, London: University of Toronto Press.

Kernberg, O. F. (1993). *Severe personality disorders: Psychotherapeutic strategies*. New Haven, CT: Yale University Press.

Lieberman, M. D. (2013). *Social: Why our brains are wired to connect*. New York, NY: Crown Publishers.

Linehan, M. M. (2014). *DBT skills training manual* (2nd ed.). New York, NY: Guilford Press.

Liou, S. (2010). Neuroplasticity. Retrieved from web.stanford.edu

Logan, C. (2009). Narcissism. In M. McMurran & R. Howard (Eds.), *Personality, personality disorder, and violence: An evidence based approach* (*Wiley Series in Forensic Clinical Psychology*, pp. 85–112). West Sussex, UK: John Wiley & Sons.

Mitchell, S. A., & Black, M. J. (1995). *Freud and beyond: A history of modern psychoanalytic thought*. New York, NY: Basic Books.

Narvez, D., Panksepp, J., Schore, A. N., & Gleason, T. R. (Eds.). (2013). *Evolution, early experience and human development: From research to practice and policy*. New York, NY: Oxford University Press.

Parker, C., Woods, D., & Gilbert, P. (2009). Outline and session by session record of Compassion Focused Group Therapy Module in the context of a local DBT program. Retrieved from www.compassionatemind.co.uk

Sacks, O. (1998). *The man who mistook his wife for a hat and other clinical tales*. New York, NY: Touchstone Books.

Salter Ainsworth, M. D., Blehar, M. C., Waters, E., & Wall, S. N. (2015). *Patterns of attachment: A psychological study of the strange situation* (Classic ed.). New York, NY: Psychology Press.

Schore, A. N. (2003). Effects of a secure attachment relationship on right brain development, affect regulation, and infant mental health. *Infant Mental Health Journal, 22*(1–2), 7–66. doi:10.1002/1097-0355(200101/04):1 < 7::AID-IMHJ2 > 3.0.CO;2-N

Shapiro, F., & Forrest, M. S. (2004). *EMDR: The breakthrough "eye movement" therapy for overcoming anxiety, stress, and trauma*. New York, NY: Basic Books.

Shay, J. (1995). *Achilles in Vietnam: Combat trauma and the undoing of character* (1st Touchstone ed.). New York, NY: Touchstone Books.

Sperry, L. (Ed.). (2016). Malingering. In *Mental health and mental disorders: An encyclopedia of conditions, treatments, and well-being*. New York, NY: ABC-CLIO.

Stromberg, J. (2013, November 22). The neuroscientist who discovered he was a psychopath. *Smithsonian Magazine*. Retrieved from www.smithsonianmag.com

Wolf, E. S. (2002). *Treating the self: Elements of clinical self psychology*. London, UK: Guilford Press.

4

THE PATHO-DYNAMICS OF TOTALITARIA

How mad leaders form followers and gain ascendance

This chapter is authored by Charles Zeiders with a treatment section added by Peter Devlin. An earlier version of the section "The Followers: Different Types and Singular Madness" appeared in "A 'Psychological Autopsy' of a Malignant Narcissist in Church Leadership: A 'Composite' Scenario with Discussion," published in The Journal of Christian Healing, spring/summer 2016, volume 32, number 1, and it is reprinted here with edits and additional discussion.

Organizations dominated by malignant narcissist leaders (MNLs) tend to become cults or high-pressure groups; this applies regardless of the social sector filled by the group. The organization may be of any size, type, or affiliation. No sort of human group is immune to the infiltrations, machinations, and power grabs of a destructive leader.

Regardless of whether the group is secular or religious, the MNL will subjugate members to the totality of his agenda, or will aspire to do so. Constituents will be persuaded to disdain non-members, scapegoat despised enemies, and conform to the worldview assigned by the malignant leader or his confederates. The organization tilts toward the ruthless with the leader seeking comprehensive control. To keep constituents compliant, the MNL will inaugurate (or a least welcome) techniques to transform members into his narcissistic extensions and psychic appendages. Psychopathologists apply such terms as *brainwashing, mind control*, and *thought reform*,[1] to identify coercive persuasion techniques (influence upon mental processes without informed consent) employed by sects, cults, and radical organizations to unduly influence and control the identity, and thus behavior, of others (American Psychiatric Association, 2013, p. 306). Recent history offers no shortage of such groupings.

However, just like not all malignant narcissists become leaders, the groups they helm also do not necessarily morph into diseased organizations. An afflicted leader may maneuver using a destructive style but not "cult-ize" the corporation or organization. Moreover, savvy officials on a board of directors may obstruct the CEO's expectation of rubber-stamping sycophants. Or, a legislative body may save a republic, impeaching the head-of-state for violating the separation of powers. An uncouth eccentric may demand that the pastor cease his haranguing and produce the financials. Checks, balances, and the people who uphold them strengthen organizational immunity against the MNL's tyranny and justly kill the totalitarian pressure to centralize power around the MNL. Due process of governance and political courage ultimately guard against the rise of night. But the psychological grown-ups, the group-members with ironic independence (those who are not group-thinkers), must speak early and often to arrest the virulence of tyranny. Sadly, a voice of resistance does not always formulate within a group, and we must consider the manipulative, high pressure systems arranged around the would-be totalitarian and his cultic enterprise.

Cult or high-pressure group: synonymous terms with a range of meanings

Definitionally, the terms *cult* and *high-pressure group* have multiple, overlapping definitions (Langone, 2015). In raw form, life defies stereotypes and academic reductionism. Just as the MNL exhibits innumerable expressions, so the term *cult* denotes a range of meanings. These over religious, political, psychological, or commercial groups feature leaders who unduly influence members, including:

- Fanatical confederacies
- Terrorist organizations such as al-Qaeda or Nordkreuz
- Unorthodox religious enterprises
- Communes run by extremists
- Multi-level marketing groups
- High-pressure sales shops
- Businesses demanding extreme conformity
- Ideological parties demanding loyalty to a "genius"
- Political groups advocating violence, radical progress, or radical reaction
- Groups intolerant of ambiguity or plurality
- Groups that locate salvation, secular or sacred, in its leader
- Dyadic or family groups, subjugated under an alpha

As with music, there may be variations on the theme.

Another definition, a sociological one, specifies a cult or high-pressure group as "an ideological organization held together by charismatic relationships and demanding total commitment" (Zablocki, 1997, n.p., as cited in Rosedale & Langone, 2015,

p. 5). Adulation from devotees empowers and inflames the criminal narcissism of a charismatic chief. This patho-dynamic of (a) a group projection of (b) libidinally charged idealization into (c) the mind of a savior figure who (d) identifies with the projection, places the organizations at highest risk for abuse, crime, and totalitarianism. Like the fictional Bishop Ladysmith-Jones in Chapter 1, the grandiosity of the MNL inflates to cosmic proportions as he identifies with the "all good" projections from lionizing believers.

How the MNL colonizes the organization

How does human dignity relate to methods of control so intrinsic to the malignant narcissist leader? Quite simply, it has to do with fear. The current species-wide developmental crisis is overwhelming, and frightened people look for saviors. Indeed, there is much from which we need saving. Global humanity faces existential threats from climate change, world war, famine, epidemics, and political incompetence. Mass migrations destabilize governments. The world currency, the U.S. dollar, is backed by insurmountable debt and military might deployable to extort recognition of the currency. The nationalist conglomerate that is China threatens the United States. And Russian expansionism threatens European security. But all of Eurasia recalls Western imperialism, exploitation, and bad faith, and African populations, like the Congolese, can credibly claim that the *heart of darkness* was a European export. For security's sake, one might contract with a confident savior and not read the mouse-print.

Fear is often the Faustian affect that announces the demise of dignity, of giving up self-sovereignty to someone with ready-answers. This is what Fromm was driving at when he wrote *Escape from Freedom* (1941), and this is what Guattari (1995) meant when he claimed that everybody wants to be a fascist. A supply of unmet human needs creates a demand for answers that are often pernicious to the soul of authentic humanity.

At local levels, cultural disruption, economic disparity, and political frustration foster trepidation and agitation. A collective conception is that no one – no system, no government, no academic, no scientist, no institution, no religion, no ideology, no culture, no society – actually knows what to do. This escalates the global quotient of dread and overwhelms mother earth's citizenry with the sense that innumerable survival threats are un-redressable by local, state, global, or corporate elites – the incompetence and bad faith of whom are obvious. Benzodiazepines (however desirable) will not address these issues. Epidemiologically, the world could not be more hospitable to the demagoguery and crank salvation of the malignant narcissist and his minions.

Susceptibility, however, need not be conceptualized on such grand scale. Openness to malignant influence can happen at any order of existence. Whether macro or micro, the human condition is a vulnerable one.

Mind control, thought reform, and "brainwashing"

A leader must assert, maintain, and enforce a critical mass of credibility (or at minimum subjugation) among his constituencies to maintain control of any group. History teaches that a leader may maintain power, not only by the crude behaviorism of killing opponents and rewarding supporters, but also through sophisticated methods of *mind control* or *thought reform*, popularly called *brainwashing*. According to West and Langone (1986), a *totalistic* group exhibits "excessive devotion ... to some person, idea, or thing and employ[s] unethically manipulative techniques of persuasion and control ... designed to advance the goals of the group's leaders, to the ... detriment of members, their families, or the community" (pp. 119–120). *Totalism*, or totalitarian control, is the terminal point of the inhuman project to possess a society or a mind. Totalism is degradation posing as dignity.

Robert Jay Lifton

Robert Jay Lifton, the psychiatrist-scholar whose oeuvre lays bare the controlling aspirations of totalitarian groups from the Cold War to the present, provided works of enduring value to discern totalistic dynamics in most guises or groups (Lifton, 2011; Hassan, 2018). Lifton isolated eight ingredients of the destructive leader's influence apothecary (see Box 4.1), and he proposed that the greater the ingredients' deployment, "the greater ... [the] ... resemblance to ideological *totalism*; and the more [a leader authorizes] ... totalist devices to change people, the greater [the] resemblance to thought reform (or 'brainwashing')" (Lifton, 1989, p. 435). Consider the frequency of the influence-ingredients listed in Box 4.1 as having a dosing effect, that is the greater the number of influences techniques, combined with aggressive application and frequency, the higher the likelihood for an individual's/group's thoughts to be "reformed" (Lifton, 2011).

Margaret Singer researched the influence techniques delineated by Lifton and found persons subjected to such techniques developed pseudo-personalities, synthetic identities split-off from the old selves (2003, p. 297). Her work culminated in *Cults in Our Midst* (2003). Lifton and Singer are among the first North American experts in thought reform techniques.

Steven Hassan

Among the second the generation mind control experts is Steven Hassan. Following his 1979 exit from the indoctrination of the Unification Church, he developed models of totalistic mind control and protocols for cult debriefing. These are conceptually similar to Lifton's but geared toward education and clinical utility.[2] Hassan's BITE model divides the essential components of mind control into quadrants populated by: *behavior, information, thought,* and *emotion*. For Hassan (2014), cults are totalistic groups arranged in a pyramidal structure; the leader enthroned atop, with trusted lieutenant immediately beneath. Together with the MNL, the lieutenants control the rank and file at the base. To accomplish this, the lieutenants engineer

BOX 4.1   LIFTON'S INFLUENCE APOTHECARY

The classic components of the mind control techniques discovered by Lifton (1989) include:

1   *Milieu Control*: is the restriction of information and communication within an environment; a plight that threatens to morph into internalized control, whereby a member introjects this technique of restriction and self-censorship.
2   *Mystical Manipulation*: refers to the MNL's claim to embody an absolute value, to know it fully, and to incarnate it. High-pressure leaders might claim to be Allah's Secretary of State, an economic savior, or any unverifiable ultimate, providentially mandated with an imperative mission. Leaders further manipulate followers through charged experiences, induced by drugs, repetitive chanting, or mass enthrallments of the Nuremberg type. Such mystical manipulations credential the leader's mad claim of ultimate status to followers.
3   *Demand for Purity*: pertains to the induction of split object relations, whereby the MNL's primitive good/evil ideation precludes the adult recognition of the moral complexities of existence, preferring to divide the world into extremes of black and white, good and evil. Such *all or nothing thinking* postulates that those in good standing with the MNL are utterly good, and those who are not, utterly evil.
4   *Confession*: orchestrated cultic rituals that include denunciations of life that exist outside the MNLs scope of approval. By denouncing pre-group existence, the subject surrenders the self to the leader and his totalist agenda.
5   *Sacred Science*: refers to the mystique of sacredness maintained around the leader and his vision. Questioning or criticizing either is represented to constituents as anathema.
6   *Loading the Language*: corresponds to Orwell's (1950) *newspeak*, which includes terms denoting the partisan seizure of language to constrict individuated analysis of the MNL or his norms. To dismiss MNL abuses, for example, loaded language might terminate mature analysis with phrases like "brilliance from on high" or "test of faith" or "executive privilege."
7   *Doctrine Over Person*: involves elevation of the leader's doctrine/ideology over any other, especially a constituent's lived experience, regardless of the latter's obvious truthfulness or veracity. Pressured from the malignant normality of the cultic milieu, critical thinkers may believe that their doubts reflect insanity, criminality, or evil.
8   *Dispensing of Existence*: pertains to the leader's claim that the legitimacy of any person or project resides only under the MNL and his vision of reality. All else is nothing, impure, or evil. Whereas the group purportedly flourishes amid the leader's perfect vision of reality, out-groups are defective, half-human, and un-entitled to exist.

Source: Lifton, 1989; paraphrase Zeiders.

group *behavior* – the style of dress, type of food, and amount of sleep, along with group bonding behaviors, like communal singing, education classes, group prayer, endless pep rallies, etc. Access to *information* is also tightly controlled. Newscasts, internet, radio, and television, together with contact with non-group family and significant others is restricted with the aim of creating an ideologically antiseptic environment. To diminish independent *thought* and facilitate cognitive susceptibility to MNL propaganda, the milieu is filled with repetitive slogans, reminders of the leader's excellence, and sound-bites designed to short-circuit critical analysis of the leader. A critical notion about the MNL, for example, would be halted by celebrating his transcendent brilliance as inaccessible to analytic inquiry. Finally, member *emotions* are manipulated by induced pleasure or pain, agony or ecstasy, depending on the level of loyalty to the MNL. Support of the MNL creates pleasure and proves an elite status, elevating loyalists to the ranks of the spiritually saved, the business lord, or political hero. But for those who lack sufficient zeal for the MNL's totalistic project, the prospect of spiritual or existential damnation (excommunication, purging, or out-group status) induces guilt, shame, and terror of non-conformity. This is Hasson' BITE model: a mnemonic summation of Liftonian mind control methods that strip authentic personhood and re-engineers the psyche to manufacture an obedient follower, one with a Singerian pseudo-personality.

Whether mediated through a socio-economic infrastructure, as in the money cult of corporate culture, or politics, or relationally, as in society's smaller totalitarian groups, mind control represents the leader's ego-maniacal effort to create a world of comprehensive psychic security for himself. It is a world that upholds his grandiosity and god drive, and renders him above the law. It is a world that justifies his cruelty, and ratifies his hatreds. The effort entails inducing loyalty and obedience to his authority, and obtaining a blank check to mandate the substance of truth, including good and evil. His "truth" is the ontological equivalent of a fiat currency. Debate or dissent is intolerable. The MNLs "think they are above the law. They think they are God on earth, and they expect everyone to just merge into what their definition of reality is" (Hassan quoted in Devega, 2018, n.p.).

Janja Lalich

Janja Lalich, a professor of sociology at California State University, Chico, rose to prominence in the 1970s in the Democratic Workers Party, a California based, radical Marxist-Leninist group. Before her exit, Lalich realized the extent of abusive control perpetrated by the chairperson and that the party was, in fact, a cult. Curious as to why she had stayed, Lalich subsequently developed the theory of bounded choice, an explanatory model of four interacting social factors (Box 4.2) that synergize to bind constituents to the leader and totalistic group norms. These dynamic dimensions seal a group from outside influence, protect them from inner doubt, and explain otherwise irrational decisions, such as group suicide, terror, and any activity born of delusional conviction.

BOX 4.2   THE THEORY OF BOUNDED CHOICE: FACTORS OF TOTALISTIC GROUP FORMATION AND MAINTENANCE

1   *Charismatic authority*: a form of authority that links the devotee to the leader with an emotional bond
2   *Transcendent belief system*: an ideology that rewards devotees with a "path to salvation" and binds devotees to the group's systems of control and influence
3   *Systems of control*: formal rules, regulations, and procedures that dictate and control the behavior of devotees
4   *Systems of influence*: informal group culture which pressures members to conform their thoughts, attitudes, and behaviors to please the charismatic leader

Source: Lalich, 2004, pp. 226–227.

At the level of individual psychology, the bounded choice model postulates that (a) the leader's charismatic authority, interacting with (b) an unquestionable, transcendent ideology, combined with (c) a hierarchical structure with the dear leader atop, and the (d) extreme socio-behavioral regimentation that shapes conformity, will culminate in the individual psyche sealing itself off from the discredited outside world. Moreover, a frightening inward sealing off occurs, as well. It is such that the follower, emotionally bonded to the leader, adheres to the MNL's irreproachable ideology, recognizes his total authority, and conforms to his totalitarian culture. The follower's capacity to make an informed choice is held in bonds. He succumbs to a state of non-self, in which he has locked out the greater world and simultaneously locked the individuated mentality of critical adulthood from his ego-state. He is twice imprisoned.

Unable to gain a footing either in the greater world or within their inner one, the follower stands in an abridged ego, with walls on either side. This triggers bouts of claustrophobic consciousness, the awareness of which is also quickly exiled from immediate consciousness. With free thought (and thus free will) so constrained, she depends upon the leader and his extensions, as a child might on parent and family. Should the leader overreach, or become ill and die by suicide, the follower will follow him even into death. Illustrating this regression, Lalich quotes one of the Heaven's Gate followers, one anxious to swallow barbiturates with vodka, in preparation to follow the UFO cult leader, Marshall Herf Applewhite, to the Mother Ship:

> I know who my [leader is]. I believe in, cleave to, trust in, and rely totally upon [him].... Once He is gone, there is nothing left here on the face of the

> Earth for me, no reason to stay a moment longer. . . . I know my classmates/
> siblings feel the same as I do and will be choosing to go. . . . I want to stay
> with my Next Level family. Choosing to exit this borrowed human vehicle
> or body and go home to the Next Level is an opportunity for me to demon-
> strate my loyalty, commitment, love, trust, and faith in [the leader].
>
> *Lalich, 2004, p. 243*

The actions of the SS officers fighting the Red Army in Berlin in 1945 provide
another example of this impaired mental state. Receiving news of Hitler's own
suicide, they stuck their pistols in their mouths and pulled the triggers, presumably following the Fuhrer to Valhalla. Totalistic groups, closed off within their social
system, shut the mind to the world and imprison the analytic self. What remains is
a true believer, which Lalich (2004) defines as "a deployable agent for the group
or leader. Living within the bounded reality of the cultic social system, the cult
member encounters no meaningful reality check" (p. 227), even unto the deaths
they think they choose.

Daniel Shaw

Daniel Shaw is another contributor to the psychodynamic understanding of mind
control in relation to malignant leadership, especially in small systems like families.
Like Hassan and Lalich, Shaw's theoretical position was formed, in part, by his own
cult involvement. When describing his experience, he said:

> I spent thirteen years of my life, including all of my thirties, as a fervent
> devotee of an Indian guru. . . . I was in a cult. . . . I had experienced her char-
> ismatic power . . . and I got hooked. Clinging to the magic . . . I submitted
> to years of abusive control. In the name of loyalty, devotion, and . . . purifica-
> tion . . . [until] the spell broke.
>
> *Shaw, 2018, p. 1*

Shaw uses the terms *malignant* and *traumatizing* interchangeably, but he prefers
to use the term *traumatizing* to identify pathogenic narcissism as a force that trau-
matizes those in proximity to it. Essential to the totalistic relational system of the
malignant/traumatizing narcissist is the disavowal of the actual purpose of his group.
Shaw contends that the goal of any such group is the maintenance of the leader's
ego-inflation and grandiosity:

> In cults . . . the stated, typically grandiose goals of the groups are not met,
> because the group's energies and resources are constantly directed toward
> the actual goal, which is always the self-aggrandizement of the leader and his
> organization through the subjugation of his followers.
>
> *Shaw, 2014, pp. 48–49*

Shaw formulated a theory (Box 4.3) in which the narcissistically disturbed family system (or similar grouping) generates either carbon–copy malignant narcissists, or true believing, self-negating followers prone to subjection. Such a system is also exemplative of larger social constructions. As in Lalich's system, Shaw's leader/follower psychodynamic is perpetuated by several interacting factors.

BOX 4.3 SHAW'S DELINEATION OF PATHOLOGICAL LEADER – FOLLOWER PSYCHODYNAMICS

1 *Intergenerational trauma.* The group leader assumes the posture of viewing dependency in followers/children as detestable. He pretends that he is utterly self-sufficient and beyond dependency. The follower/child subscribes to this message and repudiates their own dependency needs. They erect formidable, often manically energized defenses against shame and thus imitate the traumatizing narcissist. The narcissistic alpha role-models the posture of super-sufficiency and humiliates and shames vulnerability.

2 *Delusional infallibility and entitlement.* Denying any limitation, the narcissist vigilantly defends their brilliance, superiority, and omnipotence. Socially skilled and intelligent, he presents this convincingly. Those who might critique the narcissist are gaslighted into feeling mad. On some level, however, the narcissist is psychotic, feigning a super-adequacy of delusional proportions. For such an actor, limitation and neediness equate with crushing shame, castration anxiety, and inferiority. This necessitates that the destabilizing embarrassment of these repudiated aspects of self be quarantined from consciousness.

3 *Externalization of shame.* Disavowing humiliating dependency needs, the narcissist assigns this weakness to others. This defensive measure protects the traumatizing narcissist from the psychic mortification of shame. To feel alive, the leader colonizes the minds of others, using them as dumping grounds for disavowed and despised self-aspects connected to dependence, neediness, and inferiority. This externalization of shame sustains the narcissist's sense of superiority, while those he protectively identifies as inferior are frequently sickened by the forced ownership of his toxic inadequacies.

4 *Suppression of the subjectivity of the other.* Children are especially traumatized by the shame-disavowing projections of the narcissist. Striving for the superior position, the grandiose narcissist cripples individuation. Offspring remain plausible recipients of the parent's own disavowed inadequacies. Eventually, the child will either develop the counter-dependent, grandiose shame-avoidant style of the traumatizing narcissist or identify

> with the narcissist's disavowed parts and live with a sense of debilitating self-disgust. The child positively identified with the narcissist's grandiose persona will re-perpetrate the patho-dynamic. But the child negatively identified with the narcissist's shameful shadow will suffer from lasting shame and repeatedly seek salvation in relationships with other narcissists who claim to have answers, even as they reinjure the subjugated other.
>
> Source: Shaw, 2014, 2018; paraphrase Zeiders.

In Shaw's (2014, 2018) explicitly psychodynamic formulations, the perpetuation of the malignant leader/follower dynamic is incomprehensible apart from the MNL evacuating the disavowed "inferior" aspects of himself onto a vulnerable follower(s). If his follower eventually identifies with the aggressor, however, that follower will develop imperviousness to his own defense against vulnerability to inner inadequacy by protectively passing his denied self-aspects onto an in-group target or an out-group scapegoat. If the follower introjects the MNLs projective inferior self, then he contends not only with his own abandonment, but with the narcissist's disowned pain as well. Inner distress and self-loathing will predispose him to a life-long quest for a messianic or parental figure to fix their broken inner state, predicting vulnerability to the influence of malignant narcissists throughout his lifespan, unless treated.

Like Fromm, Shaw finds the MNL/follower dynamic to be essentially sadomasochistic. Anxious to maintain control of others, desperate to demonstrate omnipotence, the MNL seeks to dominate others ubiquitously. This is sadism. On the other hand, anxious to escape outer/inner worlds, feeling unworthy, incompetent, and ashamed, the follower seeks a superior leader to take over. This is masochism. Enlarging his grandiosity, feeding on followers and enemies alike, the MNL is a sadistic devourer. Inversely, the true believing followers escape their narcissistic depletion by allowing themselves to dissolve in a superior leader, one who will live their lives for them, or act adequately on their behalf. Like most psychodynamic interpretations, this is an oversimplification, but it lends itself to versatile interpretive power, with variations on the theme, depending on the psychodynamic complexities, group size, and idiosyncratic personalities involved.

Shaw reiterates Fromm's finding that mind control, for an MNL, is a doubly meaningful project. Adulating constituents assist the leader to achieve his grandiose goals, but of high unconscious import is the role of self-surrendered worshippers in staving the MNL's latent psychosis. For example, during his trial, Shoko Asahara, the deadly Japanese guru of sarin gas fame, decompensated into schizophrenia from starvation of narcissistic supplies required to feed his defensive grandiosity. To sustain his delusion of grandeur, the MNL secretly requires the veneration of others. If he loses face, he will lose his mind. Accordingly, the leader elicits worshipful surrender from at least one person, as in a cultic dyad, or a *folie a deux* – or ratification of his superiority from a mass movement. In either case, the MNL tries to prevent

> open outbreak of . . . potential psychosis by gaining the acclaim and consensus of millions of people. The best-known example for this latter case is Hitler. Here was an extremely narcissistic person who probably could have suffered a manifest psychosis had he not succeeded in making millions believe in his own self-image. . . . (After he had failed he had to kill himself, since otherwise the collapse of his narcissistic image would have been truly unbearable). . . . From Caligula and Nero to Stalin and Hitler we see that their need to find believers, to transform reality so that it fits their narcissism, and to destroy all critics, is so intense and so desperate precisely because it is an attempt to prevent the outbreak of [their own] insanity. Paradoxically, the element of insanity in such leaders makes them also successful. It gives them that certainty and freedom from doubt which is so impressive to the average person.
>
> *Fromm, 1964, p. 76*

Mind control may be coercive or consensual. It may be orchestrated or organic. But whether the extent of his base is an enraptured lover in a decrepit shack, or throngs of followers cheering beneath his balcony, mind control is vital not only to maintain the MNL's power base, but quite possibly for his sanity. Moreover, with the evolution of artificial intelligence, new forms of mind control will evolve, and new types of hero-tyrants will walk into history, hungry for recognition of their genius, hungry to devour hopeful people, hungry to feed their defenses against a core of hidden shame and madness.

The immanent threat of manipulative messiahs: a world-wide vulnerability

Modalities of influence are essential to a charismatic messiah's top-down leadership. To maintain control, he manipulates members into his organization, with no informed consent, and reforms their thoughts and sensibilities to narcissistically extend himself. It is part and parcel with his omnipotence, his omniscience, and ultimately his god drive. It is a real process and a dangerous one. Following the 9/11 terrorist attacks on the United States, at the APA's 2002 Annual Convention in Chicago, cult experts pled with the association to form a task force to study influence methodologies of destructive organizations. "Cults exist at every layer of society," opined one Stephen J. Morgan, a faculty of the American Management Association/Management Centre Europe in Brussels, Belgium. During a panel, the professor

> stressed the importance of a deeper understanding of cults in understanding terrorism. Cult leaders are usually *psychopaths* [Devlin and I find them to be

malignant narcissists] with a desire for power and often take ideas from politics, religion and psychology to fulfill their purpose, he said. Through mind control, they are able to filter their thoughts and behaviors into "fanatical faith and belief" among followers.

Dittmann, 2002, p. 30; italics added

The public health threat of the cultist, professor Morgan implied, is not only foreign, but also domestic. Subsequent to that panel, the United States and Europe have taken a menacing turn – one immediately germane to the malignant leader and his influence techniques. Although the world has many woes, escalating tolerance for intolerance is among them. Reaction to the challenges of late postmodernity menaces the liberal democracies with regressive degradation of their human-rights achievements, and it gives rise to insular fundamentalisms across the globe. Not least problematic is the scapegoating rhetoric that *dispenses with existence* and dehumanizes the Other. It is an influence technique available to any vile aspirant to power, and it is a temptation to any and all leaders desirous to maintain power. "Rally to me, and I shall protect you from the monster(s). Rally to me, and we shall kill them together. Heroically." This patho-dynamic is death to human dignity.

Varieties of vulnerability

Vulnerability to MNLs varies. Individuals in transition, perhaps disquieted from job loss or divorce, are vulnerable. Pilgrim souls, spiritual seekers, and idealists may be vulnerable. Conservative subcultures, frightened from disruptive social conditions, may champion an authoritarian demagogue. Impatient progressives may discern salvation in a New Religion or a revolutionary leader with a messiah complex. For purposes of unity, a society fatigued by political instability may embrace a visionary despot. A properly positioned MNL, rousing fear of internal fifth columnists or external conspirators, may seize more perfect control with the group's eager acquiescence. Minus individual strength of character, prophetic social voices, and enforced checks and balances, the patho-dynamics leading to malignant hegemony will continue to unfold.

Being what we are – self-interested animals, terrified of life, but desirous of ease – it should surprise no one that the wretched realities of which we write, inform the cultism of our everyday lives and our mindless complicity with its evils. What I am getting at here is a variant of the *psychopathology-of-the-average* that accepts the degenerating cult of the global *status quo* as long as the WiFi still works and the fast food remains tasty. Why should one raise an eyebrow at the steady repeal of human rights or the corporate lies about climate change? The patho-dynamics of the current culture are mad and calamitous, but not yet broken. With respect to vulnerability, any person, group, or society possesses limited immunity to destructive leaders and is predisposed to their virulence, not only by emergencies and connivances but by human nature itself.

Human nature and our contemporary circumstances

At the collective level, the possibility exists that the dominant system is destructive and organized under the principles of malignant narcissism in the form of an archetype. The liberal, for example, reacts to reaction. The conservative resents reform. The orthodox hates revision. The radical reviles graduality. And so on. But all want privilege and comfort (on some level, at least); all strive for advantage, and once satisfied, their consciences sleep like hibernating animals.

Dissatisfied people will radicalize, or submit to extremism, and the MNL will be their hero. But when history produces a system that satisfies multiple mass longings just enough − as is the growing case with *globalization*, a euphemism for the spread of the corporate totalitarian state − and former extremists enter the ranks of its beneficiaries, and the former activists will de-radicalize and regress to a social average. Conformed to a new convention, they will legitimize the new status quo with nonchalance, and de-radicalized ideological pieties muttered from armchairs. Eventually they will learn to hate questioners of the privilege they perceive themselves to enjoy, and their entitlement to that privilege, or their indoctrinated illusion that they enjoy privilege − a mindset controlled by corporate propagandists and media complicit with the corporate totalitarian state. The arrangement creates citizen-cultists for this contemporary cult of commodified culture.

The *Zeitgeist* inspires en masse self-aggrandizement, and the *Weltanschauung* makes it good. Corporate mind control experts (the marketing people, the "mad men" of high-pressure advertising firms) consign dissenters to the fringes, especially those that represent small pockets of nonconformists conspiring against the dominant one. But in any case, these manufacturers of the mass mindedness dismiss challengers as passing oddities to be taken in between amusements and side hustles.

From time to time, in different epochs, in various places, diverse subgroups unite under the spirit and worldview of malignant narcissism − it is an archetypal formation − and after destroying internal and external opponents, extend beyond their powers and kill themselves. I suspect this is the situation under the New World Order, neoliberalism, or globalism − whatever one wishes to call the corporate takeover of humanity − where pimps in suits egg buyers on to consume the world toward environmental death. The corporate totalitarian state has driven this patho-dynamic well beyond reason, and well toward extinction, and although contemporary corporate MNLs are plentiful, I question whether their elimination would alter our mass behavior without collective soul searching. Sick people do not always know that they are ill. "The fact that millions of people share the same vices," prophesied Fromm (1955, p. 14), "does not make these vices virtues, the fact that they share so many errors, does not make the errors to be truths, and the fact that millions of people share the same form of mental pathology [in the contemporary case: mass sociopathic narcissism in the corporate-sponsored or neoliberal consumer cult of self] does not make these people sane."

Just now, global humanity should not be patient with itself or the corporate totalitarian cult of consumption. There is always a way forward and sometimes people find it.

The followers: various types and singular madness

First and foremost, the patho-dynamics of any group involves people, in this case those influenced by the MNL, directly or indirectly. Those under his spell, and those suffering from it, are themselves idiosyncratically motivated, but a few generalizations might be made.

At first the MNL is not obviously destructive. Many are attracted to his style, scope, and potential. He is the solver of problems and plays the part of the long-awaited visionary. He opens his arms, inviting the chosen to his in-group. Only later will he dominate and coerce. To some his selfishness is obvious. To others, he will be ever excused by "market necessities," "genius," or "inscrutable wisdom." But he is selfish and leads to fulfill only his own purposes. He is his own ideal, the embodiment of his own ultimate value. He is selfishness personified and self-deified.

Whether his constituency is one or one billion, those under his dominion are at risk because, despite his noble platform, he takes more than he gives. Fiduciary leadership is not his forte. Catastrophe is the end point of his tenure. Combined with his susceptible followers and emergent circumstances, something goes wrong. Ascending to the Mother Ship has side effects. Invading Russia, it turns out, was really a bad idea. Shooting the technocrats destroyed the grid. But despite the bloody record, despite the "never again" slogans, despite the trail of bleached bones punctuating failed utopias, the MNL captures the hearts and souls of so many. But who actually are his people, and what gathers them under his tent?

Although the matter of followers remains one of study, a cluster of four to five subgroups, sufficiently maps this gloomy territory. Associated with the MNL will be the *normals, insiders, followers*, and *true believers* – not unlike the constructs *lost souls, authoritarians, bystanders, opportunists*, and *acolytes* (Thoroughgood, Padilla, Hunter, & Tate, 2012) delineated by others. Each subgroup succumbs to the leader's influence uniquely, for each has its distinctive character. But the arrangement a subgroup makes with a madman will be of dubious benefit to anyone.

Although my mention of subgroups might especially describe constituencies within high-pressure groups in recognizable institutions – that is, polities not exactly spun out of whole cloth by revolutionaries – the categories contribute heuristic value of broad applicability.

The normals

The *normal* category applies to people who are more, rather than less, psychologically adult and who hold a degree of super-egoic valuation for fairness and human welfare. They have legitimate concerns, and they will find that the charismatic leader empathically articulates their issues and appears to help them change their world according to their values. The normals are the first to reject a malignant narcissist's leadership. In possession of a developmentally mature sense of appropriateness, they become disillusioned as they see their values subverted by the leader's self-serving behavior and bad faith. Although these psychologically mature grown-ups may be the first to bankroll or join the leader's movement, the MNL will excommunicate, damn, or purge the well-adjusted normals who criticize him or raise issue with his methods.

The insiders

The second group aligns themselves with the leader. They bask in his glory, and he empowers them. Members of this group become the *insiders*. They may bond with the leader through a shared sense of mission, and they may personally identify with him, but they are often opportunistic. If these insiders threaten the leader's agenda or alpha rank, however, they will be sacked, defenestrated, or otherwise removed. In the Fuhrer cult of the political Volk messiah, Hitler's opportunistic architect Albert Speer and willing executioners, like Reinhard Heydrich and Adolf Eichmann, are exemplars. These actors, like insiders anywhere, may possess a degree of pathology that resonates with the MNL's, but they are smart and useful to him, and they extend his power. They benefit greatly from proximity to the mad minister. Jim Jones, David Koresh, and Tony Alamo – for that matter the Borgia and Medici popes – maintained and enlarged their enterprises through well-rewarded managers. Stalin, however, murdered his insiders on a regular basis (management styles may vary). Because insiders are instrumental to maintaining the MNL's sense of omnipotence and omniscience, they might be termed *political self-objects*.

The followers

Then there are *followers*, or those with dependent traits. Lacking ego strength and psychological adulthood, they remain loyal to the leader for a long time, or forever. At a functional level, they may believe that the leader embodies a deity – as do the infantilized North Korean victim-followers of the Kim cult. They buy into the leader's advertised omnipotence and entertain fantasies of the MNL as a mystic alleviator of their anxieties and neediness. The corporate totalitarian state also creates follower types. The corporate takeover of economics, politics, and culture undermines individual ego-strength, making some suffer from ontological insecurity and existential desperation. "One main response to such insecurity is to seek reaffirmation of one's self-identity" (Setijadi, 2016, p. 97) via the approving nod and smile of the MNL, or his proxies. Thus regressed, and thus vulnerable, psychological adulthood is hard for the followers.

In the MNL, their dependent personalities identify a parent object descended from heaven, and they are sheep for easy slaughter. Some, if they escape the orbit of the leader, will later reflect on their follower-selves as having been devoured. A patient of mine, for example, recovering from financial abuse perpetrated by a Bible cult leader, bitterly reflected, "Seasoned with Stockholm syndrome, and sprinkled with neediness, I am sure I was delicious." Followers are easy marks for the MNL. Should the regime fall, followers will suffer doubly, needing to achieve developmental adulthood, while recuperating, along with the other groups, the monetary and mental investments lost under the smoke and rubble.

The true believers

And finally, there are the *true believers*. The leader successfully acts out the true believers' own narcissism, criminality, sadism, and paranoia. Their faith in him is sacramental; that is, the MNL outwardly expresses the inward state of the true believers. Representative of their ultimate values, their leader speaks and acts for them. Like Moses, he speaks law, punishes in-group transgressors, and targets out-group evildoers for divine wrath. True believers see themselves as righting wrongs, sometimes centuries old, sometimes intergenerational, sometimes with the disagreeable man at the pub.

The thought of mediation with an out-group infuriates true believers. Forgiveness of real or imagined trespasses feels suspect; loving one's enemy violates their outrage. Most values consistent with the humanitarian epiphanies of the Axial Age, in fact, will strike this group as wrongheaded. Not always found among the MNL's officers, true believers remain loyal until late in the movement's downfall – if it falls. If their MNL overreaches – succumbing to an end stage of paranoia and sadistic violence, prior to final collapse – true believers will defend him, and his agenda, despite his moral perversity.

They are neither healthy adults, likely to defect, nor privileged opportunists, nor needy dependents. Constituents of this group symbolically fuse with the MNL. Irrational idealism, charged with enraged libido, and desired omnipotence distinguish this group. Some will remain loyal to a disgraced MNL throughout their lives. These are the smiling old Stalinists with glittering medals at the May Day parade, and the Serbian nationalist sending chocolates to Dr. Karadzic care of International Tribunal.

These constructs of convenience organize the psychosocial constituencies of destructive leaders into explanatory conceptual blocks. But no discussion of destructive leadership is complete without mention of the authoritarian personality. Associated with the rise of the demagogue, this reactive follower threatens democracy and human rights, potentially as much as the destructive leader himself.

The authoritarian personality and the cults of influence related to the rise of Donald Trump

Since the rise of Marxist-Leninism, the National Socialist German Workers' Party (NSDAP), and Italian Fascism early in the 20th century, psychological science has studied the relationship between socially authoritarian constituencies and the rise of the MNL, who thrives on an a disgruntled, violent popular following. Although associated with the right, authoritarians may be either right or left. But their championship of the MNL threatens the polis, for their leader – unstable from adulation – eventually rules for himself alone.

The demagogue: a specific type of destructive leader

Pathological political dynamics, related to social change and power, establishes the distinctive importance of the authoritarians. Like the leaders they support, grandiosity, envy, resentment, and violence-proneness are among their characteristics. The leader they cheer into power is a demagogue, often lawfully elected – but almost mandated to rule beyond the rule of law on their behalf.

> He is a politician skilled in oratory, flattery and invective; evasive in discussing vital issues; promising everything to everybody; appealing to the passions rather than the reason of the public; and arousing racial, religious, and class prejudices – a man whose lust for power without recourse to principle leads him to seek to become a master of the masses. He has for centuries practiced his profession of "man of the people". He is a product of a political tradition nearly as old as western civilization itself.
>
> *Reinhard, 1954, p. 3*

As a political creature, the demagogue worried the Greeks and the Romans, and demagogues demolished Europe in the 20th century. Demagogues tell confused populations who to scapegoat for their current difficulties. Demagogues infuse group identity with power. Leveraging popular fear and loathing from socio-economic-cultural disruption, demagogues establish a base and actualize their god drive (see Chapter 2).

Demagogues and their cults of personality are the repercussion of social decay and despair. In an enfeebled culture, demagogues may recognize each other and establish common cause, such as when elements of the American religion industry, neoliberal de-regulation of PACs, and fascist groups coalesced into cults of influence during early 21st century U.S. elections. Such arrangement's aim is to wrest power from a larger group, and the Faustian hand-holding among the church-state leaders are especially relevant here.

> Nationalism and religion are . . . "identity-signifiers" that are . . . likely . . . to provide answers to those in need. . . . [N]ationalism and religion supply particularly powerful stories and beliefs because of their ability to convey a picture of security, stability, and simple answers. They do this by being portrayed as resting on solid ground, as being true.
>
> *Kinnvall, 2004, p. 742*

Specific cults (e.g., QAnon) exist and revolve around the cult of personality that is President Trump. But, here, I address the larger scale of the effects of the demagogue. Like cult leaders, demagogues thrive on developmental crisis, when their prey are threatened by the inevitable evolution of the society or system. Demagogues tempt frightened, angry constituents with regression, and this is hard to resist. Adaptive responses involve accepting reality, metabolizing anxiety, and proactively responding. But the price of maturity is psychologically expensive.

Cognitive and behavioral resources must be mobilized with uncertain outcome. Dread must be managed until reality is accommodated by an expansion of self. For entities overwhelmed by neophobia – that is, fear of the new – regression feels less costly, and more authentic. Followers defensively apply old frames of reference to the new situation. The demagogue confirms their understandable desire for their world to be a certain way, to be the only way. Regression assumes the status of the will of god and the expression of the national in-group's exceptionalism. At the individual level, this is fixation. At the spiritual level, fundamentalism. At the political, nationalism.

The temptation to return to the nursery, or to a golden age, is not novel. Franco short-circuited Spanish modernization with Catholicized fascism. ISIS imams erected a medieval caliphate in post-modern Syria. Vladimir Putin assumed the political face of Holy Mother Russia. Jerry Falwell "fundamentalized" the Christian focus of the American Republican Party. To varying degrees, the project of all entails the provocation of popular cathexis unto themselves, their leadership, and their projects.

A degree of coercion is always necessary, but the MNL's program works best by splitting constituent object relations. The leader(s) affirms a flattering group identity: his constituents are spiritually elite. They represent the Prime Mover's in-group for the nation-state. The chieftains of the spiritually elite group fully know the divinity's agenda, and in their leadership, the divine will express. Group prejudice and neurosis guide the selection of villains. The out-group explains the in-group's unhappiness, unfortunate circumstances, and their perception of decline. Out-groups embody metaphysical and political evil. Because of this, they lack humanity, and their welfare is irrelevant. Dispensing with their existence is a social and spiritual good. Split object relations arise from "prejudice, bigotry, ethnocentrism . . . [that] involve the primal thinking apparatus: absolute categorical cognition, on one hand, and obliviousness to the human identity of the victims, on the other" (Beck, 1999, p. 15).

A particular pathological context for the rise of destructive leadership

Election data, assembled up to 2017, suggested the ubiquitous availability of cultural nationalists, in the United States and in Europe, whose disgruntlement with the status quo laid them open to church-state demagoguery. A sense of nativist superiority, combined with a desire to dominate socially inferior groups (e.g., scapegoats; protectively identified targets of group distain), held to account for perceived socio-economic disruption, predicted Trumpist-style[3] voting on either side of the Atlantic (Ivarsflaten, 2008; Pettigrew, 2017).

Returning to the specific problem of the malignant mating of church with state, this coupling sires ugly offspring and degrades both parents. Accounting for this is the fact that religion and politics alike attract a leadership personality with firm views, often forged in trauma, with an ego-identity permanently welded to an idea of ultimate good. The narcissistic defenses of the religiopolitical personality, crippled in its ability to self-reflect, render it furious at dispraise, and make it vulnerable to destabilizing grandiosity. The latter is sustained from narcissistic supplies projected from persons adoringly disposed to the prestige of ordained man of god, the candidate, or office holder.

Importantly, the followers of religiopolitical personalities are likely to be either childlike and uncritical, or angry about life with free-floating vendettas ready for thuggish cathexis on out-groups and political opponents. That psychologically injured people may predominate among the constituency is owed to the fact that the followers who are adjusted to an adult level of functioning (the normals) may question the leaders, and thus enrage the religiopolitical personality who believes he is god's gift. Moreover, questioning these followers is experienced more as sacrilege, than as an annoyance. Thus, well-adjusted people, who might otherwise contribute an adult sensibility to the project, are purged or self-removed.

The movement, drained of the human capital of psychological maturity, consists of needy people expecting the leaders to be messiahs, or angry people expecting the leaders to allow them to meet divine wrath upon citizens or groups identified with evil. Civic discourse and conventions will be disrupted by incivility and irrationality. Mentally regressed, the mob will act out. Their delinquency communicates impatience for their messianic candidate to assume power. They expect him to restore their rightful place in the national promised land.

His mandate includes reaping vengeance upon the forces of secularization, elites, sexual liberty, other religions, and economic enemies. If the messianic candidate violates law, the group will excuse him repeatedly, provided he convincingly conveys that his illegalities were in service to the religiopolitical constituents, or against their enemies, or were otherwise courageous acts of religiously inspired patriotism. He may also misinform constituents that allegations indicate that sinister enemies resort to reputation sabotage to hinder divinely ordained and effective work. Rather than as a political campaign, or party, the movement will take the tone of a religious crusade – with good and evil at stake.

Such was the case with the successful, disruptive religiopolitical candidacy of Donald Trump and his first years in office. His electability emerged from (a) real, but poorly understood, political and economic abandonment by the federal government directly related to federal fealty to the corporate totalitarian state; (b) a subcultural predisposition to alpha figures based on the authoritarian paternalism of its evangelical religious leaders; and (c) a Manichean worldview thrown into ever higher relief by secularization, economic panic, and cultural paranoia.

> [L]eaders of the Christian right have built cult followings ... embraced magical thinking, attacked their enemies as agents of Satan and denounced reality-based science and journalism long before Trump did.
>
> *Hedges, 2019*

With worldviews formed under "Christian fascist" leaders in totalistic, anti-progressive religious cult formations, the flocks of these groups, especially when stressed, seek in a political leader, what they already possess in their spiritual leaders: an alpha figure who will lead them to salvation.

The authoritarian

Professor Christopher Federico of the University of Minnesota, an expert in authoritarianism in contemporary America, responded to media queries about the authoritarian personality and the improbable election of the coarse, politically inexperienced billionaire Donald Trump as the 45th president of the United States. The enduring research classic *The Authoritarian Personality* (1950), Federico explained, inspired by Erich Fromm but spearheaded by fellow Frankfurt school colleague Theodor Ardorno, et al., provides an enduringly valid characterological construct. That construct was and remains identified by ambiguity-hatred and fascistic tendencies, as well as:

a   A preference for "clear lines of social authority, strict social norms, and social uniformity as opposed to diversity."
b   Intolerance of "those who are different (e.g., racial, ethnic, or religious minorities) or those [who] appear to deviate from traditional social norms (e.g., LGBT folks)."
c   Gravitation "toward political figures (e.g., Donald Trump in present times) which embody intolerance and willingness to attack minorities who are believed to pose some kind of social threat."

Quoted in Newitz, 2016, n.p.

In the constructs of the *true believer* and the *authoritarian* resides the base that voted President Trump to dangerous power.

The true believing authoritarians of the Christian right supported a person, whose reputation – according to their own evangelistic nomenclature – was that of a hubristic reprobate. Before his candidacy, Mr. Trump was a profiteer of vice, purveying gambling and sex in his casinos, flaunting wealth and ostentation, and demonstrably non-demonstrable in concern for humankind. But white evangelicals voted him to power anyway. In return for that power, the President was to protect white evangelicals from the forces of secularization, stem the tide of racial demographic changes, and meet their populist economic agenda.

By appointing federal judges likely to support state control of women's bodies and recognizing Jerusalem as Israel's capital, he delivered on faith-based promises. But in terms of a populist domestic budget, he betrayed his base, approving the slashing of programs supporting health care, job training, education, housing, and domestic spending for poor and middle-class families. Moreover, in keeping with the political reality that the federal government, and the dominant political parties, are part of a managed democracy obligated to the global corporate totalitarian state, the President advanced ongoing tax cuts for corporations. It was simple to do, and firmly allied him with powerful globalists. But the evangelical religious leaders continued to support him, and told their constituents to do so. The true believing authoritarians required specific defensive-symbolic gestures, and with these the President was indeed helpful. His appointment of religiopolitical jurists antagonistic to sexual liberty provided secular salvation from the religious terror of sexuality, demonized in female reproductive rights.

His persecution of South American refugees spoke to the religious groups' hatred of the new (or neophobia, characteristic of any garden-variety developmental arrest) and enlivened nativist fantasies of national dominion. His diplomatic recognition of Jerusalem spoke to the thanatological release from existential dread fantasied as a post-apocalyptic City of God. Such are the Jungian-type undercurrents that account for an unsettled group's identification of God's earthly action in the pussy-grabbing billionaire in whom they saw God's gift to the American state. The allegation that Russian espionage services subverted the American election did not deter this group after the President's inauguration. One evangelical outlet asserted that keeping Hillary Clinton "out of office was so urgent and important that it warranted some foreign intervention" (Le Tourneau, 2018). This sigh of relief, that Russian spies tanked Clinton's electability, highlights mass projective identification of Clinton as the face of sinful sex, "fema-nazism," moral relativism, abominable religions, economic rip-offs – and finally, metaphysical evil in a pantsuit.

Populism occurs when systemic failures in society injure and embitter a self-important group of large enough size. It tends toward a politics of revenge and exclusion. It can bring out the worst angels of human nature and make for leadership choices that create more problems. History will tell if this was the case with the 2016 American presidential election. A mass of authoritarian personalities in a politicalized voting block(s) may build a mandate for an MNL to fossilize social norms, enact regressive policies, and damage civil society. Such were the concerns of many, mental health professions among them, at the rise of Trumpism.

Trump's public presentation gave mental health experts worrisome thoughts. In his erratic, grandiose self-referentiality, claims to superior knowledge, envy of dictators, and displays of rage at criticism, psychiatrists saw advanced narcissism that concealed ineptitude and an unreachable, lost child. Psychiatrists saw psychopathy in his alleged crimes – campaign finance fraud, collusion with foreign agents, tax fraud, obstruction of justice, abuse of office, witness tampering, witness intimidation, illegal use of executive privilege, and contempt of Congress. In his professed belief in the Darwinian nature of relationships, distrust of associates, insistence that his predecessor had tapped his phone, and promotion of conspiracy theories, psychiatrists saw paranoia. In his predations upon women, public denigrations, and gleeful targeting of out-groups, psychiatrists saw a bullying sadist. A former fixer once said that "when it comes to his feelings for his fellow human beings, Trump 'pisses ice water' (Lange, 2016)" (Gartner, 2017, p. 96). Could such a man competently lead a superpower?

The notion that Donald Trump was an extreme character, whose ascendance to world leadership presented risk, had merit. Alessandro Nai of the University of Amsterdam – and his colleagues Ferran Martínez i Coma, Griffiths University, and Jürgen Maier, University of Koblenz-Landau (2019), authorities in political psychology, policy, and communication respectively – designed a study to profile the President. It was based on experts' ratings and used to:

(1) provide systematic empirical evidence about Trump's personality profile,
(2) contrast his profile with 21 other populist leaders and 82 mainstream

candidates having competed in recent elections worldwide, and (3) discuss the implications of such an extreme profile in terms of campaigning style and the use of negative and emotional campaigns.

p. 1

In their painstakingly controlled comparative analysis of personality traits, based on personality evidence gleaned from the campaigning styles of mostly European party leaders, Nai, Martínez i Coma, and Maier (2019), found that their reliable and valid ratings, in aggregate, demonstrated that Trump as a candidate – later president – was unique and statistically extreme. Whether compared to populist or mainstream candidates, the President was off the charts.

Consumers of these data might alternately be filled with wonder and fear – especially that the leader in question is at the helm of a declining superpower – given that populist candidates, Nai implied, are not unmeritedly viewed as abrasive, offensive egomaniacs; drunken dinner guests; thriving on aggressive rhetoric; transgressing against socio-cultural taboos; and destructive, reactionary extremists. Nai et al. explained:

> What really sets Trump – the candidate and now the president – apart from virtually all other contemporary political figures is his off-the-charts public persona. Many have commented on his callousness, his thin-skinned and mercurial reactions to even mundane affairs, and of course his monumental adoration of himself. What was missing, however, is systematic empirical evidence showing that, indeed, Trump has a unique personality style. . . . Based on ratings of national and international scholars in politics and elections, and relying on well-established measures of individual personality, we provided . . . a systematic profiling of Trump's public persona. Our approach is innovative (1) in providing a methodical personality reputation profile based on well-established inventories of human personality (Big Five [*openness v. close minded, conscientiousness, extroversion, agreeableness, emotional stability v. neuroticism*] and Dark Triad [*these are narcissism, psychopathy, and Machiavellianism, which are constructively nearly identical to the Kernbergian version of malignant narcissism*]) and (2) by applying the same measures to a wide palette of other candidates, thus allowing for consistent comparisons across candidates. Our data reveal that Trump scores very high in extraversion but extremely low on agreeableness, conscientiousness, and emotional stability; furthermore, he scores very high on the three components of the Dark Triad.
>
> Systematic comparison between Trump's public persona and the profiles of other mainstream and populist candidates shows that Trump is, indeed, off-the-charts. Compared with 21 other populists worldwide, Trump ranks as the second highest score in perceived extraversion and as the single lowest score in agreeableness, conscientiousness, and emotional stability. Trump also has the highest score of narcissism and Machiavellianism and the third highest score on perceived psychopathy.

Nai et al., 2019, p. 26

Compared to the other (mostly European) populist leaders, known to their own public as extreme, Trump is the second highest in extroversion. This bodes well for his energization when communicating to a crowd or in front of a camera. To a degree, extroversion predicts charisma. But given the high score, he cannot be counted on to listen. Compared to other bellicose populists, he rated as the least agreeable. The data suggest a contrary style and inform what many perceive to be colossal diplomatic blunders and needless antagonism of necessary allies.

Of populists from Dublin to Moscow, the ratings determined Trump to be the least conscientious leader of all. This flags alarm, and the flag is crimson. Psychodynamically, conscientiousness relates to the reality principle. Lacking self-discipline – the virtue of delayed gratification – and the ability to buckle down, focus, and engage in concerted hard work, the basic posture of psychological adulthood is absent from his leadership. This finding explains his uniformed public statements. In place of study, he pretends to have expertise he simply does not possess. A chief executive without conscientiousness or diligence amounts to the leadership of a seventh grader. As a liability to world safety, it cannot be overstressed.

Of the populist leaders, the President ranked as the least stable emotionally. Without equanimity, leadership decisions are driven by emotional reasoning and acting out. The challenges of office trigger anger, worry, and irritability – which appear to be followed by hypomanic defenses against demoralization and odd behavior like hugging the flag during rambling speeches, or punctuated by non sequiturs and jokes "about canceling the 22nd Amendment and establishing a presidency-for-life" (Steib, 2019). In this finding, previously inexplicable public outbursts – such as eruptions of rage, and rambling, elated speeches to confused supporters, are in part explained by this trait. Such instability was obvious to the European raters and was also clear to American mental health professionals. It was the latter who first raised concerns about the President's fitness to control the world's deadliest military and its nuclear arsenal, even before his January 2017 inauguration.

In terms of openness to experience, President Trump was rated average. In his ability to consider divergent options, experts found him to be neither excellent nor poor. In a political field that attracts individuals convinced of their own importance, however, President Trump scored at the top in the trait of narcissism. For the 82 nonpopulist leaders, the average narcissism rating was 2.51 out of a possible 4; for the 21 populist leaders, the average was 3.13 out of 4. For President Trump, the narcissist rating was 3.91 out of 4. The finding relates to the President's demonstrable flamboyance, attention seeking, hyper-competitiveness, reckless behavior, and overtly positive self-descriptions. Contradictions to those self-notions trigger his rage. Extreme narcissism also accounts for the President's dismissal of advice and is consistent with the problem of grandiose narcissism in which the leader has the sense that he possesses all knowledge (omniscience) and enjoys all power (omnipotent).

The patho-dynamics of America

In Chapter 2, I have linked these elements of narcissism to the notion of the god drive, a leader's impetus to enjoy the prerogatives of a divinity. History attests that leaders who fail to recognize limits leave devastation as legacies. In psychopathy, a construct like narcissism, directly connected to malignant narcissism, is associated with criminality in businessmen and politicians, and the President was rated higher than any nonpopulist leader. Compared to populist leaders, the President ranked third highest, predicting a disregard for procedure and law. Machiavellianism relates to the use of trickery and deception to achieve business or political benefit. High Machiavellianism predicts to cynical manipulation of others to achieve success. Such leaders demonstrate untrustworthiness and low integrity. In Machiavellianism, the President scored highest among all the rated leaders. Speaking to this data, Nai et al. (2019) predicted that Trump's presidency would remain in campaign mode, chaotic, and punctuated by "scandals, reckless behavior, high staff turnover, volatile communication, and a dangerous tolerance for unethical behavior" (p. 30). The prediction came true (Zogbi, 2018), and America presents to the world as an ill and troubled nation, lost in shouting matches over every conceivable matter of consequence. Many despair of solving dire matters of climate change, health care, immigration, racism, school massacres, and obvious corruption in all branches of the federal government. Trumpism correlates with a collapse in the nation's sense of reality, and if the American happiness is considered capital, as it is in Bhutan, then vast psychological sums have been lost to "Trump Anxiety Disorder" – a quirkily named, unofficial diagnosis, involving insomnia and a feeling of a loss of control "and helplessness in an unpredictable sociopolitical climate . . . [filled] with endless negative headlines" (Zogbi, 2018, n.p.). It might be humorous, except for the caveat that failed leadership, especially in the Oval Office, predicts poorly for civilization and plenary survival.

To me, such findings suggest that the President's style of relating to himself and to others – his psychodynamics – is in fact patho-dynamics, or unwell, unhealthy dynamics, and the notion bears heavily upon the American heart. As an aberration of world political leadership, the patho-dynamically extreme Donald Trump will be no doubt be studied endlessly – regardless of his legacy.

In fact, the studies are well underway.

Treatment options for survivors of cults

People who join cults are seeking meaning in their lives. They are often highly idealistic and well-educated. They may exist across the spectrum of types of followers discussed earlier in this chapter, but it's a shibboleth that cult members are emotionally damaged from the beginning and, therefore, highly susceptible to charismatic leaders. Although this may be true for some cult members, idealism, spiritual seeking, anomie, and the lack of emotional sustenance in a consumer culture are many of the other reasons people may join cults.

We live in a global society that is constantly in flux. Our kinships, cultural norms, jobs, and monetary systems are endlessly in turmoil. Toffler's *Future Shock* (1970), Bauman's *Liquid Modernity* (2000), and Baudrillard's *Simulacres et Simulation* (1981) offer ways to understand the impact on human beings of the post-industrial economy and its power to alienate us from each other. The global economy and the technology in its wake disrupt beliefs, nation states, and human connection. As a counterweight to this, cults offer community, certainty, and a transcendent belief system (whether religious, self-help, or political).

Leaving a cult can be a harrowing experience. The former cult member not only leaves friends, but, in many cases, family members. They also lose their former identity. In many cases, former cult members must rebuild themselves holistically: a new job, a new community, even a new identity or personhood. It can be a lonely and frightening experience. They have not only lost their former community, but more than likely experienced trauma from their cult leader and the cult itself.

Cults disempower followers. They do this by controlling every waking moment and every social interaction. A follower must blindly obey or be subject to harsh discipline. In George Orwell's *1984* (1950), Winston Smith's life in cultic, "high-demand," totalistic Oceania approximates what followers experience in a cult. He must display absolute devotion to a leader, and even the most intimate parts of his life are monitored and controlled by the state.

It seems like an obvious statement to recommend to former cult members that they collaborate with psychotherapists who specialize in working with their population. An experienced psychotherapist can provide support and psychoeducation that may ease the passage from cult membership. This may significantly diminish the difficulty of adjusting to a dramatically new way of being. Two websites list experienced psychotherapists who specialize in this population: www.culteduca tion.com/ and www.icsahome.com/home. Both provide lists of publications, support groups, and psychotherapists. The International Cultic Studies Association also offers recommendations for international assistance.

It is important to note that someone who has just left a cult or totalistic environment may find these websites unnerving. They have been indoctrinated, sometimes for decades, to view anyone critical of their organization as malevolent. They may feel that they are somehow betraying their former community and may feel guilty as they begin critically thinking about their previous life.

There are also anti-cult groups with different ideological and religious slants. If these groups represent a belief system of a former cult member and are not coercive, then they can offer peer support, group therapy, and psychoeducation. However, it is important that the former cult member, if she or he is to have a healthy recovery, learn about and focus on self-care, trauma informed care, and restoring personhood. These are adaptive practices, which means a Christian former cultist and a secular former cultist may both prioritize these practices.

Every human being has a different path for understanding their lives and growing from experience. For former cult members, the path, though it may be different for each person, is hard. Like many trauma survivors, sometimes looking back on an experience is painful. Eventually, it may be cathartic. When Odysseus heard a bard sing about his experiences in the Trojan War, he wept. Difficult memories invoke pain. Therefore, it is important for the former cult member to emotionally gauge how they proceed (and therefore why a psychotherapist may be of invaluable support during the recovery process).

A psychotherapist working with this population should be familiar with how cults work and the many ways they inflict trauma. The psychotherapist should be well-versed in trauma informed care. This practice can be foundational in a former cult member's recovery. The Five Guiding Principles (safety, choice, collaboration, trustworthiness, and empowerment) help the psychotherapist partner with the former cult member as well as model a benign, reciprocative relationship (Harris & Fallot, 2001). These principles are an antidote to a culture that promotes absolute devotion to a traumatizing leader. They provide a foundation of security that allows the individual to develop agency and begin the often-frightening path toward trusting and bonding with others.

There are many books listed on the websites noted earlier by former cult members who tell the story of their disillusionment and recovery. No books on the lists describe the world the former cult member may find when she or he returns to a normative life. They pass from a world of certainty into a world of relentless historical change. Displacement is commonplace. Most people know an older parent or acquaintance who feels deeply alienated and confused by contemporary culture and technology. This will also be true for the former cult member. Then, there are the other vicissitudes: aging, death, the struggle at a job, and complex intimate relationships. Martin Amis wrote that staring into a mirror as you age is like watching a horror movie.

The stressors of our Anthropocene age add to the trauma, guilt, isolation, loneliness, and possible reprisals from the former cult that a former cult member may be experiencing. There is an existential quality to this. When you lose your community, your purpose or meaning, your faith, your all-knowing leader, all that is left is anomie. A psychotherapist and a peer group that is cognizant of this struggle is an invaluable asset for the former cult member.

Conclusion

Throughout history, the human species has been subject to destructive leaders obsessed with unlimited control. Perhaps Freud's myth of the first father presiding over the primal horde represents the proto-MNL. Now the brut autocrat wears a tailored suit, but our built-in susceptibility to his charismatic self-righteousness remains. But awareness of the destructive leader's canniness, charisma, and criminality protects against the destructive aspirant gaining ascendance and enrapturing the contemporary horde. Sane authorities who say "no," the prophetic voice that calls him out, the guardians of due process, and checks and balances, go far in terms of preventing the MNL from metastasizing to others, the group, and the world. Too often events overcome the psychological defenses, or emergencies compromise the collective immune systems, and the MNL gains dominion. Whatever one might call it, he presides over a cult, a high-pressure group, a totalitarian regime. A colonizer of consciousness, he will establish systems of control, of undue influence, of brainwashing that leave his underlings ego-syntonically compliant, and even adoring, as his manipulations urge them to sacrifice their highest humanity on the altar of his exploitive messianism. Once in power, he will purge critics and develop a class of political self-objects, operators who make plausible his narcissistic omnipotence and omniscience. He will cultivate fanaticism among his true believers, and he will represent the parent-god to his most needy constituents. Although a revolutionary MNL will harvest those dissatisfied with the status quo, the demagogue will seize supporters from the authoritarians who hail his support of their fantasy that society might fossilize around their image of the good. He will relieve their existential anxiety, or permit catharsis by sanctioning their infantile hatreds via aggression against their protectively identified enemies. At the time of this writing, the democratic project is threatened. Meanwhile, globalization and neoliberalism have given birth to the Corporate Totalitarian State, successfully operating under the archetype of the MNL, the full perniciousness of which has yet to be understood but whose successful mind control techniques far surpass the dead regimes of the 20th century's communists and fascists. To uphold the dignity of others and to preserve their psychological freedom, we must preserve our own first, being in the group but not of it, and speaking our truths to power with a disciplined lack of awe for impressive leaders.

Notes

1 Despite the listing of such terms as causal of identity disturbance relevant to diagnosing an Other Unspecified Dissociative Disorder in the DSM-5, along with credible arguments for construct validity by the International Cultic Studies Association, neither American courts nor many in the mental health establishment endorse the notion that coercive control or undue influence are legally admissible or scientifically meritorious.
2 Such front-line clinical methodologies and debriefing protocols are to be found in *Combating Mind Control* (2018) and *Freedom of Mind* (2013) or via the Freedom of Mind Resource Center (https://freedomofmind.com/).
3 Here *Trumpist* refers to populist, nationalist, and nativist political blocks that tend toward religious fundamentalism, cultural conservatism, suspicion of elites, and contempt for immigrants and minorities, who seek an improved standard of living, in a nonprogressive polity led by a reliable alpha figure.

References

Adorno, T. W., Frenkel-Brunswik, E., Levinson, D. J., & Sanford, R. N. (1950). *The authoritarian personality*. New York, NY: Harper & Brothers.

American Psychiatric Association. (2013). *Diagnostic and statistical manual of mental disorders* (5th ed.). Washington, DC: Author.

Baudrillard, J. (1981). *Simulacres et simulation*. Paris, France: Galilée.

Bauman, Z. (2000). *Liquid modernity*. Cambridge, UK: Polity Press.

Beck, A. T. (1999). *Prisoners of hate: The cognitive basis of anger, hostility, and violence*. New York, NY: Harper Collins.

Devega, C. (2018, March 6). Is Donald Trump a cult leader? Expert says he "fits the stereotypical profile." *Salon*. Retrieved from www.salon.com/2018/03/06/is-donald-trump-a-cult-leader-expert-says-he-fits-the-stereotypical-profile/

Dittmann, M. (2002). Cults of hatred: Panelists at a convention session on hatred asked APA to form a task force to investigate mind control among destructive cults. *Monitor on Psychology, 33*(10), 30.

Fromm, E. (1941). *Escape from freedom*. Oxford, UK: Farrar & Rinehart.

Fromm, E. (1955). *The sane society*. New York, NY: Rinehart.

Fromm, E. (1964). *The heart of man: Its genius for good and evil*. Riverdale, NY: American Mental Health Foundation.

Gartner, J. D. (2017). Donald Trump is: (A) bad, (B) mad, (C) all of the above. In L. Bandy (Ed.), *The dangerous case of Donald Trump: 27 Psychiatrists and mental health experts assess a president* (pp. 93–109). New York, NY: St. Martin's Press.

Guattari, F. (1995). Everybody wants to be a fascist. In S. Lotringer (Ed.), *Chaosophy: Texts and interviews 1972–1977* (Semiotext(e) foreign agents series, pp. 225–250). Los Angeles, CA: Semiotext(e).

Harris, M., & Fallot, R. D. (Eds.). (2001). Using trauma theory to design service systems. In *New directions for mental health services* (p. 89). San Francisco, CA: Jossey-Bass.

Hassan, S. (2013). *Freedom of mind: Helping loved ones leave controlling people, cults and beliefs*. Newton, MA: Freedom of Mind Press.

Hassan, S. (2014, October 21). ISIS is a cult that uses terrorism: A fresh new strategy. *Huffington Post*. Retrieved from www.huffpost.com/entry/isis-is-a-cult-that-uses_b_6023890

Hassan, S. (2018). *Combating cult mind control: The #1 best-selling guide to protection, rescue, and recovery from destructive cults* (30th anniversary ed.). Newton, MA: Freedom of Mind Press.

Hedges, C. (2019, June 10). The cult of Trump. *Truthdig*. Retrieved from www.truthdig.com/articles/the-cult-of-trump-3/

Ivarsflaten, E. (2008). What unites right-wing populists in Western Europe? Re-examining grievance mobilization models in seven successful cases. *Comparative Political Studies*, *41*(1), 3–23.

Kinnvall, C. (2004). Globalization and religious nationalism: Self, identity, and the search for ontological security. *Political Psychology*, *25*(5), 741–767.

Lalich, J. (2004). Using the bounded choice model as an analytic tool: A case study of Heaven's Gate. *Cultic Studies Review*, *3*(3), 226–247.

Lang, J. (2016). Donald Trump turned his back on his closest friend when he had AIDs. *The Week*. Retrieved from https://theweek.com/speedreads/617343/donald-trump-turned-back-closest-friend-when-heard-aids

Langone, M. (2015). The definitional ambiguity of cult and ICSA's mission. *ICUSA Today*, *6*(3), 6–7.

Le Tourneau, N. (2018, September 4). Trump's base is white evangelical voters. *Washington Monthly*. Retrieved from https://washingtonmonthly.com/2018/09/04/trumps-base-is-white-evangelical-voters/

Lifton, R. (1989). *Thought reform and the psychology of totalism*. Chapel Hill, NC: University of North Carolina Press.

Lifton, R. J. (2011). *Witness to an extreme century: A memoir*. New York, NY: Free Press.

Nai, A., Martínez i Coma, F., & Maier, J. (2019). Donald Trump, populism, and the age of extremes: Comparing the personality traits and campaigning styles of Trump and other leaders worldwide. *Presidential Studies Quarterly*. doi:10.1111/psq.12511

Newitz, A. (2016, June 3). How World War II scientists invented a data-driven approach to fighting fascism: The F-scale personality test measured authoritarianism in US citizens. *Ars Technica*. Retrieved from https://arstechnica.com/science/2016/06/how-world-war-ii-scientists-invented-a-data-driven-approach-to-fighting-fascism/

Orwell, G. (1950). *1984* (Signet classics). New York, NY: New American Library/Penguin Group.

Pettigrew, T. F. (2017). Social psychological perspectives on Trump supporters. *Journal of Social and Political Psychology*, *5*(1), 107–116.

Reinhard, L. (1954). *American demagogues: Twentieth century*. Boston, MA: Beacon Press.

Rosedale, H. L., & Langone, M. D. (2015). On using the term "cult." *ICSA Today*, *6*(3), 4–6.

Setijadi, N. (2016). Globalization and nationalism: Perceived self, identity, and the search for ontological security (analysis of the identity negotiation process of expats in Jakarta). In *Proceeding of the 3rd Conference on Communication, Culture and Media Studies* (pp. 97–103). Retrieved from https://pdfs.semanticscholar.org/39e4/c2b4e07bfe933e1a04c2370d-39f90d92a98b.pdf

Shaw, D. (2014). *Traumatic narcissism: relational systems of subjugation.* New York: Routledge.

Shaw, D. (2018). Authoritarianism and the cultic dynamic: Traumatic narcissism in American politics. *Public seminar books.* Retrieved from www.danielshawlcsw.com/publications/

Singer, M. T. (2003). *Cults in our midst: The continuing fight against their hidden menace* (revised & updated ed.). San Francisco, CA: Jossey-Bass.

Steib, M. (2019, June 16). Trump says his supporters might "demand" he serve more than two terms. *New York Magazine Intelligencer.* Retrieved from http://nymag.com/intelligencer/2019/06/trump-says-his-supporters-might-demand-more-than-two-terms.html

Thoroughgood, C. N., Padilla, A., Hunter, S. T., & Tate, B. W. (2012). The susceptible circle: A taxonomy of followers associated with destructive leadership. *The Leadership Quarterly,* 23(5), 897–917.

Toffler, A. (1970). *Future shock.* New York, NY: Random House.

West, L. J., & Langone, M. D. (1986). Cultism: A conference for scholars and policy makers. *Cultic Studies Journal,* 3(1), 117–134.

Zablocki, B. (1997). A sociological theory of cults. Presented at the annual meetings of the American Family Foundation, Philadelphia, PA.

Zogbi, E. (2018, July 28). Therapists coin new term: Trump anxiety disorder. *Newsweek.* Retrieved from www.newsweek.com/therapists-report-rise-anxiety-trump-was-elected-1046687

5

A TOTALITARIAN SAMPLER

The mad leader in context of the cultic organization

No formula exists to organize the maddening variabilities among malignant narcissist leaders (MNLs) and their organizations. High-pressure groups populate every section of the globe and all segments of society. Indices of dangerousness flux according to group size. All such groups espouse divergent visions and missions and vary from insular to evangelical. Some are hate groups. Some are "love" groups. Some make money. Some steal it. Any stressed demographic is naively vulnerable to messianic seduction, resigned submission, or zealous radicalization. But the merit of reducing such phenomena to ideal categories is to mentally model the danger when confronted with it. Whether analyst, academic, or citizen, the knowledgeable person has capital to invest against the deflation of wits triggered by evil in social form. To recognize social "evil," one must know something about it, and the categories from which spring variations on the terrible theme.

Cults, high-pressure groups, and (would-be or accomplished) totalitarian regimes are all apt terms for the organizations that fall under the broad and specific categories discussed in this chapter. Depending on the category of the group, and the ideal with which the destructive leader has mentally identified, a high-pressure group may constellate around variant content: social action, self-improvement, health, leadership, UFOs, salvation, enlightenment, money, career, virtue, or vice. Cults do not have to be exclusively religious, and totalitarian groups are not solely political. But common cultural elements exist among cult categories and subcategories (see Chapter 4). Such include obsequious reverence for the leader, elitism, manipulation of constituents, a sense of group victimization (or of being grossly misunderstood, or of being incomprehensible due to group genius), intense group disciplines, insistence on obedience, strict regulation of members, scapegoating of critics and competitors, sexual exploitation, economic exploitation, and maximal manipulation via affection, rejection, praise, menace, denigration, or shaming (Singer, 2003).

Supreme devotion to the charismatic leader and his transcendent agenda is ever the preferred group culture of the MNL.

Categories of cults

The broad categories of vulnerable organizations are the very groupings which comprise society itself: the spiritual/human potential, the commercial, and the political. In the spiritual realm, the leader presents as the functional equivalent of god or an ultimate guru. In the commercial realm, the leader presents as "the one" with unsurpassed savvy regarding all matters financial. In the political category, the leader presents as the perfect politician who possesses the gifted integrity to uphold the body politic in effective purity.

Of course, no leader or organization presents in an ideal form. A corporate enterprise might have a political or religious dimension, a spiritual group might also possess a financial or power agenda, and some political groups thrive off religious fanaticism or cold cash. Thus, in practice, a high-pressure group might overlap these categories, as depicted in the Venn diagram in Figure 5.1. Most groups fall predominantly into one category but overlap variously with the other categories.

The vignettes that follow this section have headings above them. The headings provide the proper name of the destructive leader and the high-pressure group,

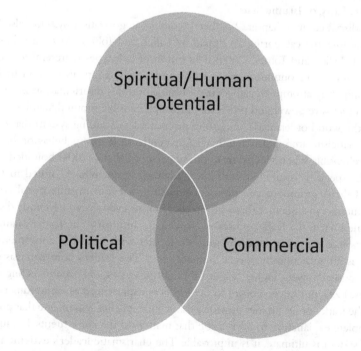

FIGURE 5.1 Diagram of broad and overlapping categories for defining totalistic groups

followed by the predominant category into which the group falls, followed by lesser categories of which the group's predominant category overlaps. Another way to think of this taxonomic protocol is as a brief rank order system that highlights broad categories that a group inhabits from most to least prominent. Thus, if a heading read, "Adolf Hitler and the NSDAP: a predominantly political high-pressure group, with spiritual/human potential and commercial group sub-features," the indication would be that Hitler is the leader, the Nazi Party is the cult/high-pressure/totalitarian group, and that group's purpose – and thus category – is first political (e.g., political parties seek power foremost). But overlapping with the NSDAP's predominant category is the spiritual/human potential category (e.g., to unlock the mythic power of the *Ubermensch*), and overlapping to a lesser degree the commercial, or economic, category (e.g., to enrich the NSDAP, Reich, and Volk with the resources extorted from weaker out-groups).

Within the overlapping broad group categories any number of specific, zealous groups might be categorized and explored. Cultic groups running on spiritual libido might include those specifically devoted to the Christian Bible, Eastern religion, or more generally to self-actualization. High-pressure groups running on acquisitive energies appear as multi-level marketing scams, Bernie Madoff-style mutual fund enterprises, or Enron-type corporations. Would-be totalitarian political groupings include reactionary, revolutionary, and absolutist movements, as well as parties devoted to extreme ideas of justice such as the Aryan Nation, Democratic Workers Party, or Islamic State.

As discussed in Chapter 2, other credible categorization systems also exist. For example, the categories developed by Lalich and Tobias (2006) are shown in Box 5.1. Lalich and Tobias' (2006) delineation of cult types represents another of any number of taxonomic options to organize such groups in relation to MNL leadership. Any attempt to categorize *totalitaria* prevents disorientation in the mad world of abusive power and previously incomprehensible group dynamics.

In the world of *totalitaria*, the group promotes a self-sealing system that engenders fanaticism among its members. Apparently mad group behavior becomes comprehensible when viewed from the vantage of Lalich's (2004) bounded choice model, especially combined with psychodynamic principles. As noted in Chapter 4, Lalich's group-analytic protocol stipulates that four organizational components interact in a manner that a group complex, or even shared psychotic disorder, is formed. First, the leader possesses charismatic authority. The leader's narcissism projects into the group, and the group resonates with it. To the constituents, the leader is an authentically special human being. The leader's core narcissism foster's "unusual powers, highly original thought processes, and ecstatic feeling states" (Oakes, 1997, p. 172). Exposure to the leader is experienced as extraordinary. Second, the leader or his proxies provide a transcendent belief system, one that provides a complete explanation to everything that matters to the constituents. Because the belief system is ultimate, it is unprovable. The charismatic leader's extreme narcissism gives rise to schizotypal thought processes that form the core of revolutionary doctrines, or "complete" conventional ones. A conceptual map for transformation,

BOX 5.1 CATEGORIZATION OF CULTS BY LALICH AND TOBIAS

Eastern cults

Eastern cults are characterized by belief in spiritual enlightenment and reincarnation, attaining the Godhead, and nirvana. Usually the leader draws from and distorts an Eastern-based philosophy or religion, such as Hinduism, Buddhism, Sikhism, or Sufism. Sometimes members learn to disregard worldly possessions and may take on an ascetic and/or celibate lifestyle. Practices and influence techniques include extensive meditation, repeated mantras, altered states of consciousness, celibacy or sexual restrictions, fasting and dietary restrictions, special dress or accoutrements, altars, and induced trance through chanting, spinning, or other techniques.

Religious cults

Religious cults are marked by belief in a god or some higher being, salvation, and the afterlife, sometimes combined with an apocalyptic view. The leader reinterprets Scripture (from the Bible, Koran, Talmud, or Cabala) and often claims to be a prophet, if not the messiah. Typically the group is strict, sometimes using such physical punishments as paddling and birching, particularly of children. Often members are encouraged to spend a great deal of time proselytizing. Included here are Bible-based, neo-Christian, Islamic, Jewish or Hebrew, and other religious cults, many of which combine beliefs and practices from different faiths. Practices and influence techniques include speaking in tongues, chanting, praying, isolation, lengthy study sessions, faith healing, self-flagellation, or many hours spent evangelizing, witnessing, or making public confessions.

Political, racist, or terrorist cults

Political, racist, or terrorist cults are fueled by belief in changing society, revolution, overthrowing the perceived enemy, or getting rid of evil forces. The leader professes to be all knowing and all powerful. In some cases, adherents may be more drawn to an extreme ideology rather than a leader per se. Groups tend to operate as secret cells. Often the group and/or individuals are armed and engage in violent activities, including arson, kidnapping, bombing, and suicide bombs. Such groups typically meet in secret with coded language, handshakes, and other ritualized practices. Members consider themselves an elite cadre ready to go to battle. Practices and influence techniques include paramilitary training, reporting on one another, fear, struggle or criticism sessions, instilled paranoia, violent acts to prove loyalty, long hours of indoctrination, or enforced guilt based on race, class, or religion.

Psychotherapy, human potential, and mass transformational cults

Psychotherapy, human potential, mass transformational cults are motivated by belief in striving for the goal of personal transformation and personal improvement. The leader is self-proclaimed and omniscient, with unique insights, sometimes a "super-therapist" or "super-life coach." Practices and techniques include group encounter sessions, intense probing into personal life and thoughts, altered states brought about by hypnosis and other trance-induction mechanisms, use of drugs, dream work, past-life or future-life therapy, rebirthing or regression, submersion tanks, shame and intimidation, verbal abuse, or humiliation in private or group settings.

Commercial, multi-marketing cults

Commercial, multi-marketing cults are sustained by belief in attaining wealth and power, status, and quick earnings. The leader, who is often overtly lavish, asserts that he has found the "way." Some commercial cults are crossovers to political and religious cults because they are based on ultra-conservative family values, strict morals, good health, or patriotism. Members are encouraged to participate in costly and sometimes lengthy seminars and to sell the group's "product" to others. Practices and influence techniques include deceptive sales techniques, guilt and shame, peer pressure, financial control, magical thinking, or guided imagery.

New Age cults

New Age cults are founded on belief in the "You Are God" philosophy, in power through internal knowledge, wanting to know the future or find the quick fix. Often the leader presents herself or himself as mystical, an ultra-spiritual being, a channeler, a medium, or a superhero. New Age groups, more so than some of the other types, tend to have female leaders. Members rely on New Age paraphernalia, such as crystals, astrology, runes, shamanic devices, holistic medicine, herbs, spirit beings, or Tarot or other magic cards. Practices and influence techniques: magic tricks, altered states, peer pressure, channeling, UFO sightings, "chakra" adjustments, faith healing, or claiming to speak with or through ascended masters, spiritual entities, and the like.

Occult, satanic, or black-magic cults

Occult, satanic, or black-magic cults are generated through belief in super-natural powers and sometimes worship of Satan. The leader professes to be evil incarnate. Animal sacrifice and physical and sexual abuse are common; some groups claim they perform human sacrifice. Practices and influence techniques include exotic and bizarre rituals, secrecy, fear and intimidation, acts of violence, tattooing or scarring, cutting and blood rituals, sacrificial ritu-als, or altars.

One-on-one or family cults

One-on-one or family cults are based in belief in one's partner, parent, or teacher above all else. Generally an intimate relationship is used to manipu-late and control the partner, children, or students, who believe the dominant one to have special knowledge or special powers. Often there is severe and prolonged psychological, physical, and sexual abuse. Practices and influence techniques include pleasure/pain syndrome, promoting self-blame, induced dependency, induced fear and insecurity, enforced isolation, battering and other violent acts, incest, or deprivation.

Cults of personality

Cults of personality are rooted in a belief that reflects the charismatic per-sonality and interests and proclivities of the revered leader. Such groups tend to revolve around a particular theme or interest, such as martial arts, opera, dance, theater, a certain form of art, or a type of medicine or healing. Practices and influence techniques include intense training sessions, rituals, blatant ego-centrism, or elitist attitudes and behaviors.

Source: From: Lalich and Tobias, 2006. Reprinted with permission.

the transcendent belief system, whether economic or spiritual, is viewed by con-stituents as a salvation path. Adlerian psychoanalysis finds that fictional finalism, or guiding beliefs leading to the fulfillment of an ultimate aim, must be analyzed to fully comprehend behavior. Third, systems of control involve the formal constitu-tion of the group, the charter, laws, protocols, precedents, and so forth. In a monas-tery, ashram, or human potential group, this would be the rule of life, official forms of devotee polity, or informed consent documents. In a business, the prospectus-like documents, or the explicit definition of financial value, along with the formal terms for advancement fill this function. In a political group, the charter, documented reactionary/revolutionary/centrist agendas and rules of due process constitute this item. Systems of control involve the *explicit* codes of conduct. Fourth, systems of influence involve the social style of the group, how the group interacts with itself, in such manner that inner and out behavior is shaped by what is tolerated or taboo, rewarded or restricted, permitted, or poisonous. Systems of influence involve the implicit codes of conduct.

In the vignettes that follow, I am especially interested in the charismatic authority of the leader and how that authority – supported by a group myth of his extraordinariness, a transcendent belief system, systems of control, and influence – drives leadership and group behavior in a way that damages the leader, his group, and often, sadly, society itself.

Bhagwan Shree Rajneesh and the Rajneesh movement: a predominantly spiritual/human potential high-pressure group, with commercial and political sub-features

Founded by the Indian mystic Bhagwan Shree Rajneesh (1931–1990), alternately known as Osho, the Rajneesh movement was an Eastern cult that drew on ideas and methods from Eastern religions, heterodox philosophy, Tantra, Dynamic Meditation (meditation based on hyperventilation, violent catharsis, and relaxation), and sexual freedom. Also influential in the Rajneeshian repertoire were experience-based psychological techniques drawn from the Western psychological school of the Human Potential Movement. Throughout the 1970s the movement was headquartered in Poona, India, and from 1981 until Rajneesh's indictment and deportation from the United States in 1985, in Rajneeshpuram, a former ranch converted into an ashram in Oregon.

In India he compared himself to the great spiritual teachers, Loa Tzu, Buddha, Jesus Christ, Bodhidharma, and Muhammad. But by 1985, he claimed to have surpassed all former spiritual masters. "I myself have come to where you cannot go any higher . . . a moment of spiritual growth which is untranscendable" (Rajneesh, 1985, p. 197). He later claimed to have transcended even the untranscendable and to represent a milestone in evolutionary spiritual consciousness (Clarke, 1988, p. 34). When Rajneesh came to the United States from India in 1981, he proclaimed, "I am the Messiah America has been waiting for" (Storr, 1996, p. 57). He was worshipped as a god by his devotees, and is reputed to have impacted many who met him as a beneficent master with a radiant, knowing presence.

Psychiatric sources depict Rajnesh as sickly as a child with odd charisma, manifesting depression, anorexia, and a death wish – demonstrating signs and symptoms consistent with narcissism, criminality, cruelty, and an Oedipal-style flouting of authority. During his childhood, Rajneesh was indulged by his grandmother and won her support to undermine his father's failed disciplinary attempts (Clarke, 1988). Despite claiming that his psycho-somatic-spiritual illnesses evaporated in a Buddha-style enlightenment at age 21, Rajneesh concealed personality problems, bipolarity, ill health, and habitual polysubstance use throughout his life (Storr, 1996).

Known as the "sex guru," Raneesh's early disciplines included often sadistic group sex with the goal of enlightenment. Other practices included repetitive chanting, jumping, meditation, and micro-managed busyness leading to devotee infantilization. Ex-cultists and mental health professionals concur that the spiritual exercises demanded of devotees enfeebled their egos and bonded them to the god Rajneesh in an appalling group regression.

With devotees worldwide, the Bhagwan Rajneesh initially presided over a monetized spiritual empire with headquarters in Pune, India. Evidence of tax evasion, sex slavery, and drug trafficking caused Rajneesh to immigrate to Oregon in the United States where he continued to preside over a diversified criminal enterprise. The dangerousness of this enterprise was revealed in a biological weapons attack against Oregon locals opposed to Rajneeshpuram expansion, planned assassinations of U.S. officials, and uniformed guards toting machine pistols to intimidate state and federal officials during investigations.

Especially troubling was the Bhagwan's prophesy that two-thirds of humanity would perish in a nuclear holocaust, or in the global AIDS epidemic, which had been foreseen by Nostradamus. He also predicted that an earthquake would unleash along the San Andreas Fault. During a raid at the close of Rajneesh's American career, federal officials were ashen-faced to discover stockpiles of biological weapons and a top-secret research project tasked with weaponizing the AIDS virus. Experts opined that Rajneesh intended to trigger the very apocalypse he had prophesized, with the aspiration to then preside over a new world populated by his grandly-worthy *sannyasins*, or Homo Novus, a Rajneeshian version of the *Ubermensch* or Superman of proto-Nazi philosophy (Carter, 1990). Like cult leaders Shoko Asahara and Charles Manson, along with President Robert Mugabe, the Bhagwan Rajneesh admired Adolf Hitler and complained that he and Hitler were misunderstood in their aspiration to design a new humanity (McCormack, 2018).

Rajneesh tasked his chief of staff, Ma Anand Sheila, with implementing his plans, which included the securing of land, zoning, and self-government rights from the state of Oregon and the federal government. The ends were to justify the means. Rajneesh insisted his movement required this land and self-governance to build a Noah's Arc of consciousness from which his devotees would emerge to erect a new order upon the post-apocalyptic earth ("Rajneesh," n.d.). Also, tasking underlings with implementing illegal schemes is a means by which both gurus and mob bosses maintain plausible deniability.

Following deportation from the United States in 1985, Rajneesh evinced paranoid ideation, alleging that U.S. authorities had irradiated him in prison. Resettled in India, he attributed his crashing health to evil magic inflicted from disloyal followers. He died at an ashram in Pune, India, in early 1990. Just as the federally indicted master demonstrated the *all-good/all bad* object relations indicative of the MNL (see Chapter 2), so his surviving followers are split regarding whether their late lord was a god or a beast.

Tony Alamo and the Alamo Christian foundation: a predominantly spiritual/human potential high-pressure group, with commercial and political sub-features

Together with his wife Susan, Tony Alamo (1934–2017) ran an exploitive, paranoid, hateful Christian fundamentalist cult that propagandized its ministry as saving street people from marginalization and penury. The Alamos preyed upon their followers' faith in the duo as direct messengers from God and their desire to help the less fortunate. The ministry began in San Francisco in the 1960s, when Tony Alamo, a failed singer, met and married Susan, a failed actress-turned-evangelical con artist. Alamo's bride drew disciples by preaching horrific sermons about the torments of hell and presenting herself and her husband as salvation figures. Once they joined forces, the couple became stars in the religion industry, and after her death from cancer, Alamo continued to use her model. This model swindled and manipulated people through a successful television show and a coveted product line made popular by celebrities.

Although Alamo did indeed provide for the homeless – and the needy and spiritually lost – offering them room and board, disciples were actually enslaved in workhouse conditions, toiling unpaid in Alamo's businesses, the most lucrative of which was manufacturing designer jackets, popular with rock stars such as Michael Jackson. Evincing the god drive (see Chapter 2), Alamo conflated his voice with the God he professed to worship and believed that his pronouncements carried divine authority. Participating in his paranoid worldview, his congregants proselytized that the American presidents and Roman popes were antichrist devils. Alamo's disciples ratified their pastor's conspiracy theories with acclamation, underpinned with the holy terror of his displeasure.

Alamo threatened any who tried to defect with damnation. Reports exist of Alamo's disciples, living like prisoners or citizens in a totalistic regime, at times disallowed to leave church compounds unless accompanied by a minder or "body guard." Further, any who offended Alamo was subject to debilitating physical beatings. There were cases when, in the midst of brutal beatings, mothers would tell their confused, suffering children that they deserved the beating simply because God's messenger desired it. But Alamo's abuses did not go fully unopposed. In 1990, after losing in court to a damaged plaintiff, Alamo was forced to pay 1 million dollars to a Miller family for ordering four adult men to restrain one of their minor children and beat his buttocks 140 times until blood burst from the child's smashed tissue. Nevertheless, the grip Alamo had on his disciples was profound (Langone & Eisenberg, 1993; *Ministry of Evil*, 2019).

In 1982, Susan Alamo died of cancer, and Tony decompensated. For six months, he kept her body on display, surrounded by praying church members, while he tried to raise her from the dead. Eventually, he interred her ripened remains in a heart-shaped mausoleum. He commenced with criminal behavior, including tax violations, functional enslavement of his devotees, and sexual abuses of his disciples, which included biblically rationalized child rape. Preached as a revelation, Alamo proclaimed that God divulged to him that the age of consent began at puberty. When the federal government caught Alamo transporting minors across state lines for unlawful sexual purposes, the polygamist pedophile was sentenced to 175 years for charges related child sexual abuse (Lancaster, 2018; Tony Alamo, 2019, January 28).

Before his death in federal custody in 2017, Alamo wrote to Presidents Clinton, Bush, and Obama, urging each to visit his cell, so that "I might share with you all my visions, plans, and strategies not only to uproot evil from the earth, but to bring happiness, comfort, and peace to the world by resolving the most complicated issues facing humanity" (Alamo, 2011, n.p.). No record exists of a response from the Oval Office, the envied power of which Alamo formerly attributed to the Christian devil.

Although the minister's legacy continues, it is one of pain and cosmic confusion. Reflecting on her leader's incarceration, burdened by memories of theologically rationalized child-rape, impoverishment, and beatings, a girl-refugee from his cult wrote, "All that I knew was gone. . . . He was a false prophet. [Hence], everything he told me was a lie. If everything he told me was a lie, then where was God?" (quoted in Clancy, 2018, n.p.).

Keith Raniere and NXIVM: a predominantly commercial high-pressure group, with spiritual/human potential and political sub-features

Keith Raniere's followers adored him as an enlightened genius, supreme executive coach, and the most ethical man in the world. At the peak of his influence, he messianically claimed to generate self-actualized business leaders tasked to save humanity from global catastrophe.

According to his father, Raniere indicated grandiosity at the age of 7 or 8. Scoring in the gifted range on an intelligence test, Raniere changed and his father witnessed a shift in the boy's character. "[I]t was almost like a switch went off. And suddenly, overnight, he turned into, like, Jesus Christ. And that he was superior and better than everybody, like a deity"[1] (Bloch, Goldhar, Elash, & Pizer, 2018, n.p.). By age 13, Raniere's followers claim, the coaching-genius achieved enlightenment. In adulthood, Raniere said he knew the past lives of his followers (Ling, 2018). Raniere's claim to superpowers is not uncommon among destructive leaders. Depending on the actor's balance of sociopathy to schizotypy, his claim is either a fraud or delusion, but either way it creates a mystique.

During adolescence, he embarked upon polyamorous relationships, but each woman was sexually dedicated solely to Raniere. For unclear reasons, he developed an attraction to near-emaciated women. That Raniere cared for his alcoholic mother following his parents' divorce may have born upon his sexual consumption of women and motivation to enslave them. His predation was, perhaps, Raniere's attempt to create a corrective emotional experience for himself, one to offset affection deprivations common to addicted households. Rather than acting as the servant to an out-of-control woman, he would be the master of fully controlled women – recompensed by becoming the dominant male of Freud's primal horde theory.[2]

That he was well spoken, widely read, and candidly idealistic enabled him to become an accomplished seducer. These endowments contributed to the success of his Executive Success Program (ESP) which, according to the FBI, Raniere offered under his umbrella company NXIVM; these provided expensive coaching programs. Presumably to proclaim his place at the forefront of human evolution and business practice, Raniere adopted the alias "The Vanguard"; upon receipt of his teachings, students were to turn to portraits of "The Vanguard" and offer it thanks. ESP/NXIVM taught students to remain loyal to Raniere's "technology" and "science" and avoid "suppressive," unenlightened persons. Raniere told students to control as much of the world's money as possible – for humanity's sake. Evaluating Raniere's ESP, a forensic psychiatrist explained that exhausting training hours, restricted relationships, group secrecy, hyping of "The Vanguard," paramilitary rituals, and mandatory contact with Raniere's coaches amounted to indoctrination without informed consent (Hochman, 2003). He further opined that Raniere made unproven scientific claims, covertly pressured clients to conform, and hid the profit motive behind messianic pretentions; this, along with the self-coronation of the leadership, supported the conclusion that the group was high pressure and cultic.

The psychiatric unmasking of Reniere's practices illustrates the manner by which the destructive leader absorbs his clientele's wealth while supporting a grand vision of himself as transcendently virtuous.

> ESP [Raniere's Executive Success Program] is presented as a means of saving the world from "hunger, theft, dishonesty, envy and insecurity." After stating this, participants are urged to "pledge" to enroll people in ESP. . . . Prior to the world being saved, the only guaranteed result of recruitment and continued seminar enrollment is up-front revenue generation. . . . Members are encouraged to advance in "rank," which requires, among other things, more courses, which means more fees for ESP.
>
> *Hochman, 2003, n.p.*

To punish the above "suppressive" findings, Raniere's organization unsuccessfully litigated against Doctor Hochman, and other critics. Hyper-aggressive litigation against critics is an intimidation strategy Raniere may have lifted from Scientology or the playbook of notorious New York City attorney Roy Cohn, McCarthy-era which hunter and mentor of Donald Trump.

Rumors and media reports suggested that Raniere preyed upon women and underage girls, practiced business shadily, charged fees for self-aggrandizing ceremonies, and played god with the lives of his clients. Yet, his charisma impelled actresses and heiresses to join his organization and devote their energies to this humanitarian savior. He drew attention from the world's elite when he hosted the Dali Lama at one of his Albany events in 2009. Raniere was gifted as promoting himself as a messianic visionary; he compared himself to Einstein and Ghandi, drawing connected people into his cult, like the Seagram's heiress Clare Bronfman, to help him build his network and bankroll his schemes ("Nxivm," 2019).

Like many MNLs, Raniere eventually overreached and his profound persona failed to protect him – not simply from whistleblowers, but from the authorities. According the FBI, Raniere conspired with a top female lieutenant to entice women to join a secret sorority within NXIVM. The women were to sexually service Raniere and be exploited for organizational profit. The sorority was misrepresented as a mentorship opportunity, rather than a batch of sex slaves whose ego strength would be eroded by "readiness drills" involving sleep deprivation, dietary restrictions, and pain-inductive practices, like freezing showers and stress positions. Victims of the sorority, called DOS, told the FBI that they were blackmailed with life-destroying information in Raniere's possession, like explicit photos and scandalous confessions. They were told that these would be publicly released if they failed to comply with Raniere's demands. Federal investigators also learned that DOS stood for "'Dominus Obsequious Sororium,' which translates to 'Master Over the Slave Women'" (United States of America v. Keith Raniere, 2018, p. 6). The FBI alleged that Raniere organized DOS as a sadomasochistic pyramid scheme: "DOS operates as a pyramid with levels of 'slaves' headed by 'masters.' Slaves are expected to recruit slaves of their own (thus becoming masters themselves), who in turn owe service not only to their own masters but also to masters above them in the DOS pyramid" (p. 6). At the top of the pyramid, Raniere exercised ultimate control of the women, with additional control provided by lower-ranking slaves who enslaved others. Raniere was the only man involved.

Especially deleterious to his narcissistic mask was the FBI's revelation of a sadistic ceremony of flesh burning, one that devolved DOS women from human beings into Raniere's possessions, like chattel.

> Many of the DOS victims were branded in their pubic regions with a cauterizing pen in a process that took twenty to thirty minutes. During the branding "ceremonies," slaves were required to be fully naked, and the master would order one slave to film while the others held down the slave being branded. . . . RANIERE [sic] acknowledged to one DOS victim that his initials are incorporated into the brand as a form of "tribute." . . . Masters told their slaves after the branding ceremonies that the videos of the branding ceremonies and photographs of the women with their brands were additional pieces of *collateral* [an item designated for the purpose of blackmail against noncompliance or defection].
>
> *United States of America v. Keith Raniere, 2018, pp. 11–12; italics added*

Raniere was arrested in Mexico where he had fled to escape federal authorities. He was extradited to the United States and imprisoned. Ruled a flight risk, he was denied bond and charged with sex trafficking, sex trafficking conspiracy, and conspiracy to commit forced labor. The media firestorm swirled with wild reports, including that Raniere was a megalomaniac with aspirations of world domination, that he had designs to install a NXIVM puppet in the Mexican presidency (Zimmerman, 2018), and that a video surfaced in which Raniere seemed to admit to having people killed. All the while, news crews filmed investigators carrying computers from NXIVM offices and public derision of Raniere and NXIVM reached circus levels. Guilty pleas from Raniere's former acolytes emerged after federal prosecutors indicted Raniere for sexually molesting underage girls and producing child pornography (Saul, 2019), ultimately leading to a jury finding him guilty on seven counts of racketeering, sex trafficking, conspiracy, wire fraud, and other offenses ("Keith Raniere's Nxivm," 2019).

Coeval with such spectacle and speculation, Raniere's hold on once-enamored disciples collapsed. One disillusioned disciple offered her insight to the press, stating that she recognizes that "Vanguard isn't the smartest man in the world, with a plan to save humanity with his teachings. Vanguard is just Keith, a middle-aged guy from Albany who likes to control women" (Bloch et al., 2018, n.p.).

Roger Ailes and Fox News: a predominantly political high-pressure group, with commercial and spiritual/human potential sub-features

When Roger Ailes (1940–2017) resigned from Fox News in 2016, he was president and CEO of that organization. During his tenure, he supervised the for-profit indoctrination of white conservative evangelicals and other constituents of the voting American public. Despite his network's claim to fair and balanced reporting, political scientists and media critics viewed the network under Ailes' control as a politically partisan outlet at war with liberal politics, fulminating a widespread reactionary sensibility among its viewers that chiefly promoted the interests of the American Republican Party.

Some scholars question if Ailes' Fox News amounted to an institutional extension of the Republican Party (Azari, 2016). Contemporary psychoanalysts, like Shaw (2018), viewed Fox as a nationally deranging, propagandistic hate group[3], and the former Executive Director of Professional Practice of the American Psychological Association wrote that "Fox is a danger, because it is a cult and uses the same destabilizing psychological techniques cults use to undermine the independent functioning of minds they want to control" (Welch, 2010). Commenting on Ailes' networks' successful mind control efforts, high-pressure group expert Hasson (2016), after viewing the investigative documentary *Brainwashing My Dad* (Senko, 2015), observed, "In documents highlighted by this film, Ailes and his associates admit that they [were] only interested in communicating the messages of the Republican party and actively look[ed] for ways to infiltrate the American public with these messages" (Hasson, 2016, n.p.). Under the masquerade of news, Hasson contended, Ailes presided over a mind control network that used catch phrases, fear induction, and narrative devices likely to trigger dopamine release to bind viewers' distorted worldview to one desired by political and commercial interest groups. Rather than journalism, Ailes' project perpetrated undue influence and cultic indoctrination upon the voting public.

Ailes weaponized his media platform to create a formidable reproduction of his own defenses – a media world in which one's insecurity is attributed to dangerous social elements which must be crushed in order for security to be restored. During his career, he acted as media advisor to Richard Nixon, Ronald Reagan, and Donald Trump. Raised in an Ohio factory town by parents who eventually divorced, Ailes alleged his abusive father taught him to withhold trust, while his hemophilia hindered stereotypical male development via sports and rough and tumble play. This may have contributed to a life-long sense that he had something to prove, and drove a defensive grandiosity. Fear for his physical security, combined with an unconscious sense of male inadequacy, may have contributed to a paranoid trait:"His hemophilia confirmed and expanded the right-wing vision he grew up with – the notion that every threat was lethal, and had to be met with no mercy" (Gleiberman, 2018, n.p.).

From the 1960s until early 1996, Ailes excelled in media positions, political advising, and campaign work for Republican candidates of the American right. Known for having studied Nazi public relations techniques to promote Richard Nixon (Turan, 2018), Ailes was appreciated as a Machiavellian king-maker by the American right. In the second half of his career, Ailes swung into damage control over offensive statements perceived as anti-Semitic. In 1996, he accepted Rupert Murdoch's offer to lead Fox News.

Once in control at Fox, Ailes promoted a style of journalism criticized for its reactionary politics, cultural conservatism, and intolerant bias, verging on active odium of targeted out-groups, according to documentations (Senko, 2015) and media commentators (Taibbi, 2017; Sullivan, 2018). As a leader, Ailes tolerated no broadcaster unreflective of his worldview. Some have described Fox News as a cult; an eyewitness to Ailes' totalitarian management style remarked that many of the "People who've worked there [at Fox News] . . . are aware of the kind of repressive aspects of the workplace. But they're incredibly well-paid, and Roger was famous for taking care of [his] people" (McCarthy, 2018, n.p.). But it was not his inhumane politics, but instead his sexual misconduct that destroyed his ability to lead.

Ailes fired those who bucked his subjugation, and he exploited his power to enjoy the coercive Don Juan-ism indicative of the phallic narcissist. Female broadcasters were further objectified as a ratings strategy. Ailes pressed them to wear short skirts on air and to exhibit their cleavage and legs, and "He started ruining the careers of innocent, highly capable women because they wouldn't engage in *quid pro quo* sex with him" (Ehrlich, 2018, n.p.). Ailes ended one woman's career "overnight," and when she eventually did testify, her statement was described as "harrowing, not for its explicitness (she declined Ailes' offer) but rather for its savagery" (Ehrlich, 2018, n.p.).

Accused of running Fox as a private propaganda network for far-right conservatives eager to scapegoat liberals, Ailes ran his private life with the same split political object relations. At the height of his power, despite unprecedented political influence, he went to war against the tiny municipal government of Cold Springs, New York, where he had purchased a house. Ailes' assault upon the liberal locals showed the news chief "determined to make this blue town run red with the blood of those who stood in his way . . . a man who saw even the smallest conflict as a blood feud" (Ehrlich, 2018, n.p.).

One correspondent reported that, under Ailes, Fox News was "like a surveillance state"; he directed the engineering people "to place close-circuit cameras in various locations that allowed Ailes to monitor the goings-on in offices, studios, green rooms, the back entrance of the network's midtown Manhattan headquarters, and Ailes's homes" (Grove, 2016, n.p.). The same article alleged that the news chief may have ordered illegal spying on liberal reporters. Opining on the legacy of the Citizen Kane-like man depicted in Alexis Bloom's 2018 documentary *Divide and Conquer*, a critic described Ailes as domineering and arrogant, and a practitioner of "Orwellian malevolence . . . who dragged the playbook of fascist propaganda, for the first time, into the white hot glare of televised democracy" (Gleiberman, 2018, n.p.).

Quite possibly echoing Ailes' opinion of himself, his wife once asserted through a publicist that her propagandist husband was more important than the United States. Sex scandal, mounting allegations, and contention with Fox's owners – the well-known Murdoch family – culminated in Ailes' ouster (officially he resigned) in 2016. Briefly he assumed an advisory role to President Trump and, following a fall and head injury, died of complications related to hemophilia – Ailes' lifelong reaction formation against which, some believe, gave rise to the domineering arrogance of his leadership style, and explains why he "armored his vulnerability in the tactics – and belief systems – of a bully" (Gleiberman, 2018, n.p.).

Marshall Applewhite and Heaven's Gate: a predominantly spiritual/human potential high-pressure group, with commercial and political sub-features

Marshall Herf Applewhite (1931–1997) was a pilgrim of sorts. His salvation plan for transcending his sexual shame, unresolved grief, and fear of death involved asexual bonding with co-leader Bonnie Nettles[4] and preaching that virtue, combined with ascetic living, could result, under his supervision, in escape from earthly pain aboard an extraterrestrial space craft.

> Applewhite had been theologizing, proselyting, and preaching a blend of Christian astrology and outer space fantasy since the 1970s. Applewhite promised his disciples that they would evolve into spiritually superior, bald aliens by severing all links to modern society and human desires. Heaven's Gate suicide cult members not only shunned sex, but approximately a third of the men in the cult chose castration, following Applewhite's personal example.
>
> *Olsson, 2005, p. 89*

Applewhite's early life offers no foreshadowing that he would end his days as a homicidal eunuch ordering his 39 followers to swallow phenobarbital with vodka chasers, their ticket to a spacecraft traveling behind the Hale-Bopp comet.

Much of the destructive leader's development was normal, and Applewhite was once a man with promise. The son of a Presbyterian preacher, Applewhite aspired to his father's profession, but he eventually opted to pursue his talent in music. Throughout the decade of the '60s the musician married, sired two children, and circulated among roles as performer, choir director, and music teacher. But the MNL's repression of his ego-dystonic same-sex desire was unsuccessful. Applewhite was burdened from a series of homosexual scandals, one which resulted in his firing from the music department at the University of St. Thomas, Houston, Texas. In the aftermath of an affair with a male music student, a humiliated Applewhite was hospitalized for depressive symptoms, sexual conflicts, and coronary issues.

In the hospital, he renewed acquaintance with a former student, now his attentive nurse, Bonnie Nettles. (Another version of how the cult leaders connected is that they met in Applewhite's theater class (Bearak, 1997).) Like Applewhite, Nettles may have found sexuality a disappointment, or frightening, and the two merged in a way that utterly precluded the messiness of a physical relationship. Following Applewhite's discharge, they became a couple of sorts. Applewhite provided compelling teaching, delivered via charismatic preaching, and Nettles inspired confidence as the quiet leader with a steady hand on the rudder. Witnesses describe them as exuding a magnetic presence. By the early '70s the two cut ties with their families, left Houston, and traveled the United States.

By 1975, their cult reached peak popularity: followers paid rapt attention for information about a rendezvous with salvific spacemen, and NBC considered basing a show on the couple, tentatively titled *The Mysterious Two*. In 1984, just before succumbing to cancer, Nettles wrote to her daughter that she expected immanent transportation from the planet on a spacecraft, a defensive fiction that effectively denied the reality of her approaching demise. With Nettles' death, Applewhite lacked the support he required to maintain his narcissistic equilibrium, and keep his fear of sex and death at bay. To cope, he had himself castrated and continued to teach his space theology, leaving an empty chair for the late Nettles whom Applewhite pretended was spiritually present.

> He projected a total renouncement of sexuality into the delusional theology of his New Age religious cult and asexual merger with Bonne Nettles. He attempted to reverse his personal sexual failures by preaching abnegation of sexuality to his followers, as if it were some superior spiritual plateau paralleled only by the ancient Gnostics. When Bonnie Nettles died, Applewhite's failed salvation efforts through their spurious healing merger imploded. He escalated his extraterrestrial, delusional denial of death into his own soft-sell version of a group suicide as a special escape to better worlds.
>
> *Olsson, 2005, pp. 97–98*

Applewhite fled from his fear of sex and death, of shame and annihilation, by inventing a science fantasy that he was the reincarnation of an extraterrestrial Jesus, that suicide with him would result not in erasure, but evolution. Members of

Heaven's Gate were to keep clear of Luciferians who symbolized any "dark force" that threatened Applewhite's version of reality.

They were to become themselves by abandoning themselves. Family ties were cut. Finances were delivered to the leader. They ate the same food, wore unisex clothing, and sported a sexless group hairstyle. They changed their names, and they read only approved texts. To avoid ideological impurities that might arise from a Luciferian source, the would-be space people travelled in pairs. In short, Heaven's Gate disciples mirrored Applewhite's desperate, grandiose flight from the discomfiture that accompanies psychological adulthood (see Chapter 4). Stripped of individuality and mental adulthood, their childlike adoration buoyed Applewhite above his debilitating shame and fear, and supported the group notion that they were exceptional space pilgrims, instead of immature fantasists (Ross, 2014), like people who might make a religion from comic book superheroes or Star Trek cinema characters.

In March 1997, in the neighborhood of Rancho Sante Fe outside San Diego, the Heaven's Gate organization committed group suicide. Under Applewhite's directions, they went to dinner *en masse*, ordered the same meal, took the same barbiturates, drank the same alcohol, and expired with the same plastic bags over their heads. This was the fruit of Applewhite's leadership and the last behavioral evidence of a collective bounded choice born of Applewhite's charisma, salvation plan, high pressure rules, and cult culture. While grandiosity, mind control, and group paraphrenia account for much of this sad phenomenon, it cannot be discounted that, beyond a happy ascent to the mother ship, Applewhite's thanatological motivation may have been darkly informed by the contempt he felt toward a world so intimidating that he simply could not confront it on the terms of a grown man. By leaving his own and his followers' corpses to stink in the fallen adult world, he criminally expressed his narcissistic rage to a planet that found him special neither as a musician nor as a reincarnated space Christ.

Marcus Wesson's Christo-Vampire family cult: a spiritual/ human potential high-pressure group, with few political or commercial features

Marcus Wesson (b. 1946), an unemployed former soldier who was compelling and well-spoken, presided over a family cult. He subjugated his relatives and children with rage, charm, and the special status he had in the eyes of God — whose favor was demonstrated in the revelation of the profound rightness of practicing vampirism, Christianity, and incest. Forcing his children to recognize his divinity and call him *Lord*, Wesson dominated family life. He quite literally enjoyed a captive audience of sexually abused women and girls (one wife he wed at age 8), sons traumatized from 30-day beating schedules, and older women who were enslaved to his whims, including a restricted diet and belief in his made-up religious claims.

On March 12, 2004, Wesson achieved dubious distinction as Fresno's worst mass murderer. The 57-year-old was arrested and convicted for the sexual abuse and murder of nine of his own children, including three toddlers, four children under 9 years old, a teenage girl, and a 24-year-old woman. Media reports depicted Wesson as a self-styled patriarch who ran a family cult based on Christianity and vampirism to which he required his isolated family adhere. During his trial, the media further described him as a "domestic dictator" who "espoused a home brew of evangelical Christianity, the occult and sexual mania" (Ryan, 2005, n.p.). He "began telling people that God was speaking through him and that the end of time was near" and that he "had to keep his divine knowledge 'anonymous'" (Ryan, 2005, n.p.), thus home-schooling his children and declining to hold a job.

He was described by his son as psychotic, delusional, and narcissistic. During home-schooling, he taught his student children that he was God's messenger. Wesson admonished his children that the Bible mandated incest, and that disagreement with his will was sin that would be met with ruthless corporal punishment. Living conditions were described by surviving children as prison-like, depressing, and hopeless. Treating himself to excellent food, Wesson restricted his family's intake and forced them to feed from trash cans. One daughter recounted that Wesson molested each daughter by the time they were 8 or 9 years old in preparation for "marriage" at the time of puberty. Paranoid, Wesson characterized authorities as Satan and prophesized that one day representatives of the devil would come for them, sporting a blue uniform and a badge. His children were indoctrinated to believe that the ordained response to that apocalyptic moment involved submission to fatal shooting by the eldest woman, who would then herself die by suicide. In this manner their souls would be saved.

Despite the coercive threat of divine judgment, two of Wesson's nieces, whom he had raped, announced their intension to defect from his dominion and take their incestuously sired children with them. An argument ensued and the police were called. Authorities mistakenly believed that Wesson would cooperate, and they allowed him to enter his home where he activated the murder-suicide pact. Ordered to deliver the younger children from the "Satan" embodied by the police, one of Wesson's adult daughters shot her younger siblings dead, and then, in obedience to her lord Wesson, fatally shot herself (Ross, 2014, pp. 97–100). Wesson stacked the corpses of his murdered children in a heap and emerged from the house dripping with their blood. Weapons drawn, officers incapacitated and cuffed him, entered the house, and found his victims stacked from youngest to oldest. In addition to the carnage, officers beheld a significant number of antique coffins, an indicator of Wesson's thanatological preoccupations and vampiric fantasies. Six police chaplains were called to the crime scene to support the shaken officers, some of whom later went on administrative leave for mental health reasons following the investigation (Jobling, n.d.).

> Marcus Wesson was charged with nine counts of murder and fourteen counts of sexually abusing his daughter and nieces. He was the father of all the murdered children. Some of the children were the result of incestuous relationships with his daughters. "They were exterminated, one after the other," Lisa Gamoian, the prosecutor, said at Wesson's trial in 2005. "In this family, he was Christ himself, the ultimate authority figure who determined life and death."
>
> *Ross, 2014, p. 99*

The man who led a family cult based on his infallible vision of an incest-positive, vampire-based Christianity was found guilty on all counts and sentenced to death in San Quinton.

To understand the crimes derived from Wesson's malignant narcissism, it is necessary to mention that his father, an alcoholic, likely under-mentored and over-shamed his son, while his fanatically devout Seventh Day Adventist mother may have rationalized her inability or refusal to protect young Marcus as virtuous martyrdom. His damaged development can be located in his reaction formation against unconscious inadequacy born of lovelessness and toxic shaming – hence, the god drive. Declaring himself the mouthpiece of God, he fashioned unassailable adequacy and defended against the persecutory parents. Through his spiritual and sexual enslavement of his daughters, or "wives," he achieved revenge upon the birth mother who failed to protect him and shamed him with Seventh Day Adventist theology. He ensured that even the mildest opposition from his new "wives" signified sin against God incarnate whom Wesson claimed to be. This was also a means to triumph over his father, even as he identified with him.

Wesson's vampire cult theology is psychodynamically revelatory. It points to the oral privations Wesson likely suffered at the breast in his infancy. Certainly, neither parent would have been exemplary in sharing the milk of human kindness. Or perhaps Wesson's temperament made incorporation of their supplies impossible. In any case, the vampire fantasy, which became his transcendent belief system, demonstrates an attempt to repair the injury to his under-nourished core. The vampire sucks something nourishing that sustains him. So does the infant suckling.

Oedipally, Wesson presents as having cathected incestuous libido upon his mother, while he felt threatened by his alcoholic father. To ensure safety in incestuous sexual gratification in his adulthood, he declared himself a god, whose pronouncement alone could make a wrong right. But he also identified with the aggressor, and he brutally beat his sons, telling them that they must never become sexually interested in the women. In this way, he enjoyed the sexual liberty he envied in his own father, and he neatly exemplified Freud's mythic father of the primal horde, who keeps the women to himself and subjugates the envious sons through brute force.

Wesson was a destructive leader. His vampiric attempt to fix his childish, broken mind resulted in perversion of his leadership, spirituality, sexuality, object relations, and legacy. Especially tragic are the lives of his surviving family members; they are left to sort out their confusion and mourn the dead.

Shoko Asahara and Aum Shinrikyo: a spiritual/human potential high-pressure group, with political and commercial features

The blind guru Shoko Asahara (1955–2018) degenerated into destructive madness and meticulously coordinated a nerve gas assault in the Tokyo subway. Despite his loss of temporal sight, Asahara claimed to see the future and preached to his followers that he envisioned an apocalypse which was desirable for them to actualize through terrorism in service to providence.

On March 20, 1995, headlines across the world announced that a deadly gas had been released into the Tokyo subway system, killing twelve citizens and seriously injuring five thousand more. Within days, the evidence accumulated about the perpetrators pointed toward Aum Shinrikyo, a Japanese-based international cult led by forty-year-old Shoko Asahara, with a membership of ten to thirty thousand people and a net worth of more than a billion dollars. Charges against Asahara and some of his disciples included murder, kidnapping, and manufacturing and stockpiling lethal chemicals. Later, the remains of lawyer's known for fighting Aum, along with the remains of the lawyer's wife and fourteen-month-old son, were unearthed. These individuals had been missing since 1989.

Singer, 2003, pp. 339–340

Shoko Asahara was a spiritual megalomaniac, who murdered his critics and wanted to rule Japan and the world. Asahara galvanized his followers with the promise of remaking the post-apocalyptic world according to their counter-cultural fantasies. (Such dreams are almost always fear-avoidance strategies.) The MNL guru and his followers shared a blend of adolescent rebellion, magical thinking, and self-aggrandizing fantasy that suppressed their dread of the maturational rigors required to reach psychological adulthood. Asahara seduced them with the delights of the *puer's* Neverland utopia, an alternate reality in which followers avoid becoming their despised parents and enjoy super-status in an empire of elites, a fantasized alternate world where self-esteem is guaranteed by all the rights and privileges of in-group status on a cosmic level.

Born into Japanese post-war devastation in 1955, Shoko Asarhara entered the world with infantile glaucoma; he was partially blind in his right eye and utterly blind in his left. Sent to a special school with blind students, Asahara exploited his partial sight to attain social power, but he was disliked for extorting money from his peers and lost school elections due to his reputation as a bully. Denied admittance to Tokyo University, Asahara practiced acupuncture, purveyed fraudulent cures, and suffered the disgrace of jail time and bankruptcy.

In 1984 at the age of 29, following time spent in prison, Asahara embarked for India where for he studied Buddhist enlightenment (Olsson, 2005). Returning to Japan, the mystic declared a new religion, petitioned for legal status, and recruited a following of financially fit, young professionals with technical educations. Dismayed by the post-war culture of drudgery and workaholism, his followers were promised collective meaning and individual enlightenment if they adhered to his polyglot doctrine of Buddhism, Hinduism, and esoteric Christianity. In exchange for surrendering their wealth to Aum Shinrikyo, reading Asahara's books, ingesting hallucinogens, wearing brain wave helmets, and practicing celibacy and fasting, the disciples were promised to survive a poison gas attack from the United States instigated by Freemasons and Jews. Such promises attracted a following.

Just prior to launching their nerve gas attack, Asahara's organization boasted up to 40,000 adherents globally and enjoyed revenue from subsidiaries, like coffee shops and computer assembly factories. Discipline was enforced by Asahara loyalists, who kidnapped defectors and murdered the guru's detractors. Although Asahara declared himself to be the Christ (Asahara, 1992), his narcissism, grandiosity, and audacious criminality also expressed along temporal lines; according to Japanese authorities, the guru was impatient for the Doomsday scenario that would kill 90 percent of the world's population and leave him, and Aum Shinrikyo, in charge of the new age. Thus, he ordered the gas attacks, operating under the delusion that his chemical terrorism would overthrow the government of Japan and elevate him to Emperor.

The master's decision to fulfill his own prophesy did not usher in a post-apocalyptic golden age; instead, 12 people died and 5,000 others were injured from their sarin gas attack. Asahara and his top disciples were arrested and charged with responsibility for a terrorist attack. Aum Shinrikyo, once a 40,000-strong organization, was disgraced and withered to a fraction of its size, and Shoko Asahara was hanged by the Japanese government in 2018 (Lifton, 2000; Olsson, 2005; Van Biema, 1995). It was observed that prior to his death, the loss of narcissistic supplies from worshipful sycophants caused a mental breakdown, characterized by observable psychosis.

Conclusion

In his public remarks about destructive leaders and MNLs, Devlin (2018) frequently refers to *the theft of utopia* (also discussed in Chapter 6). His is an apt phrase that points to the disappointment experienced by all who long for a better life, or a better world, promised by a charismatic, confident leader, whose animal magnetism and riveting speech are so convincing and so reassuring that, at times, a kind of peak experience occurs. The individual or the group bonds with a dangerous narcissist with a messiah complex. They will credential his transcendent worldview, however preposterous, and lose their self-sovereignty to the laws and customs he inflicts upon his followers. In spiritual groups, the devotee will eventually find that the promised heaven is an actual hell. In commercial groups, the anticipated good life culminates in crushing poverty or prison time. In political groups, the utopian dream unfolds in a totalitarian nightmare, in which one's very thoughts are subject to party inspection. In whatever category of social grouping, the "all good" leader is a potential malignancy. Let us check the imbalance of his "goodness" with the skepticism and whole object relations of the appropriately cynical adult.

Notes

1 When queried by the media, one of Raniere's former mistresses attributed these words to the leader's father.
2 All such leaders in this book might be credibly interpreted in light of Freud's primal horde theory. Devlin and I discuss this further in Chapter 7.

3 An acknowledged expert in traumatizing narcissism and cultic techniques of undue influence, mind control, and totalitarian processes, Shaw (2018) lumped Ailes' Fox into "the Goebbels-inspired media" and referred to Fox News as a "de facto state news outlet" (p. 3), distinguishing Fox from the objective news organization that was its persona under Ailes' command.

4 A former Baptist married to a Houston businessman from 1949 to 1973, Bonnie Nettles left her spouse and four children to travel about with Applewhite as the mother-figure of their jointly established UFO cult. Fascinated with spiritualism and séances, Nettles sometimes made decisions based on interlocutions from a disembodied 19th-century monk named Brother Francis. Her worldview and decision-making drew from astrology, theosophy, and divination. She came to believe that she and Applewhite were the two witnesses referred to in the Book of Revelation by St. John the Divine. Early in their movement, Nettles prophesized that she and Applewhite would be killed, reanimated, and beamed aboard a spacecraft in demonstration of their extraordinary claims. Nettles also supported Applewhite in the notion that he was Jesus Christ or Christ's successor (Balch & Taylor, 2002; Bearak, 1997; Zeller, 2014). After her death, Applewhite revised his theology such that Nettles resided "in the Evolutionary Level above human (the 'Kingdom of Heaven') . . . [and] made it clear . . . that Hale-Bopp's approach is the 'marker' . . . [for] graduation from the Human Evolutionary Level" via group suicide (CNN, 1997, n.p.). Thusly, Applewhite and his crew would reach the spaceship trailing the Hale-Bopp comet and evolve in space with Nettles (Chryssides, 2016).

References

Alamo, T. (2011, January 3). From Pastor Tony Alamo to the President of the United States. Retrieved from www.alamoministries.com/content/english/letters/tothepresident.html

Alamo, T. (2019, January 28). *RationalWiki*. Retrieved from https://rationalwiki.org/wiki/Tony_Alamo

Asahara, S. (1992). *Declaring myself the Christ: Disclosing the true meanings of Jesus Christ's gospel.* Shizuoka, Japan: Aum Publishing Company.

Azari, J. (2016). How the news media helped to nominate Trump. *Political Communication, 33*(4), 678–679.

Balch, R. W., & Taylor, D. (2002). Making sense of the Heaven's Gate suicides. In D. G. Bromley & J. G. Melton (Eds.), *Cults, religion, and violence* (pp. 209–228). Cambridge, UK: Cambridge University Press.

BBC News. (2019). Keith Raniere's Nxivm sex cult trial: What we learned. Retrieved from www.bbc.com/news/world-us-canada-48401061

BBC News. (2019, April 20). Nxivm: Seagram heiress Clare Bronfman pleads guilty in "sex cult" case. Retrieved from www.bbc.com/news/world-us-canada-47996207

Bearak, B. (1997, April 28). Eyes on glory: Pied pipers of Heaven's Gate. *New York Times.* Retrieved from www.nytimes.com/1997/04/28/us/eyes-on-glory-pied-pipers-of-heaven-s-gate.html?sec=health&pagewanted=1

Bloch, J., Goldhar, K., Elash, A., & Pizer, D. (2018, September 12). The making of Vanguard: The story of how NXIVM's Keith Raniere went from gifted child to self-help guru to accused sex-cult leader. *CBC News.* Retrieved from https://newsinteractives.cbc.ca/longform/the-making-of-the-vanguard

Bloom, A. (Director). (2018). *Divide and conquer: The story of Roger Ailes* [motion picture]. United States: Magnolia.

Carter, L. F. (1990). *Charisma and control in Rajneeshpuram: The role of shared values in the creation of community.* New York, NY: Cambridge University Press.

Chryssides, G. D. (Ed.). (2016). *Heaven's Gate: Postmodernity and popular culture in a suicide group.* New York, NY: Routledge.

Clancy, S. (2018, May 6). Reaching "daylight": New book focuses on the children who survived Tony Alamo and his cult. *Arkansas Democrat Gazette*. Retrieved from www.arkansasonline.com/news/2018/may/06/reaching-daylight-20180506/

Clarke, R. O. (1988). The narcissistic guru. *Free Inquiry*, 8(2), 33–45.

CNN. (1997, March 27). Mysterious couple known as "The Two" may be behind suicide cult. Retrieved from Cult Education Institute website: https://culteducation.com/group/968-heaven-s-gate/9559-mysterious-couple-known-as-the-two-may-be-behind-suicide-cult.html

Devlin, P. (2018, April 5). Seminar Roundtable. *On Dangerous Character*. Washington Hospital, Washington, DC.

Ehrlich, D. (2018, September 13). "Divide and conquer: The story of Roger Ailes" Review: A damning documentary about the monster behind Fox News. *IndieWire*. Retrieved from www.indiewire.com/2018/09/divide-and-conquer-the-roger-ailes-story-review-tiff-1202003374/

Gleiberman, O. (2018, September 29). Film review: "Divide and conquer: The story of Roger Ailes": A documentary about the rise and fall of Roger Ailes, the dark guru of Fox News, paints a fascinating and distressing portrait of insatiable power. *Variety*. Retrieved from https://variety.com/2018/film/reviews/divide-and-conquer-the-story-of-roger-ailes-review-1202961176/

Grove, L. (2016, September 2). Exile: The downfall of Roger Ailes step by step. *Daily Beast*. Retrieved from www.thedailybeast.com/the-downfall-of-roger-ailes-step-by-step?ref=scroll

Hasson, S. (2016). Roger Ailes, FOX News, right-wing talk shows, and undue influence techniques. *Freedom of Mind Resource Center*. Retrieved from https://freedomofmind.com/roger-ailes-fox-news-right-wing-talk-shows-and-undue-influence-techniques/

Hochman, J. (2003, February). A forensic psychiatrist evaluates ESP. Retrieved from www.culteducation.com/group/907-nxivm/6047-a-forensic-psychiatrist-evaluates-esp.html

Jobling, I. (n.d.). The crime the media chose to ignore. *Murderpedia*. Retrieved from https://murderpedia.org/male.W/w/wesson-marcus.htm

Lalich, J. (2004). Using the bounded choice model as an analytic tool: A case study of Heaven's Gate. *Cultic Studies Review*, 3(3), 226–247.

Lalich, J., & Tobias, M. (2006). *Take back your life: Recovering from cults and abusive relationships*. Richmond, CA: Bay Tree Publishing.

Lancaster, G. (2018, May 7). Tony Alamo (1934–2017). *Encyclopedia of Arkansas History & Culture*. Retrieved from www.encyclopediaofarkansas.net/encyclopedia/entry-detail.aspx?entryID=4224

Langone, M., & Eisenberg, G. (1993). Children and cults. In M. Langone (Ed.), *Recovery from cults: Help for victims of psychological and spiritual abuse*. New York, NY: W.W. Norton.

Lifton, R. J. (2000). *Destroying the world to save it: Aum Shinrikyō, apocalyptic violence, and the new global terrorism*. New York, NY: Henry Holt.

Ling, J. (Host). (2018, September 3). Sex, money, and Nazis. *Undercover* [Audio podcast]. Retrieved from www.cbc.ca/player/play/1317913667800/

McCarthy, T. (2018, December 7). "It's easy to make someone a monster": Behind a Roger Ailes documentary. *The Guardian*. Retrieved from www.theguardian.com/film/2018/dec/07/divide-and-conquer-roger-ailes-documentary-alexis-bloom

McCormack, W. (2018, March 27). Outside the limits of the human imagination: What the new documentary "Wild, Wild Country" doesn't capture about the magnetism and evil of the Rajneesh cult. *The New Republic*. Retrieved from https://newrepublic.com/article/147657/outside-limits-human-imagination

Oakes, L. (1997). *Prophetic charisma: The psychology of revolutionary religious personalities*. Syracuse, NY: Syracuse University Press.

Olsson, P. A. (2005). *Malignant pied pipers of our time: A psychological study of destructive cult leaders from Rev. Jim Jones to Osama Bin Laden.* Baltimore, MD: Publish America.

Rajneesh. (n.d.). *Wikipedia.* Retrieved from https://en.wikipedia.org/wiki/Rajneesh

Rajneesh, S. (1985). *Glimpses of a golden childhood.* Rajneeshpuram, OR: Rajneesh Foundation International.

Ross, R. A. (2014). *Cults inside and out: How people get in and can get out.* North Charleston, SC: CreateSpace Independent Publishing Platform.

Ryan, H. (2005, May 19). Child brides and vampire names: Bizarre the norm in mass murder trial. *Court TV.* Retrieved from CNN.com: www.cnn.com/2005/LAW/04/22/wesson/

Saul, E. (2019). Nxivm member admits to enslaving woman in a locked room for 2 years. *New York Post.* Retrieved from the Cult Education Institute website: https://culteducation.com/group/907-nxivm/34741-nxivm-member-admits-to-enslaving-woman-in-a-locked-room-for-2-years.html

Senko, J. (Director). (2015). *The brainwashing of my dad.* JSenko Productions in association with Cinco Dedos Peculias presents a film by Jen Senko and Matthew Modine. Retrieved from www.thebrainwashingofmydad.com/

Shaw, D. (2018). Authoritarianism and the cultic dynamic: Traumatic narcissism in American politics. *Public seminar books.* Retrieved from www.danielshawlcsw.com/publications/

Singer, M. T. (2003). *Cults in our midst: The continuing fight against their hidden menace.* San Francisco, CA: Jossey-Bass.

Storr, A. (1996). *Feet of clay: Saints, sinners, and madmen – A study of gurus.* New York, NY: Free Press Paperbacks.

Sullivan, M. (2018). A Roger Ailes biopic immortalizing him as an evildoer? Yes, please. *Chicago Tribune.* Retrieved at https://www.chicagotribune.com/opinion/commentary/ct-perspec-hollywood-roger-ailes-fox-biopic-0529-20180523-story.html

Taibbi, M. (2017). Roger Ailes was one of the worst Americans ever: Fox News founder made this the hate-filled, moronic country it is today. *Rolling Stone.* Retrieved at https://www.rollingstone.com/politics/politics-features/roger-ailes-was-one-of-the-worst-americans-ever-111156/

Turan, K. (2018, December 6). Review: The rise of Fox News is told through the man who made it happen in "Divide and Conquer: The Story of Roger Ailes." *Los Angeles Times.* Retrieved from www.latimes.com/entertainment/movies/la-et-mn-divide-conquer-roger-ailes-review-20181205-story.html

United States of America v. Keith Raniere. (2018, February 14). Complaint and affidavit in support of arrest warrant. U.S. District Court, Eastern District of New York. Retrieved from www.justice.gov/usao-edny/press-release/file/1046381/download

Van Biema, D. (1995, April 3). Japan's prophet of poison: Shoko Asahara. *Time.* Retrieved from http://content.time.com/time/subscriber/article/0,33009,982760-4,00.html

Welch, B. (2010, March 18). Fox News is not just biased: It's a cult. *Huffington Post.* Retrieved from www.huffpost.com/entry/fox-news-is-not-just-bias_b_337961

Zeller, B. E. (2014). *Heaven's Gate, America's UFO religion.* New York, NY: New York University Press.

Zimmerman, A. (2018, August 9). Megalomania: Inside the NXIVM sex cult's secret plot to take over Mexico. *Daily Beast.* Retrieved from www.thedailybeast.com/inside-the-nxivm-sex-cults-secret-plot-to-take-over-mexico

6

THE PERVERSION OF UTOPIA

Malignant narcissist leaders and the transcendental

Tyranny has been written about since the beginning of recorded history. The earliest recorded story is about a tyrant named Gilgamesh, who was a legendary Sumerian king and the first epic hero in world literature. Tyrants are as diverse as humanity, but they always rule – whether group, sect, or nation state – with absolute power.

In his book *Tyrants: A History of Power, Injustice, and Terror* (2016), Waller Newell distinguishes between three types of tyranny: the garden variety, the reformer, and the millenarian. The garden variety tyrants seek power for personal gain. They are transactional. They exploit a nation (or a human being) for money, sexual pleasure, and shiny objects. The reformers, on the other hand, seek power to change their nation or society. They engage in large building projects, improve schools, and rarely use violence wantonly. Kemal Ataturk might be a prototypical reform tyrant. Then, there is the millenarian tyrant. Newell believes they are a modern phenomenon. For Newell, the ascendency of the millenarian tyrant begins with the French Revolution. Garden variety and reformer tyrants existed before the French Revolution and continue to resurface, but with the rise of Robespierre and the Jacobins a new form of tyranny appeared.

Newell describes this new form of tyranny as characterized by the willingness of a leader to commit mass murder in the service of a utopian vision. It is "driven by a utopian aim in which society is to be transformed from being unjust, materialistic, and selfish in the present to being spiritually pure, selfless, and communal in the future" (Newell, 2016, p. 264). These leaders also espouse an egalitarian reorganization of society, have no regard for individual liberty, and pit themselves against an outside enemy. They are willing to sacrifice hundreds, thousands, or even millions to achieve a New Jerusalem or a worker's paradise.

This description is also mirrored by Daniel Chirot in his book *Modern Tyrants* (1994). He writes that modern dictators like Mao, Hitler, and Stalin were worshipped "in ways no mortal has been since the great religious prophets of the past,

Jesus Christ, Buddha, and Mohammed" (Chirot, 1994, p. 2). These leaders believed they had a profound understanding of the human condition and that only they could *free* humanity from human suffering and the vicissitudes of existence. They believed they could radically upend social norms and societies and remake them. Eric Hoffer characterized the modern millenarian tyrant as possessing:

> audacity and a joy in defiance; an iron will; a fanatical conviction that he is in possession of the one and only truth; faith in his destiny and luck; a capacity for passionate hatred; contempt for the present; a cunning estimate of human nature; a delight in symbols (spectacles and ceremonials); unbounded brazenness which finds expression in a disregard of consistency and fairness; a recognition that the innermost craving is for communion and that there can never be too much of it; a capacity for winning and upholding the utmost loyalty of a group.
>
> *Hoffer, 1964, p. 105*

It is important to acknowledge that these tyrants – addressed later in this chapter as malignant narcissist leaders (MNLs) – have altered the course of global history. The life of Jan of Leiden (perhaps the prototype of the modern tyrant) resembles the trajectory of many charismatic MNLs who were adrift before rising to pre-eminence. In this chapter, I analyze his rise and fall as well as that of Antônio Conselheiro, Adolf Hitler, David Koresh, Credonia Mwerinde, and Hong Xiuquan.

It is almost too easy to ignore their humanity and portray them with the sobriquet "evil" – easy because their pathology is so destructive. In his book *On Evil* (2010), Terry Eagleton writes that evil is the antipode of the human bonds of mutuality and tenderness. According to Eagleton, it is, in fact, anti-human (Eagleton, 2010). Nevertheless, the leaders portrayed throughout this chapter are deeply human even though their humanity is bent. A better word for their pathology would be *agony*. Although they inflict suffering on others, they too suffer deeply. Disavowing their humanity and portraying them as demons only inflates the MNL beyond the realm of the merely human. If they are seen as they truly are – pathetic, dependent, stunted, pompous, and cruel – then the nimbus of sacredness around them attributed by their followers disappears.

The rise of the modern tyrant

Newell believed this new form of tyranny deserved to be classified as a "category of psychology" (Newell, 2016, p. 24). This new category manifests in adulthood as cluster B diagnoses such as narcissism and antisocial personality. Their combination or comorbidity is often called malignant narcissism (Fromm, 1964). It has been widely written – beginning with Fromm and Kernberg – that these men and women lack empathy; have bloated, grandiose egos; predate upon other human beings; and demand adulation. They are often unaware that their grandiosity is a mask for self-loathing, self-doubt, and fear. Their extreme narcissism is like air blown into a balloon. It inflates a shriveled self. We can only guess that these malignant narcissist leaders (MNLs) had childhoods that were emotionally and developmentally stunted, and that the malignant narcissism they enacted was rooted in this trauma and deprivation.

MNLs are also charismatic. In their case, this charisma means they are special, at least to their followers, and they exist separate from the mundane and ordinary human beings. According to Max Weber (1968), who first defined the concept of *charisma*, the charismatic leader embodies the transcendental and appears to his or her followers as chosen by God or history to achieve a millenarian plan. They are a god or god's authority on earth. It is this spiritual authority that cements the millenarian leader's authority over their followers. It feeds their need for adulation. It also allows them to place the mask of God over their self-doubt and psychic chaos.

The MNL often appears within millenarian or transcendental movements. Once they establish themselves as leaders of the movement, they inspire followers to surrender themselves to the leader's millenarian plans. This begins a profoundly deep and disturbing relationship. The followers are psychically eaten by the MNL; they surrender and lose their identities and become players in the leader's psychic enactment of a personal pathology.

Jan of Leiden

Jan of Leiden (also known as Jan Beukels or Brockelson) was born into poverty and out-of-wedlock. He had artistic aspirations as an actor and dramatist. Before he arrived in Munster, he had drifted between trades, although he is best known as a tailor. He was a gifted orator who held radical millenarian beliefs. But, more importantly, when he had his moment to lead, he ruled as a brutal tyrant who wielded a transcendental belief system like a hammer (Arthur, 1999). Under Jan of Leiden's reign, a new category of leadership, perhaps embryonic, appeared. It is easy to dismiss Jan of Leiden as mad, as writers and pamphleteers did in the 16th century. But Jan may well be the progenitor of a new kind of leader: one with authority rooted in transcendentalism (millenarianism) and who rules through totalistic deindividuation and terror. Jan's authoritarian reign was not the New Jerusalem that Anabaptist preachers and theologians originally envisioned.

In 1535, he declared himself King of the World in the town of Munster, an independent German principality in the province of Westphalia and just north of Cologne. At the time, Jan was the leader of the town of Munster, or, rather, the Anabaptist movement within the walls of the town. The Anabaptists were under siege, and they had expelled the bishop, all Catholics, and all Lutherans. They had established leadership under first Jan Matthys and then Jan of Leiden. The town was surrounded by mercenaries loyal to Franz Von Waldeck, the ousted Catholic bishop of Munster who wanted his city returned to him.

The Anabaptist movement had begun years earlier during the Protestant revolt. Although they lacked a unitary theology, they shared several practices and beliefs within their sect. Anabaptists believed that the conversion and baptism to Christian belief must be undertaken in adulthood when an individual is old enough to decide. They were literalists who believed in the primacy of the New Testament over ecclesiastical tradition and allegiance to the state. This belief incited Luther, Zwingli, and many other Protestant leaders to urge genocide against the Anabaptists. Anabaptists had an egalitarian or communal streak. All types of work, whether peasant, artisan, or merchant, served God. Therefore, class distinctions should be eradicated. They were filled with apocalyptic fervor because the New Jerusalem was imminent. The movement began in the wake of the German Peasant's War of the 1520s, which might have jaded the Anabaptists against any demand to a higher earthly authority (Naphy, 2011).

By the time Jan led the Munster Anabaptists, many of the Anabaptist leaders had been executed or, more rarely, imprisoned. In 1529, at the Diet of Speyer, both Catholics and Protestant leaders had declared genocide against all Anabaptists. This triggered relentless, sadistic persecution of the Anabaptists and their leaders by both Catholics and other Protestants alike. Itinerant, messianic, Anabaptist prophets became prominent. One such prophet, Verna Baumann who was a servant in north-eastern Switzerland, declared herself to be Jesus Christ.

> Many people flocked to see her, confessing their sins; but then "Verena herself told the people that she was to bear the Anti-Christ, but shortly afterward she said she was to bear the child mentioned in Revelation 12. She called herself at one moment the great whore of Babylon, but immediately afterward the living Son of God. She also appeared naked in front of the crowd and reproved them for having lewd ideas."
>
> *Waite, 2007, p. 31*

Into this bloody and dire moment stepped Jan of Leiden. Before his ascension to his throne, his predecessor was the Dutch baker and Anabaptist Savonarola, Jan Matthys. Jan of Leiden was one of Matthys' aide de camps. Under Matthys, the Anabaptists burned books and paintings – including the paintings of the Westphalian school – in bonfires and extinguished them forever. On Easter Sunday, Mathys charged on horseback against Bishop Von Waldeck's mercenary army in the belief that God would protect him and reward him in battle. He and 12 disciples who rode with him were slaughtered and dismembered. Matthys' head was impaled on a pike and his genitals were nailed to one of Munster's gates.

Jan of Leiden quickly declared himself leader before a crowd outside St. Paul's Cathedral with a Marc Antony-like oration: "God willed that Matthys should die. . . . His time had come, and God has let him die. . . . God shall raise up unto us another prophet who shall be greater and higher than was even Jan Matthys" (Friedrich, 1986, p. 168). When "a murmur from protest arose from the crowd" Jan retorted

> Shame on you, that you murmur against the ordinance of the Heavenly Father! Though you were all to join together to oppose me, I shall still reign,

> not only of this town but over the whole world, for the Father will have it
> so; and my kingdom which begins now shall endure and know no downfall!
>
> Cohn, 1970, p. 272

Jan dismissed the elected city council and appointed 12 elders (after the 12 tribes of Israel) to sanction his new laws. He instituted a new, tightly controlled regime with extreme consequences for not following its mandates. In a city besieged and on the brink of famine, Jan rode a white horse through the narrow, cobbled streets to his throne in a procession of courtiers and wives. The Munster craftsmen smelt Jan a gold crown, gold medallions, a gold scepter, and a gold sword sheath and belt, and built him a throne. He "decreed the death penalty not only for murder and sedition, but for blasphemy, spreading scandal, adultery, avarice, fraud, lying, criticizing one's parents, or even complaining" (Friedrich, 1986, p. 169).

> A rebel who had managed to escape was torn from the arms of his wife and
> children and quartered, still alive, with halberds. The executions were performed
> in small doses so that the pedagogic effect would be more lasting. Each day ten
> rebels were killed. For weeks, the victims' cries of pain echoed through the city.
>
> Orsini, 2011, p. 164

He created Commissars and a Chekha (i.e., secret police) to crush dissent. He divided these men and assigned them different sections of the city, the New Jerusalem, a phrase used by the prophet Ezekiel that refers to a messianic kingdom where the Holy Temple will be rebuilt.

> Terror, long a familiar feature of life in the New Jerusalem, was intensified
> under Bockleson's [Jan of Leiden's] reign. Within a few days of his proclama-
> tion of the monarchy ... all who persisted in sinning must be brought before
> the king and sentenced to death. They would be extirpated from the Chosen
> People, their very memory would be blotted out, their souls would find no
> mercy beyond the grave.
>
> Cohn, 1970, p. 275

As king, Jan also held the office of public executioner and sometimes beheaded those who he deemed to have transgressed God's law.

Terror was used as a method of subjugation. According to Norman Cohn, women were the first Munster citizens to be executed for crimes against the New Jerusalem. These crimes (e.g., ridiculing a preacher or denying a husband sexual intercourse) seemed to enforce male (or more specifically Jan's) domination. Jan also shrewdly chose bodyguards from men who had drifted into Munster and had little or no relationship with Munster citizens. These bodyguards were free to execute anyone they wished. Every citizen of Munster was a potential victim of his regime.

This terror and paranoia was a forerunner of Stalin's more contemporary "Great Terror" and Mao's "Red Terror." Jan of Leiden may be a historical avatar for the modern totalitarian state. His rule parallels the later subjugation methods of both cult and totalitarian leaders. He sought a radical reorganization of society. The Anabaptists had always held strict puritanical beliefs on sex. Infidelity was a capital offense in Munster before Jan came to power. However, once Jan became leader of Munster, he declared that every citizen must be married and decreed polygamy not just legal but a law every citizen must obey.

Sexual experimentation wasn't unique amongst religious sects. In the early 15th century, a sect that was an offshoot of the Taborite movement "declared the chaste were unworthy to enter their messianic Kingdom." They practiced free love, and chose to be naked in order to be in a state of innocence (Cohn, 1970, p. 220). Unlike this neo-Adamite sect, the polygamy in Munster was governed by a leader and it reveals Jan's totalistic control of Munster's citizens, even their deepest intimacies. Jan had one of his acolytes, a pamphleteer and would-be prophet, decree polygamy a law that everyone in Munster must accept. When a blacksmith named Heinrich Mollenbecke led a revolt against this decree, Jan had the rebels tortured and beheaded. Jan himself married 16 young women, including the former wife of Jan Matthys, the purportedly beautiful Divara, whom Jan had anointed his queen.

Then there was Jan's dramatic performances of his transcendental powers and use of oratory as a political tool. Cohn and others write that Jan was extraordinarily attractive, at least to people in the 16th century, and he was remarkably eloquent. He created outdoor show pieces and parades that demonstrated his power. On one occasion, he demanded the citizens of Munster gather in the cathedral square if they heard three trumpets. The trumpets sounded, blown by Jan's own acolyte Dusentshur. The citizens gathered. And according to Dusentshur's prophecy (though he was controlled by Jan), the men of Munster would have supernatural powers and the citizens of Munster would march outside the city gates and slaughter the Bishop's mercenary army. Instead, Jan appeared surrounded by his court. He stated that the gathering was a loyalty test, and it probably was. It was also a visual means of displaying his power. Other malignant narcissist tyrants have used gatherings, rallies, and parades as methods to assert their power. Jan's gifts for dramatic spectacle are evocative of Leni Riefenstahl's propaganda films of the 1930s or Mussolini upon a horse raising his arm in the Roman salute.

Jan's reign of terror ended when two dissidents, fearful of their fate in Jan's bloody, famine-stricken New Jerusalem, slipped away and fled to join the Bishop's mercenaries. They informed the Bishop and his generals of weaknesses in Munster's walls. The mercenaries stormed one of these weak spots and eventually Munster itself. Queen Divara was beheaded and Jan was "attached to a pole by an iron-spiked collar, his body was ripped with red-hot tongs for the space of an hour. He died after his heart was pierced with a red-hot dagger" (Orsini, 2011, p. 165).

Is it appropriate to compare Jan of Leiden with other MNLs? Or to portray him as a prototype for our contemporary cult leaders and dictators? Aren't there significant historical, cultural, and societal differences between them? Or, can't they all be described as irrational and mad and then tossed into the dustbin of history?

I argue that Munster's fall, as well as Jan's, parallels the fate of other tragic and disastrous millenarian movements. There have even been sieges that resemble Munster's extraordinary moment in European History and there have been leaders who unmistakably resemble Jan. Much has been written about these movements and their leaders, but less has been written about the similarities these leaders share and their followers' intense devotion to them.

Hong Xiuquan

If Hong Xiuquan never existed, China – and the world for that matter – might be dramatically different. Hong Xiuquan, leader and prophet of the Taiping Rebellion, in which millions of Chinese perished, failed the notoriously difficult imperial exams numerous times. In the aftermath of one of these failures, he declared himself the brother of Jesus Christ and proceeded to establish in modern-day Nanking, the Taiping Heavenly Kingdom (Platt, 2012). Hong Xiuquan followed a similar path to that of Jan of Leiden, except on a more epic scale.

Hong Xiuquan was a crestfallen village schoolteacher when he failed his final attempt at the imperial exams, which had only a 1 percent passing rate. He subsequently began preaching a theology that "pursued a land reform program that represents the most radically egalitarian in recorded history" while he simultaneously and contradictorily "declared himself the emperor of the Taiping" (Landes, 2011, p. 204).

Like Jan of Leiden, Hong attempted to establish a theocracy with strict laws that were antipodal to the existing social order. In Hong Xiuquan's Heavenly City, men and women – even married couples – lived separately and sex of any kind was prohibited. This prohibition did not apply to Hong, however, who had a harem of concubines living with him in his palace.

But his millenarian vision of a Heavenly Kingdom included Hong as a member of the Heavenly Family and brother to Jesus, posing a major threat to the Qing Dynasty. It led to an army from the Qing Dynasty besieging and destroying Taiping in 1864. Approximately 30 million people perished during Hong Xiuquan's rebellion – more than any rebellion in human history and a number equivalent to the population of the United States in 1860.

Antônio Conselheiro

At the end of the 19th century, an event similar to the siege and downfall of Munster occurred in Brazil. An itinerant prophet, Antônio Conselheiro (or "the Counselor"), established a millenarian religious community that he called Canudos in northern Bahai, a rural region of Brazil still known for hardship and poverty. Conselheiro preached "that same extravagant millenarianism, the same dread of the Anti-Christ's appearing amid the universal wreckage of life. The nearing of the end of the world" (Da Cunha, 1944, p. 127).

Nevertheless, in some ways Conselheiro was Jan of Leiden's antithesis. In *Rebellion in the Backlands*, Euclides da Cuhna's definitive book documenting the siege at Canudos, he portrayed Conselheiro as a

> somber anchorite with hair down to his shoulders, a long tangle beard, an emaciated face, and piercing eyes, a monstrous being clad in a blue canvas ... his withered epidermis was as wrinkled as an old broken and trampled over his lifeless flesh.
>
> *Da Cunha, 1944, pp. 127–131*

Unlike Jan of Leiden, whose Lucullan lifestyle continued to the final demise of Munster, Conselheiro reportedly starved himself to death because of the brutal misery of the defenders of Canudos. In the aftermath of the downfall of Canudos, Brazilian soldiers found his emaciated body.

And yet, Jan and Conselheiro are also cut of the same cloth. Both men were raised in harsh poverty and lost one of their parents. Both men were autodidacts. Both men were charismatic orators. Both men preached and prophesized a millenarian theology that was also critical of the ruling state. Both men established radical communities that were opposed to the extant social order. Both men were skilled in governing multitudes of followers.

However, unlike Jan who was sadistically violent to his followers, Conselheiro turned violence inward. According to da Cunha's account, Conselheiro tortured himself with harshirts and fasts (Da Cunha, 1944). This masochism makes Conselheiro unique amongst this type of leader, but, but still placed under the rubric of malignant narcissism. Kernberg argued that masochism happens in a therapeutic setting when a narcissist's fantasy of grandiosity is challenged. Masochism gives the narcissist a feeling of restored power and control and triumph over others for they alone inflict pain upon themselves (Kernberg, 1993). A human being must have extraordinary power in order to inflict such pain upon themselves.

Adolf Hitler

Another millenarian leader, Adolf Hitler, shared common traits with Jan of Leiden and Conselheiro. Anthony Arthur notes in *The Tailor King: The Rise and Fall of the Anabaptist Kingdom of Münster* that Jan of Leiden and Adolf Hitler share biographical similarities and traits. They were charismatic orators, antinomian thinkers, and failed artists. Furthermore, they required

> the indoctrination of children through early education and military training; the substitution of the group for the individual and the family in terms of loyalty and obligation; the inclusion of the chosen and the exclusion of the rest; elaborate ceremonies, marches, and public gatherings; symbols and slogans; and abrupt promotions and demotions, appearances and disappearances.
>
> *Arthur, 1999, Chapter 13*

In his compelling book *Explaining Hitler* (1998), Ron Rosenbaum writes that Hitler invokes an archetype in our culture for human evil. But the genocidal scale of Hitler's millenarian actions sprang from a man who was corporeal and mortal. Rosenbaum makes this point with the photograph on the cover of his book: a baby picture of Adolf Hitler. Even this man who is now a universal symbol of evil began life like any other human being.

David Koresh

In 1993, David Koresh's destructive life ended on a smaller scale than that of Hong Xiuquan. Koresh also struggled and drifted before claiming special prophetic powers. He too was a gifted orator and was sexually profligate with his followers, even accused of statutory rape. He demanded chastity amongst his male acolytes and annulled marriages while he had sex with his female followers. He named his harem "The House of David," and female members who became pregnant left the father's name blank on forms (Newport, 2006).

The details of his childhood are murky. He claimed to have been sexually abused and that his mother was a prostitute (his mother, Bonnie Haldemann, denies this). He dropped out of school in the eleventh grade because he had difficulty reading, possibly having dyslexia. He was an aspiring musician, played in rock bands, and failed at building a record label business. He joined and then became leader of a millenarian offshoot of the Seventh Day Adventists. Like Jan of Leiden, Koresh's leadership was preceded by the death of an older leader, Lois Roden.

The ATF and FBI's 51-day siege at Waco ended in the immolation of Koresh and his followers. The subject of this siege is now part of American popular culture and narrated in a TV mini-series. His death follows in a long tradition of these deaths. At the end, the leader dies while under assault either at or near the end of their reign.

Credonia Mwerinde

The largest mass suicide or murder by a religious movement occurred in 2000 and was perpetrated by a little-known Ugandan religious movement, The Movement for the Restoration of the Ten Commandments of God, founded and led by Credonia Mwerinde. She had also drifted through life assuming many occupations, including as owner of a bar and brewer of banana beer. Ugandan authorities suspect that she poisoned her three brothers in order to inherit their property before having a religious epiphany. This epiphany occurred in a cave near her home. She envisioned that she directly spoke to the Virgin Mary who told her to spread the word of God. Standing at the entrance of the cave was a large megalith-like stone that Mwerinde claimed portrayed the Virgin Mary turning her back to a fallen world (Atuhaire, 2003). While in the cave, she reported Marian visions as well as visions of Jesus Christ.

Mwerinde's millenarian movement – a sect of the Roman Catholic Church – was imbued with a mystical culture in which leaders and followers were given extravagant titles such as Mwerinde's, Eykembeko kya Yuda Tadeo (The Building of Judas Thadeus). What is striking about Mwerinde is not so much her personal charisma, although she is described as flamboyant, but her domination of those who followed her. Her sobriquet was "The Programmer." She designed an indoctrination program for followers that isolated them from their families and society. As Atuhaire writes in his book on the religious movement, *The Ugandan Cult Tragedy* (2003), entry into the movement was totalistic; followers sold all their possessions and cut familial ties. Mwerinde forbade sex between spouses, permitted followers one meal each day, and, at times, even forbade speech.

She, like Jan of Leiden, also promised her followers a spectacular event that would make the movement famous. Mwerinde and the upper echelon of the movement had the group prepare with a week-long feast for the end of the world, which was to occur December 31, 1999. When the end of the world proved to be another ordinary day, members began to openly question Mwerinde's authority. Mwerinde responded to this affront to her authority by fomenting the murder/suicide of her followers. By March 2000, over a thousand followers had died by poison or immolation.

Utopia and its perversion

In his definitive book on millenarianism, *The Pursuit of the Millenium*, Norman Cohn writes that Jan of Leiden and his religious dystopia are a forerunner of more modern attempts to create radically alternative societies that are tied to the transcendental. This might be a French revolutionary's egalitarian nation state, a Marxist utopia, an Aryan Elysium, or a Theocracy awaiting end times. Cohn argues that millenarianism only appears at specific moments when communities and kinship ties are torn.

When the siege of Munster took place in the 16th century, Christianity, which was the foundation for European society for hundreds of years, was fragmenting. In the 19th century, Western industrial society, spurred by the science of the Enlightenment, further disrupted traditional communities and culture not only in Europe, but throughout the world through imperialism and colonization. Urban life then became the dominant milieu for humankind and was, as described by writers like Frederic Engels in *The Conditions of the Working-Class in England in 1844* (1987), brutal and impersonal. Social fragmentation became an even more pervasive phenomenon in the 20th century with the War to End All Wars, the economic calamity of the Depression, World War II, and the multitude of genocidal catastrophes. In *The Origins of Totalitarianism* (1975), Hannah Arendt described this quickening fragmentation between the two world wars: "Every event had the finality of the last judgement, a judgement that was passed by neither God nor by the devil, but looked rather like the expression of some devil" (Arendt, 1975, p. 267).

In the latter 20th and now 21st centuries, social fragmentation and dislocation continued at a dizzying pace. In *Future Shock*, Alvin Toffler wrote: "Change is avalanching upon our heads and most people are unprepared to cope with it" (Toffler,

1970, p. 12). The postmodern world economy dislocated human beings from each other and further splintered community. Human beings then yearned "for the security of togetherness and for a helping hand to count on in a moment of trouble" (Bauman, 2003, p. VIII).

Social chaos, fragmentation, and dislocation are the social conditions that the millenarian leader needs in order to thrive. When human communities and bonds sever, as they now have for most of global humanity, millenarian leaders may fill the vacuum. They offer a totalistic, communitarian, transcendental vision and ideology that attract followers who face "the uncanny frailty of human bonds, the feeling of insecurity that frailty inspires, and the conflicting desires that feeling prompts to tighten the bonds yet keep them loose" (Bauman, 2003, p. VIII).

The millenarian leader uses this anomie to prey upon the poor, the wealthy, and the bourgeois. They prey upon every race, class, and religion. Their followers can be anyone. Scientists made sarin gas for Shoko Asahara; Catholic priests were leaders in the Movement for the Restoration of the Ten Commandments of God; TV actresses recruited sex slaves for Keith Rainiere. Atuhaire sums up the follower psychology in the foreword to his book: "In a state of deprivation, worry, uncertainty, rejection and lies, an individual may easily be driven to extreme conditions of acceptance of an alternate route, no matter how ridiculous it might sound to the world around" (Atuhaire, 2003, p. VII).

Once the millenarian leader ascends to a leadership role, their vindictiveness and paranoia reigns too. A tyrant must always be hypervigilant. As Seneca warned Nero, no matter how many men or women they murder, tyrants will never kill their successors. However, unlike other types of tyrants, the millenarian tyrant embodies a transcendent belief system. As avatars, their pathology becomes unfettered; their cruelty becomes capricious. They use millenarian ideological and spiritual beliefs to justify the dehumanization of their followers. They then play with them like murderous children.

Stalin had a murderously whimsical temperament. In his canonical book on the 1930 purges, *The Great Terror* (1990), Robert Conquest writes that the reasons Stalin decided to execute or reprieve were often senseless and vindictive. In 1927, Dr. Vladimir Mikhailovich Bekhterev, a highly esteemed neuroscientist of international renown, examined Stalin. Although the reason for the examination is uncertain, Dr. Bekhterev mentioned to colleagues later in the evening that he had just examined a paranoiac (never mentioning Stalin's name). The following day, Bekhterev suddenly and mysteriously died. Stalin then ordered that Bekhterev's name and corpus be removed from Soviet schools and publications (Haycock, 2019). And yet, a university student who was going to be jailed for throwing a dart at a portrait of Stalin sent an appeal to Stalin. Stalin responded by not only exonerating the student but praising him for his marksmanship (Montefiore, 2004).

Jan of Leiden, too, created a terror state rooted in a sadistic whimsy. Unlike Stalin, Jan sometimes publicly executed his victims. When one of his wives disagreed with him, he publicly beheaded her, then danced around her bleeding corpse. Moreover, he shares another trait with modern leaders: paranoia and hatred directed toward a single enemy. For Stalin, it was the Trotskyites. For Mao, it was the bourgeois. For Pol Pot, it was Cambodian ethnic and religious groups. For Jan, it was Jews, the clergy, and the rich. For Oceania (the superstate depicted in *1984*), it was Emmanuel Goldstein. This enemy, whose malevolence and threat to the state is often imaginary, unites followers in a sacred war. The creation of an enemy is also a violent manifestation of the leader's own paranoia and fear. There are often sound reasons for a dictatorial leader to be paranoid. However, if you combine these fears with a psychological fear or anxiety that your grandiosity covers up a mundane, self-loathing, and inadequate wretch, then a leader's paranoia can become extreme and violent.

It is important to note without a transcendent and millenarian edifice, none of these leaders would have been able to thrust themselves into leadership and act out their pathologies. The perversion of utopia – a heaven on earth – would be impossible.

Conclusion

Cohn recounts that if you wish to trace the beginnings of a millenarian movement, the origin will be a social catastrophe. The irony is that the postmodern world may be an ongoing global debacle for communities and kinship. Whether social scientists and others believe there is a global crisis in loneliness, the discussion alone points to a social phenomenon afoot (Cacioppo & Cacioppo, 2018). Whether it's global capitalism that turns workers into transitory cogs-in-the-machine or communication technology that both connects and isolates humankind, the consensus is that we are becoming increasingly isolated. This is the playground for Jan of Leiden and other MNLs. Psychoanalyst and former cult member Daniel Shaw stated in a recent podcast on IndoctriNation that he believes that cult leaders are increasingly forming smaller cults. However, this does not mean a diminution in the growth of cults; instead we may be living in a golden age for cults (Bernstein & Shaw, 2019). The MNL is in historical ascendency.

The severity of this phenomenon is significant. Instead of seeking practical, material goals, followers become playthings in a paranoid leader's millenarian fantasy. They surrender their individuality to a future golden age that never happens. When a malignant leader's failed promises lead to disaffection by their followers, murderous violence can ensue. The malignant leader, on the other hand, must maintain the illusion of their omnipotence for reasons that are deeply rooted in their personal pathology. According to Daniel Shaw, their dependency on their followers is deeply ambivalent and conflicted (Shaw, 2003). They both need adulation to fuel their stunted egos and, whether aware or not, abhor this dependency. The leader then acts with sometimes extraordinary cruelty toward his or her dependents.

Three cages hang from the Lambert Cathedral in Munster. One of those cages held Jan of Leiden's corpse after he was executed. It has hung there since his death. That empty cage may be a more appropriate memorial to MNLs than Lenin's tomb or Franco's Valley of the Fallen. For, in the end, these leaders, as powerful as they may become and as charming or charismatic as they might seem to be, are deeply disturbed and capable of ugly, destructive outcomes for those around them.

References

Arendt, H. (1975). *The origins of totalitarianism.* New York, NY: Harcourt Brace Jovanovich.

Arthur, A. (1999). *The tailor king: The rise and fall of the Anabaptist Kingdom of Münster.* New York, NY: St. Martin's Press.

Atuhaire, B. (2003). *The Uganda cult tragedy: A private investigation.* Cambridge, UK: Janus Publishing.

Bauman, Z. (2003). *Liquid love.* Cambridge, UK: Polity Press.

Bernstein, R. (Host), & Shaw, D. (Interviewee). (2019, March 13). Emotional vampires: Narcissists and cult leaders in relationships. *IndoctriNation* [Audio podcast]. Retrieved from www.rachelbernsteintherapy.com/indoctrination-podcast/

Cacioppo, J.T., & Cacioppo, S. (2018, February 3). The growing problem of loneliness. *Lancet, 391*(10119), 426.

Chirot, D. (1994). *Modern tyrants: The power and prevalence of evil in our age.* Princeton, NJ: Princeton University Press.

Cohn, N. (1970). *The pursuit of the millennium.* Oxford, UK: Oxford University Press.

Conquest, R. (1990). *The great terror: A reassessment.* New York, NY: Oxford University Press.

Da Cunha, E. (1944). *Rebellion in the backlands* (Trans. S. Putnam). Chicago, IL: University of Chicago Press.

Eagleton, T. (2010). *On evil.* New Haven, CT: Yale University Press.

Engels, F. (1987). *The conditions of the working-class in England in 1944: With a preface written in 1892.* London, UK: Penguin Classics.

Friedrich, O. (1986). *The end of the world: A history.* New York, NY: Fromm International.

Fromm, E. (1964). *The heart of man: Its genius for good and evil.* New York, NY: Harper & Row.

Haycock, D. A. (2019). *Tyrannical minds: Psychological profiling, narcissism, and dictatorship.* New York, NY: Pegasus Books.

Hoffer, E. (1964). *The true believer: Thoughts on the nature of mass movements* (6th ed.). New York, NY: Harper and Row.

Kernberg, O. F. (1993). *Severe personality disorders: Psychotherapeutic strategies.* New Haven, CT: Yale University Press.

Landes, R. (2011). *Heaven on Earth: The varieties of the millennial experience.* New York, NY: Oxford University Press.

Montefiore, S. S. (2004). *Stalin: The court of the Red Tsar.* New York, NY: Alfred A. Knopf.

Naphy, W. G. (2011). *The Protestant revolution: From Martin Luther to Martin Luther Jr.* New York, NY: Random House.

Newell, W. (2016). *Tyrants: A history of power, injustice, and terror.* New York, NY: Cambridge University Press.

Newport, K. G. (2006). *The Branch Davidians of Waco: The history and beliefs of an apocalyptic sect.* New York, NY: Oxford University Press.

Orsini, A. (2011). *Anatomy of the Red Brigades: The religious mind-set of modern terrorists.* Ithaca, NY: Cornell University Press.

Platt, S. R. (2012). *Autumn in the heavenly kingdom: China, the West, and the epic story of the Taiping civil war.* New York; Canada: Alfred A. Knopf.

Rosenbaum, R. (1998). *Explaining Hitler: The search for the origins of his evil.* New York, NY: Random House.

Shaw, D. (2003). Traumatic abuse in cults: A psychoanalytic perspective. *Cultic Studies Review*, 2(2), 104–131. Retrieved from www.leavingsiddhayoga.net

Toffler, A. (1970). *Future shock* (9th ed.). New York, NY: Random House.

Waite, G. K. (2007). *Eradicating the devil's minions: Anabaptists and witches in Reformation Europe, 1525–1600*. Toronto, Canada: University of Toronto Press.

Weber, M. (1968). *On charisma and institution building* (Select papers, edited and with an introduction by S. N. Eisenstadt). Chicago, IL: University of Chicago Press.

7

ZEIDERS AND DEVLIN DIALOGUE

Etiology, sexuality, and a primal horde of horrible insights useful for research

Introduction

Throughout this dialogue, we discuss the formation of the revolutionary personality, noting that trauma and abuse are instrumental to the revolutionary personality. Although we debate the relevance of Oedipal issues, we find that the leader's identification with the aggressor and his narcissistic defenses – like grandiosity and scapegoating – account for much of his malignant behavior and destructive tenure. The catastrophic absence of nurturant love, combined with soul murder, are vital to comprehending the malignant narcissist leader (MNL) at an etiological level. Complexities of the MNL's sexual life are discussed in terms of pseudo-attachment, phallic narcissism, and sado-masochism. An appreciation of a destructive leader's sexual style may open a window to understating certain executive decisions. Whether tyrant or cultist, the sexual style of the MNL is ultimately sadomasochistic, with the self-surrender associated with genuine love conspicuously absent. Freud's primal horde theory is mentioned as an especially useful poetic to describe of the nature of power and destructive leaders who attain it. We argue that just as the primal father ruled via brute force to exploit the horde and rule for his sexual and other enjoyment, so does the MNL. The primal father, however, was prehistoric and precultural, while the MNL requires some sort of legitimacy. So, to self-justify, the MNL identifies with an ultimate value. He is a beast marketed as a god. Adding to Freud, we theorize that primal mothers also exist, and in them their awestruck followers find solutions to unmet needs, if even in fantasy. Destructive leaders Charles Manson and Jan of Leiden are interpreted in light of primal horde theory, neurotheology, and the banality of evil. We argue that the MNL's destructive leadership stems from not coming to terms with embarrassment over the frailty inherent in the human condition. Pol Pot and other actors are interpreted in this light. They were administrative incompetents whose malignant coping against their own finitude destroyed cultures and societies. Such actors leave a legacy not of terror, but also of horror, which is defined clinically and explicated referencing such works as Conrad's *Heart of Darkness* and Francis Ford Coppola's *Apocalypse Now*.

Zeiders and Devlin dialogue

Zeiders: Well, Devlin, let us begin our dialogue with a summation of the political *totalist*, the sort to whom you cogently attribute the *theft of utopia*: during formative years, a future despot will develop a revolutionary trait from an Oedipal complex emergent from power conflicts with father figures. Early conflicts with the father prefigure antagonism of the state. The actor envies the power of the aggressor because of wrecked attachment, resentment from neglect, or shame/contempt derived from physical and sexual trauma. But on the heels of this envy comes identification with the aggressor's power position. At the same time, the actor develops an appreciation for grievances that might be shared by others within the culture. Profound narcissistic defenses form against the agony implicit in the abandonment depression, soul murder, and betrayal rage. From such narcissistic defenses, replete with grandiosity, combined with a preexisting gift for oratory, a magnetic charisma emerges that attracts positive public attention. During political crisis, the MNL comes to the fore as a revolutionary who understands his nation's plight. His ego inflates commensurate with the narcissistic supplies provided by the masses. He identifies with the masses and they with him. Fed from public acclaim, the destructive leader's consciousness swells with egomania. His self-appraisal burgeons into morbidly obese grandiosity. The MNL and his followers collectively fantasize that providence ordains him a man of genius, one mystically destined to save the people. Due to the depth of the Oedipal complex, he brokers no limit to his prepotency. He shares no power, nor tolerates criticism without fury. He sovereignly knows the will of the people, and he, mystically, is the people. But he is also identified with the aggressor, the one(s) who injured him in childhood, and his political enemies are father-like objects or targets upon whom he evacuates his unresolved sense of weakness. These identifications are unconscious, but they manifest in partial adaptation of the overthrown regime's expressions of power. Having metaphorically castrated the father by overthrowing the former regime, the MNL dons the garments of the defeated father. Consciously and ideologically the MNL remains the champion of the people. Unconsciously, he is the god and father of the nation, entitled to transfigure the nation as his genius demands. The man of the people becomes a man without limits. As the movement matures, bureaucrats transform the MNL's revolution into a new establishment; he settles into allowing his propagandists to sustain his cult of personality. His regime revolutionizes society but is illiberal; only the demigod fathoms pure policy. He annihilates those who fail to grasp this. But he also purges many who are loyal, because he trusts no one. Regardless of his revolution's fate, he will ever scapegoat those he destroys as enemies of the people. Until his death, suicide, or deposition, he will never admit to morphing into a magnification of that which he hates – the persecutor.

Devlin: Zeiders, you describe an MLN with precision and theoretical rigor. It's also a Miltonian description. Except here we have Zeiders' Satan, not Milton's Satan. The MNL described by Zeiders is a maelstrom of psychoanalytic complexes, narcissistic cruelty, and demoniac splendor. He is also male. Yet, one of the most murderous cult leaders in the past 30 years was a woman named Credonia Mwerinde. To paraphrase Albert Speer: one seldom recognizes the devil when *her* hand is on your shoulder. Contrary to the literature, my contention is that women are just as bad as men. To say otherwise is sexist. Just as the male leader can be virtuous or vicious, so can the female leader.

Then, there is the question of the devil. Or Western culture's atavistic need to portray certain human beings as symbols and personifications of evil. Is the MNL, the human being, the *Homo sapien*, who encompasses many of the traits described earlier, radically evil? Or are the cult leaders, tyrants, and totalitarian dictators we have portrayed in this book both banal and deeply human (so human we recognize slivers of ourselves in their destructiveness)? Do we obfuscate and caricature these destructive human beings by endowing them with almost superhuman psychological malevolence? And if we endow them with this power and charisma, do we then also endow them with a majesty or greatness (that might even feed their narcissism)?

When MNLs are described by historians, psychologists, and other writers, one loses the quotidian of these leaders' lives. Most of these leaders were bores. Does anyone think Stalin was a sparkling dinner guest (although in his biography of Stalin, Simon Sebag Montefiore (2003) writes he could sometimes muster charm)? Or does anyone imagine Bhagwan Rajneesh didn't drone on and on as he gave audience to his followers? There is a famous exchange between Hannah Arendt and Karl Jaspers in 1946 (years before Arendt would publish *Eichmann In Jerusalem*) (Arendt & Jaspers, 1992). She writes to Jaspers that the Nazi crimes are so terrible that they are beyond any nation's ability to address them. Jaspers responds that we need to see the Nazis (however, this applies to all the MNLs in this book) as banal and trivial. He warns against the danger of mythologizing the Nazis. Arendt replies that, yes, she too rejects mythologizing and demonizing, but that doing so is extraordinarily difficult because their crimes were extreme. How then do you make sense of such malevolent excess?

Therefore, despite my qualms, Zeiders, your description of MNLs is important because it frames the fearful, yet very human, symmetry of the MNL. Indeed, it would be egregious not to attempt to understand such destructive behavior. You and I have common ground in several areas. An abundance of research now exists on attachment and its power over the development of our personalities. Even before Bowlby (1982) and Ainsworth, Blehar, Waters, and Wall (2015), the psychoanalyst Rene Spitz's 1945 study of *hospitalization* (a pediatric diagnosis that describes how infants wither when they lack human connection in hospitals) and Harry Harlow's (Harlow, et. al., 1965) poor rhesus monkeys sadly illustrated the emotional stunting that occurred when primates, both rhesus and human, lose or never have the "good-enough" caregiver. Because of these studies, there is a consensus that infant and childhood deprivation may lead to the diminishment of empathy and a person's ability to be pro-social. Most of what has been written about MNLs describes, in different ways, childhoods of abuse, deprivation, and chaotic families. Whether an Oedipal complex or some other disruption plays a role in their lack of development is an open, but worthy, debate.

Furthermore, we agree that narcissism is a significant characteristic, though not the only one (human beings are complex), in the makeup of the MNL. In Freud's 1914 essay, *On Narcissism* (Gay, 1995), he famously writes that if human beings don't love, then they fall ill. Because their childhood deprivation (I personally like Shengold's (1989) term: *soul murder*) both stunts their empathy and shrivels their ego, MNLs lack the ability to love in a pro-social and holistic way (although this is always on a continuum). Their powerful, incessant need for adoration combined with antisocial traits are foundational to their personalities. This is also foundational to your description of them, Zeiders.

Zeiders: Your Freudian point is well-taken, Devlin. Evidence for the compromised ability of the MNL to freely love manifests in the sexual life of the MNL, which is variant but often deviant. Often the sexual life of the MNL will be characterized by heterosexuality, begrudged tolerance for marriage, self-serving affairs, and promiscuity of the entitled, Don Juan type. Destructive leaders fitting this profile include Henry VIII and Benito Mussolini. Theirs is the sexuality of the phallic narcissist, characterized by Wilhelm Reich (1972) by a superficial posture toward women, and a haughty superiority that

> overlays insecurity and a wish to be attractive. The phallic narcissist's relationships are always infused with sadistic characteristics and are disturbed by a typical derogatory attitude toward the female sex.
>
> *quoted in Post, 2015, p. 146*

King Henry, whose inspired methods of torture anticipated the dungeons of Stalin's NKVD and Hitler's SS (Newell, 2019, p. 121), fits Reich's description. The domineering monarch had no shortage of hubris, wives, mistresses, or disposable partners. When the monarch's partners fell into the beam of his paranoid projections, the devalued sex objects were subjected to the official apparatus of state justice, involving torture, show trials, and capital punishment.

Like the Tudor King, Mussolini exhibited a degree of compulsive sexual behavior, which involved self-aggrandizing consumption of sex objects and sadistic objectification of women. "He rationalized his hobby as a sexual predator by declaring that no superman of his attainments should be confined to one woman" (Tyson, n.d., n.p.).

For these destructive leaders, their sexual lives indicate not only primal sexual vigor, but also a venue for the MNL to overcome the castration anxiety and fear of impotence that plagues their leadership activity. Psychodynamic theory teaches that this Hemingway-esque style of exaggerated masculinity masks Oedipal fears, dreadful inadequacy, and possibly homophobia.

A significant underpinning of the MNL's sex life is neediness. Sexual behavior configures so that the sex object, once consumed, nourishes the leader's sense of value. In this instance the MNL expects sex on demand – as the pleasure principal countenances only immediate gratification – as well as praise for performance. He is unaware that he cannot regulate his self-esteem without feeding on an external resource. For such a leader, sex objects are multi-purpose objects, often disposable, that discharge tension and strengthen the narcissistic fortress, which is the destructive leader's ego adorned in grandiose persona. This type of sex life can be found in destructive political, commercial, and spiritual leadership.

Further, an application of theory to the MNLs supports the hypothesis that psychophysical agitation from the unusual stressors of leadership drive sexual acting out as a form of stress reduction. Sexual sadistic behavior is a reenactment of trauma. Here the meaning of the sexual act exists as a re-enactment, in which the sexuality has a relational meaning. In such cases, sexuality is intertwined with the aggression (Juni, 2009). For yet another MNL, narcissism and sexual masochism intertwine. Theoretically non-intuitive, intelligibility for the masochistic MNL derives from considering that the "masochistic injuries are an affirmation of distorted narcissistic fantasies" (Cooper, 1989, p. 541).

In a masochistic sexual encounter, the MNL achieves gratification via the fantasy that he heroically withstands an assault; the assault affirms the leader's victim status, and it obliquely justifies radical, destructive action against enemies. Endurance of sexual punishment strengthens the MNL's comic book dream that he holds of himself: he is a Superman who cannot be overcome. Sexual masochism also represents a return of the repressed (e.g., that is the MNL's hidden sense that he is a shame, a human tumor, a misshapen soul) ritualistically addressed and expunged through degradation, pain, and orgasm. A rare MNL may combine sexual masochism with exhibitionism. For example, the corporate executive who crawls about in a dog collar before onlookers at a sex club draws a narcissistic remedy from the spectators' impressed gaze. It is one that medicates against the burden of the horrific core material by converting his spectacle into a source of narcissistic supply. "Only a superman could subject himself to such humiliation and then rise phoenix-like as I have," is his fantastic inner slogan about the matter. Even in masochism, this sexual style is characterized by a self-aggrandizing power dynamic rather than by a relational one. Of course, I offer this politicized physical behavior as a psychodynamic insight, not as a DSM determination.

It is important to realize that professional and sexual behavior operate as overlapping dynamics. For example, Hitler's self-loathing, ego dystonic homosexuality, and unmanly impotence were projected onto his gay Storm Troopers in the party purge known as the Night of the Long Knives. This literal purge symbolically purged these elements of Hitler's shameful sexual problems. Similar dynamics may partially account for his genocidal anti-Semitic policies. Self and other hating, Hitler enlisted several women to abuse him during sex acts. That these women attempted suicide suggests that contact with Hitler's inner disturbance during sadomasochistic sex play was so overwhelming that they preferred death to the affective witnessing of the dictator's diabolical phenomenology. Like many MNLs, Hitler contended with his sexual conflicts in both his personal and professional behavior (Waite, 1977). Any window into the dynamics of a leader's sexual life opens insight into the psychological complexity behind his executive decisions.

Devlin: The polyamorous characteristics of the MNL are about dominance and control, yes, but also about their inability to form mutual, pro-social bonds with other human beings. As Freud wrote on narcissism, the type of energy human beings define as love is never directed outward (or inward) (Waite, 1977). This is true for a gay, straight, or bisexual MNL. They need to control others so they can control the narrative of their idealized superiority. They subjugate others, sometimes sadistically, to hide their self-loathing and inadequacy. The most important point in the sexual practices listed by you, Zeiders, is the power dynamic and the erasure of the humanity of the sexual partner. During Stalin's reign, the security czar Laverntiy Beria kidnapped teenage girls from the streets of Moscow and raped them at his villa (now the Tunisian embassy). David Koresh raped girls as young as 11 years old. John Humphrey Noyes, like Jan of Leiden, preached against monogamy, yet he raped 12- and 13-year-old girls. The list of these crimes and transgressions by MNLs is endless. The question remains: Why?

Sex between human beings is an intimate act. It can be laden with deep emotional meaning or it can be transactional. It should always be consensual and never coerced. MNLs have a powerful and prevailing need to totally control other people's lives, reaching to their most intimate interactions. If you control another human being at this, possibly the deepest, level, you are approaching that level of control. Then, this emphasizes the antisocial or sociopathic vein in the MNL's make-up. The MNL has extraordinary difficulty viewing another human being as a human being. In her or his mind's eye, other people are cogs in a machine that worships the MNL. Human beings, therefore, exist to feed the MNL's narcissism and physical and sexual needs.

Why, then, the sexual sadism? An MNLs sexual sadism fits sadly and neatly into their profile. MNLs enact their psychological chaos outwardly as well as inwardly and catch other people in their psychic whirlwind. Although there are many theories on sexual sadism, enacting a violent sexual fantasy that includes controlling and dominating the other person is a frisson and arousal for the sadist. It is important to note that when this is consensual and does no harm to either person, then it is something completely different. Also, impotency and sexual dysfunction are unimportant here. It's the subjugation and domination that matter. To truly surrender to a love object might even be something for which an MNL yearns, but the actor's defenses will only allow such engagement in a quasi-form; ritual submission trumps real surrender.

Your point on sexual masochism reminds me of the 19th-century Brazilian prophet, Antônio Conselheiro. Although the harsh circumstances of his life make him the most sympathetic leader we have discussed, he tortured his body with a passionate intensity that resonates with your discussion of the MNL's view of himself or herself as "a human tumor, a misshapen soul." There is very little discussion of masochism and its comorbidity with malignant narcissism, so you are offering an important insight.

Zeiders: In the course of our collaboration, Devlin, both of us have run headlong into Freud's social creation myth. For me Freud's *primal horde theory* is rich, not so much as a provable theory, but as an interpretive template with which to organize the tomes on tyranny and misery now overflowing in our libraries.

Here are two encapsulations of his psychodynamic creation story, and they are far from Edenic. The Eden story pertains to genesis, but Freud's myth pertains to patho-genesis.

> The original human social organization is the "primal horde" ruled by a powerful adult male; this adult male fucks all the women and kills any other man who challenges his authority or touches his women. The first moment in human development is . . . tyranny of the most absolute kind, an order formed on the basis of unmediated violence.
>
> *Kinnucan, 2013, n.p.*

Society's origins lie in human prehistory when early *Homo sapiens* began living

> in large groups, [and] the primal horde [was] . . . dominated by one older male, who could monopolize all females. . . . This tyrannical father was murdered and then eaten by the resentful young males, his sons, who then possessed all females, including their mothers and sisters. The murdered father was then symbolized in the totem animal, which holds the authority within the horde. Through the sacrifice of the totem animal, the sons could try to allay their burning sense of guilt.
>
> *Beit-Hallahmi, 2014, n.p.*

On an archetypal level, the malignant narcissist in leadership remains a terrible fact, and the primal father's role may be filled by an individual, or an organization that operates according to similarly sick dynamics. With strength comes power, and with power comes authority, and with authority comes the ability to fashion reality according to self-serving fantasy. Government, corporations, and religious institutions gather allegiances from constituents, as did the proto-human primal father through his brute strength, and inflict their versions of right-wrong, humane-inhumane, good-evil that legitimizes their power in whatever form or fulmination. Such titles as CEO, Fuhrer, President for Life, Brother Number One, and Archbishop all smack of power assemblage, and prerogatives of Freud's primordial tyrant father. Notions of exceptionalism, greatness, and mastery are ideological shorthand for a party that has assumed the power position of the primal father. But regimes are both born and killed in blood. To steal and enjoy the father's pleasures, the primal horde killed him, but then they suffered guilt and fear, so they devised types of self-justifications to exonerate and to legitimize themselves.

Freud saw this in the ancient totem fetish, the precursor of ideology, theology, and economic theory. This erection of a value system that justifies power is essential to powers' survival. It allays the superstition that the father haunts and readies for retaliatory spiritual assaults, and dissuades the next cohort of envious sons from overthrowing the present hoarder of power, because that power is – in a word – legitimate. In modern history, the *ideal* is the conceptual totem to which power points to justify itself. Only the primal father ruled in a state beyond good and evil, ruling utterly by might, with his legitimacy completely irrelevant. Unneedful of justification, the

> primal father's rule alone is free of . . . the appeal from power to justice. . . . His power is simply his capacity to kill. His reign is certainly not just, but neither is it *unjust*, and here he has the advantage over all the governments since his day.
>
> *Kinnucan, 2013, n.p.*

History is choked with people and polities that stand in proxy for the primal father. These aggrandize the leader and his followers, which is narcissism; they ideologically justify massive rights violations, which is criminality; they gain pleasure from atrocity, which is sadism; and they contain the polity's dread of blowback in expensive police and military spending, which is paranoia. Even organizations that are not nation states similarly organize themselves. Our condition appears such that we cannot escape malignant narcissism.

One way to conceptualize the MNL is as an iteration of the primal father, the strong man, who after his murder by his sons, remained powerful as a god, an overarching force that persisted in cogency and determined social behavior. He is the face of an archetype. The MNLs about which we have written, Devlin, assume the role of the primal father, but with the added psychodynamic dimension that they are needful of an ideal, an idea of themselves presented as good, an ultimate value. This self-idealization excuses their re-use of primordial power. Identification with the primal father, then, is power. Identifying with an ideal renders that power magically good. The primal father is a beast. The ideal is a god. The MNL is a beast marketed as a god.

Devlin: What is significant for me is the interplay between the MNL and her or his followers. Because of the MNL's pathological narcissism, they sacralize and idealize themselves and allow their followers to project their transcendent beliefs upon them (MNLs need adoration like we need food, sleep, and oxygen). Many of the historians who have written about MNLs believe they are a modern phenomenon that began with the French Revolution (see Chapter 6). However, sacralizing a leader has an atavistic quality. As far as we know, sacralizing leaders has existed as long as human communities have existed. However, it's not always so patriarchal. Women cult leaders have led some of the most violent cults. Silvia Meraz Moreno, Valentina De Arande, Credonia Mwerinde, and Clementine Barnabet are a rogue's gallery of deeply malignant human beings. And as you invoke patriarchal names for these leaders like "strong men," many of these female leaders call themselves "mothers." Joyce Green changed her name to Ma Jaya Sati Bhagavati; Sheela Patel changed her name to Ma Anand Sheela. I would argue that if women had had a Torture Room of One's Own, then they would be well-represented in MNL history.

However, I agree with you, Zeiders, on the primordial quality of this. Neuroscientists think that spiritual beliefs are hard-wired and processed in the left parietal lobule of the brain. Maybe, this spiritual or transcendent capacity allows the MNL to exploit someone's devotion and faith. And the primal horde theory works better as a myth than it does as an actual period of our pre-literate history. Myth and stories are ways of bringing immediacy and texture to our understanding of the human condition. However, does not even the primal horde theory boil down to an individual asserting power and dominance over others?

Zeiders: Indeed, it does, Devlin. Your chapter on Mr. Green (see Chapter 3) interested me in that, as an MNL, the subject demonstrated strict control of his drug posse and enforced his control by wrapping it up in quasi-religious rituals. Mr. Green told you that he ordered his lieutenants to follow his rituals and rules strictly, while he held himself above even his own law. In turn, this reminded me of the symbolic castration inflicted on male Branch Davidians via enforced celibacy by David Koresh, while the prophet himself enjoyed every woman as his "wife." Mr. Green and David Koresh held followers under their power by might and ritual. So, your neurotheological point is well-taken. Yet, both MNLs were above even their own law, demonstrating their specialness to the in-group and out-groups alike. But sometimes the MNL bonds his group, his horde, to him by sharing his limitlessness with them, by baptizing the forbidden and making it ultimately right. Ernest Becker (1973) explored this troubling aspect of human nature in the Manson Family. In this case, Manson elevated himself beyond good and evil, but shared that transcendence with the group by celebrating Eros in group sex, and Thanatos in murder. Perhaps the only thing more frightening than an MNL who is above the rules, is the MNL who takes his self-surrendered followers there to the fullest extent.

> [Charles Manson] filled the description of Freud's "primal father": he was authoritarian, very demanding of his followers, and a great believer in discipline. His eyes were intense, and for those who came under his spell there is no doubt that he projected a hypnotic aura. He was a very self-assured figure. He even had his own "truth," his megalomanic vision for taking over the world. To his followers his vision seemed like a heroic mission in which they were privileged to participate. He had convinced them that only by following out his plan could they be saved. . . . It seems obvious from all this that Manson combined the "fascinating effect of the narcissistic personality" with the "infectiousness of the unconflicted personality." Everyone could freely drop his repressions under Manson's example and command, not only in sex but in murder. The members of the "family" didn't seem to show any remorse, guilt, or shame for their crimes. . . . What makes them so terrible is that they exaggerate the dispositions present in us all.
>
> *Becker, 1973, pp. 137–138*

To what extent do you find that any of these dynamics, Devlin, might apply to Jan of Leiden and his devotees?

Devlin: You hit a bull's-eye here. Jan of Leiden brutally reorganized the Anabaptists in Munster into an upside-down kingdom, radically reorganizing social relations. He instituted polygamy in Munster in a sexually unliberated century, to say the least. A group of Anabaptists resisted this, and they were brutally murdered. Again, you rightly point out, this debasement before a leader, surrendering their personhood to him or her, is a common thread with cult and totalitarian leaders. Poor Winston Smith (Orwell, 1950) is a literary example of a human being who is forced to subjugate his personhood (in extremis, of course). It is hard to know what the Anabaptists in Munster were thinking. Jan of Leiden ruled with a murderous iron fist. However, when the Munster walls were finally breached, the Anabaptists fought valiantly. So, it's possible many followers of Jan of Leiden still believed in his sanctity even at the end.

I wrote the chapter on Mr. Green because I believe that there is a complexity and continuum with MNLs. Because Western culture is partially embedded in Christianity, it's almost impossible for those operating within Western culture, as Hannah Arendt wrote to Karl Jaspers, not to project the motifs and symbols of evil onto human beings (Kohler & Saner, 1992). Are we willing to accept the MNL on the continuum of our humanity or do we place deeply malignant people in an almost supernatural realm? Erich Fromm wrote in the *Anatomy of Human Destructiveness* (1973) that there are, with every generation, human beings who are so destructive they exist beyond the pale of our ability to understand. You may agree with Fromm. I, on the other hand, am uncertain. I'd like to believe that even the most destructive human beings one can imagine are still human. Writers from Johann Hari (2018) to Terry Eagleton (2011) to the social psychologist Matthew Lieberman (2013) write about our need for connection, how this connectivity defines our humanity. MNLs need this connectivity too. Except, of course, it is sadistic and authoritarian. I am tempted to portray these deeply destructive human beings as simply evil, but I always resist these thoughts. I am reminded of the debate between Rollo May and Carl Rodgers on human evil (May, 1982). Rodgers argued people are destructive because of the culture they live in. May argued we are the culture. The worm, human evil, is in the apple, humanity (this is my clichéd metaphor, not May's). I obviously agree with May. Maybe (no pun intended) a touch of the MNL exists not only in the night, but in all of us. This is extreme behavior on a human continuum.

Zeiders: Now, when you said, "I'd like to believe that even the most destructive human beings one can imagine are still human," Devlin, you moved me to seek what I might share with an MNL. And what I find is creaturely embarrassment, the embarrassment that is part of my human condition. To be human is to fall short, to have my ideal self exceed my ability to actualize it, to fail in terms of fully achieving my perfect personhood. As therapists, and as human beings, we know that humility is the solution to this problem. But for the MNL, this adjustment to self-limitation is impossible.

The destructive leader lives in unconscious, holy terror of his core-level shame, deformity, and inadequacy. Throughout his career he spends immense energies defending against narcissist injury. Shame is the shadow of his grandiose persona, and any experience that threatens to expose his psychic deformity to the full light of his consciousness is hypervigilantly detected and ruthlessly addressed. Like the maniac, the malignant narcissist thrives on the expansiveness of the fully funded self-image. But disruptions to the plausibility of superiority threaten the destructive leader with exposure to his lovelessness, ugliness, and incapacity. He cannot find a way to come to terms with himself. Threats to the narcissistic mask, either from criticism or failure, are met with defensive eruptions.

I think one of the ways in which MNLs uphold their defensive grandiosity is by unconsciously comporting themselves after the style of the primal father they overthrow, or by living out the fantasy that their domination represents the birth of history. Pol Pot, you know, did both. Brother Number One effectively established himself as communist royalty (Becker, 1998), and when his Khmer Rouge army sacked Phnom Penh in the spring of 1975, he set the Cambodian calendar to Year Zero. Although his aristocrat-envy was an unconscious thought-crime against his own proletarian revolution, the creative destruction he ordered of pre-Khmer Cambodian society was so incompetent, so botched, that the Year Zero was the beginning of a near apocalypse for the Cambodian people, a genocidal nightmare brought forth from Pot's grandiosity, paranoia, and moral blindness.

Devlin: This is also a point where we agree to agree. If MNLs have the opportunity, they attempt to reconstitute a city or territory or nation, but actually create a dystopian society. Often it is something unimaginably horrible. Jan of Leiden and many of the other leaders mentioned in Chapter 6 created alternative societies that ripped the fabric from the preceding society.

Pol Pot is another leader whom I could have included in that chapter on the perversion of utopia. He and the Khmer Rouge attempted to create a millenarian society. This is a motif in secular revolutions since the beginning of the French Revolution. Edmund Burke (2019) wrote that the French Revolution was a "digest of anarchy." But I would argue that he was mistaken. Like the Jacobins before them, Pol Pot and the Khmer Rouge's millenarian scheme to create an egalitarian, agrarian state had psychological roots.

Many of the members of the Khmer Rouge, like many Bolsheviks and Jacobins, were idealists who believed in the goodness and efficacy of creating a new world. In the past, these idealists might have joined a convent, monastery, or similar practice (and I am, by no means, saying these practices can't be coercive). But, once in a group like the Khmer Rouge, they "convert" to the ideology of the group. As you know, Robert Jay Lifton has written about this "conversion" process in his book *Thought Reform and the Psychology of Totalism: A Study of "Brainwashing" in China* (1989). However, when I think of these party members, I always think of Rubashov in his cell in Koestler's *Darkness at Noon* (2006), awaiting his next round of interrogation.

What is fascinating, Zeiders, as you mention above, is once a leader has a stranglehold on power, they become absolute rulers, and their party members become the aristocracy. The ideas of the revolution become twisted and used to destroy both real and unreal opposition. However, they don't always imitate the preceding ruling class. Stalin and Mao were not exactly fashion plates. And their power was in many ways more absolute than their predecessors, because they destroyed classes of people, whether they posed a threat or not. Effectively, they destroyed civil society.

Zeiders: Wiping out classes of people is horrifying, Devlin, so the psychology of horror deserves a place in our study of malignant narcissism. I would say that horror is an affective cousin of the terror found in post-traumatic stress. But horror itself is integral to understanding the MNL's dehumanizing approach to individual and mass object relations, and the emotion of horror benefits his domination project.

Inflicted at the behest of the MNL, horror is panicked, phantasmagoric revulsion within human consciousness such that the victim(s) suffers:

- the eruption of an abyss behind ordered reality,
- the return of the repressed,
- catastrophic boundary intrusion,
- loss of self via political indoctrination,
- loss of self via spiritual possession,
- chaotic subjectivity,
- un-addressable physical rot,
- existential necrosis,
- psychotic love,
- psychotic hate,
- and especially the dehumanization of the self, or other,
- combined with the loss of the sense that the universe cares for one's person or people.

Much that is referred to as *terrorism* could be re-termed *horrorism*. While *terrorism* inflicts death upon life, *horrorism* inflicts the inhuman upon the human. Horror destroys the notion of the valued human subject. Horror affronts the human being with irrelevance; the dehumanization of the human subject is the great perversion of the malignant narcissist in leadership.

Part of the horror of the MNL's personality is their dehumanization of themselves. In the self-apotheosis that is their god-drive (see Chapter 2), they pervert the face of their humanity, much in the same way that a botched plastic surgery might leave a once-beautiful face ever mutilated, and obviously so, and hideous to those who behold its countenance. Further, through mind control techniques (see Chapter 4), the MNLs render their constituents as distorted as themselves. Via the inhumane instrument of power, the MNL disfigures, mangles, and butchers the humanity of any object unfortunate enough to be split-off into the dark realm of the bad object or out-group.

In the psychobiography of the Romanian Prince Vlad Draculi (1431–1477), or Vlad Tepes, or Vlad the Impaler, one finds paternal abandonment, anal rape, and forced silence to be sufficient horrors to form a malignant leader whose aristocratic entitlement, paranoia, and sadistic revenge orientation, in turn, raised horror to the level of a negative ethos for political and military leadership (Dan, 2014).

To become a *horrorist*, the MNL suffers horror-infliction from an empathy-less aggressor, suffers catastrophic dehumanization, and develops self-loathing, and rage, that may become traits. To compensate, and to evacuate these afflictions, they strive for power, project self-loathing onto targeted bad objects, and experience sadistic euphoria by acting out rage in the vengeful mutilation of the humanity of the enemy. If the MNL cannot work through primary trauma (and what tyrant goes into analysis), the horrific acting out will become habitual. Kellerman (2014, p. 65) also provides a draft of this dynamic in relation to tyrant-personalities with God-complexes. Horror is a component of the MNL phenomenon.

At the conclusion of Coppola's Vietnam war movie *Apocalypse Now* (1979), the rogue officer Colonel Kurtz lived as a god of war and thrived like a primal father on horrific abasement of his friends and enemies. Killed on behalf of the American military by the assassin Major Willard, Kurtz's final words were "The horror. The horror." This might demonstrate the return of the repressed and affective phantasmagoria as the final experience of a life horribly lived. But given the profundity of the MNL's defenses, I doubt that actors like Kurtz experience this sort of natural justice other than in cinema.

Devlin: In Conrad's *Heart of Darkness* (2016), Kurtz does become a god to the Congolese surrounding his station. His famous last words appear purposely ambivalent. Was Kurtz referring to his own behavior or King Leopold's horrific colonial practices, or something else entirely? In the end it depends on the reader's interpretation. What are missing are stories from the Congolese. Throughout the novella, they are depersonalized and abject. Only the Europeans have personalities. The horror for me is the dehumanization of the Congolese. Kurtz is incidental.

I imagine if I met Kurtz in the flesh, he'd be a scary, annoying bore. We know almost nothing of his background. He has a fiancée but appears to have abandoned her for the ivory trade. We are told he is a talented artist and musician. But is this true or did Kurtz proclaim it? He more than likely combines the makeup of the malignant narcissist: sociopathy and narcissism. But is he really that impressive? He achieved domination over the local Congolese because he had superior technology. When Marlowe finally meets him, he is less than his hype. Kurtz proclaims everything surrounding him belongs to him. He proclaims as he is dying that he will return to the Congo and carry out his ideas (whatever they are). Marlowe finds him comical and pathetic.

In Coppola's *Apocalypse Now*, Colonel Kurtz is also a mysterious figure with an overachieving curriculum vitae. Yet, when Willard finally arrives at Kurtz's lair, he finds an obese, psychotic blowhard with delusions of divinity. Despite this, the horror you describe is more explicit. Kurtz is already deeply mad. Moreover, he is quite open about the horrors that shaped him. He describes an attempt to inoculate a Vietnamese village and the horrific aftermath in which he beheld that the Viet Cong had amputated each child's arm that the Americans had inoculated. He also describes his profound disillusionment with the establishment he served. We know this type of military betrayal has a classical lineage with Achilles' rage against Agamemnon's betrayal of Achilles.

What is pertinent to MNLs is that, in Colonel Kurtz's fictional case and in Vlad's historical case, historical circumstances shaped their characters. Vlad's sadism proved, if briefly, to be a successful military tactic. He was deeply disturbed and sadistic, but was he a narcissist? Did Vlad have a god-drive? Do these military leaders fit the MNL profile completely? Conrad's Kurtz does have a god-drive. He does take advantage of the Congolese with superior technology. His depredations fit tragically with other horrific depredations that actually occurred in the Belgian Congo.

The horror seems to exist within these individuals, but also within a greater society that shaped them. However, human beings make up society; it's not a discrete entity separate from us. With these MNLs, they are almost acting within norms – although your point that Vlad shocked even his bloody contemporaries needs to be considered. Their malignancy also exists within the greater society. Dostoevsky (2002) wrote that without God, everything is permitted (this quotation is part of a soliloquy by Ivan Karamazov). I disagree. *Homo sapiens* permit what they permit. We are violent messy animals and need to acknowledge that MNLs are born from the violent messy world we have created. That is the horror.

Conclusion

Our topic is a horrible one indeed. Our discussion has covered such ground as the formation of the revolutionary personality and its ascendance to destructive power. We have reviewed the disturbing sexual aims of MNLs and how those aims might influence executive decisions. We appropriated Freud's primal horde theory, added a primal mother, and found the myth apt to describe power relations between cult leaders and devotees. To justify the brutality that enforces their authority, cult leaders declare themselves to be gods, or otherwise worm toward apotheosis. Of course, such divinity is a destructive fiction that MNLs invent to actualize their god-drive, their megalomanic flight above the embarrassing limitations they share with us all. But when they land from this flight, it is often a crash with biblical destruction, preceded and accompanied by unimaginable horror. To the extent that value exists in our reflections, it is in the underscoring of the importance of retaining a permanent skepticism of the magnetic person who has answers, and knowing that the line between righteous indignation and hatred is thin.

References

Ainsworth, M, Blehar, M., Waters, E., & Wall, S. (2015). *Patterns of attachment: A psychological study of the strange situation* (Classic ed.). New York, NY: Psychology Press.

Arendt, H., & Jaspers, K. (1992). *Correspondence 1926–1969* (Trans. R. Kimber & R. Kimber). New York, NY: Harcourt Brace.

Becker, E. (1973). *The denial of death*. New York, NY: Free Press.

Becker, E. (1998, April 28). Pol Pot remembered. *BBC News*. Retrieved from http://news. bbc.co.uk/2/hi/programmes/from_our_own_correspondent/81048.stm

Beit-Hallahmi, B. (2014). Primal horde theory. In D. A. Leeming (Ed.), *Encyclopedia of psychology and religion* (2nd ed., n.p.). Boston, MA: Springer.

Bowlby, J. (1982). *Attachment and loss* (2nd ed., Vol. 1, *Attachment*). New York, NY: Basic Books.

Burke, E. (2019). *Reflections on the revolution in France*. London, UK: Anodos Books. (Original work published 1790)

Conrad, J. (2016). *Heart of darkness* (Ed. P. B. Armstrong, Fifth Norton Critical ed.). New York, NY: W.W. Norton. (Originally published 1899)

Cooper, A. (1989). Narcissism and masochism: The narcissistic-masochistic character. *Psychiatric Clinics of North America, 12*(3), 541–542.

Coppola, F. F. (Director, Producer). (1979). *Apocalypse now*. United States: United Artists.

Dan, P. (2014). Psycho-biographical considerations about Vlad the Impaler also known as Dracula. Retrieved from www.academia.edu/10342218/Psycho-biographical_considerations_about_Vlad_the_Impaler_also_known_as_Dracula

Dostoevsky, F. (2002). *The brothers Karamazov* (Trans. R. Pevear & L. Volokhonsky). New York, NY: Farrar, Straus and Giroux.

Eagleton, T. (2011). *On evil*. New Haven, CT: Yale University Press.

Fromm, E. (1973). *The anatomy of human destructiveness*. New York, NY: Fawcett.

Gay, P. (Ed.). (1995). On narcissism: An introduction. In *The Freud reader* (pp. 545–561). New York, NY: W.W. Norton.

Hari, J. (2018). *Lost connections: Uncovering the real causes of depression – and the unexpected solutions*. New York, NY: Bloomsbury.

Harlow, et. al., (1965). Total social isolation in monkeys. *Proceedings of the National Academy of Science of the United States of America, 54*(1), 90–97.

Juni, S. (2009). The role of sexuality in sadism: Object relations and drive theory perspectives. *American Journal of Psychoanalysis, 69*(4), 314–329.

Kellerman, H. (2014). *Psychoanalysis of evil: Perspectives on destructive behavior* (SpringerBriefs in Psychology). New York, NY: Springer.

Kinnucan, M. (2013, July). The political theology of Sigmund Freud. *Hypocrite Reader*, (30). Retrieved from http://hypocritereader.com/30/theology-freud

Koestler, A. (2006). *Darkness at noon: A novel*. New York, NY: Scribner.

Kohler, L., & Saner, H. (Eds.). (1992). *Hannah Arendt Karl Jaspers: Correspondence 1929–1969* (Trans. R. Kimber & R. Kimber). San Diego, CA: Harcourt Brace.

Lieberman, M. D. (2013). *Social: Why our brains are wired to connect*. New York, NY: Crown Publishers.

Lifton, R. J. (1989). *Thought reform and the psychology of totalism: A study of "brainwashing" in China*. Chapel Hill, NC: University of North Carolina Press.

May, R. (1982). The problem of evil: An open letter to Carl Rodgers. *Journal of Humanistic Psychology, 22*(3), 10–21.

Newell, W. (2019). *Tyrants: Power, injustice, and terror*. Cambridge, UK: Cambridge University Press.

Orwell, G. (1950). *1984* (Signet Classics). New York, NY: New American Library/Penguin Group.

Post, G. (2015). *Narcissism and politics: Dreams of glory*. New York, NY: Cambridge University Press.

Reich, W. (1972). *Character analysis* (3rd, enlarged ed.). New York, NY: Farrar, Straus & Giroux.

Sebag Montefiore, S. (2003). *Stalin: The court of the Red Tsar*. New York, NY: Vintage.

Shengold, L. (1989). *Soul murder: The effects of childhood abuse and deprivation.* New York, NY: Fawcett Columbine/Ballantine Books.

Spitz, R.A. (1945). Hospitalism: An inquiry into the genesis of psychiatric conditions in early childhood. *The Psychoanalytic Study of the Child, 1,* 53–74.

Tyson III, J. (n.d.). Mussolini's sex life. *Schuylkill Valley Journal Online.* Retrieved from www.svjlit.com/features/svj-online-mussolinis-sex-life-issue-7/

Waite, R. G. L. (1977). *The psychopathic god: Adolf Hitler.* New York, NY: Basic Books.

INDEX

Note: Page numbers in *italics* indicate figures.